Praise for **THE DEV**

"Fascinating, deeply researched ... This ... compelling characters. ... Pomerantz h... story and human behavior." —*Kansas City Star*

"A mesmerizing tale ... A fascinating and thoroughly delightful read. Rating: A-Plus." —*Bridge Bulletin*

"Fascinating ... bound to appeal to bridge players and true-crime fans and should also win admirers from anyone interested in American social history." —*Richmond Times-Dispatch*

"Truly a panorama of the era, full of wonderfully colorful characters, significant historic detail, and astute social commentary." —Georgia Public Broadcasting

"A thrilling story that illuminates a forgotten yet essential slice of American history. Masterfully reported, beautifully written, and all but impossible to put down ... An unforgettable read." —Jonathan Eig, author of the *New York Times* bestseller *Luckiest Man: The Life and Death of Lou Gehrig*

"Consistently absorbing and entertaining ... *The Devil's Tickets* is a triumph." —Howard Blum, author of the *New York Times* bestseller *American Lightning*

"I was completely absorbed by *The Devil's Tickets*. ... Anyone who's played bridge, or ever been the least bit curious about the game's appeal, will love this book." —Bob Hamman, eleven-time Bridge World Champion

"Excellent stuff!" —Pope Brock, author of the *New York Times* bestseller *Charlatan*

"Riveting. ... A wonderful story of a bygone era that will stay etched in your mind. Pomerantz writes with a fabulous style. This is a must-read not only for all bridge players but for anyone who cares about life in the fast lane in days gone by." —Barbara Seagram, owner of the Barbara Seagram School of Bridge

"A delight to read." —Louis Sachar, author of the National Book Award–winning *Holes*

A Barnes & Noble Book Club's "Featured Selection"

ALSO BY GARY M. POMERANTZ

Where Peachtree Meets Sweet Auburn:
A Saga of Race and Family

Nine Minutes, Twenty Seconds:
A True Story of Tragedy and Triumph

Wilt, 1962:
The Night of 100 Points and the Dawn of a New Era

THE Devil's TICKETS

A VENGEFUL WIFE, A FATAL HAND, AND A NEW AMERICAN AGE

GARY M. POMERANTZ

BROADWAY PAPERBACKS | NEW YORK

BROADWAY

Published in the United States by Broadway Paperbacks, an imprint of
the Crown Publishing Group, a division of Random House, Inc., New York.
www.crownpublishing.com

Broadway Paperbacks and its logo, a letter B bisected on the diagonal,
are trademarks of Random House, Inc.

Originally published in hardcover in the United States by Crown Publishers, an imprint of
the Crown Publishing Group, a division of Random House, Inc., New York, in 2009.

Library of Congress Cataloging-in-Publication Data

Pomerantz, Gary M.
The devil's tickets / Gary M. Pomerantz.
p. cm.
1. Bennett, Myrtle, d. 1992. 2. Reed, James A. (James Alexander), 1861–1944.
3. Culbertson, Ely, 1891–1955. 4. Murder—Missouri—Kansas City—Case studies.
5. Man-woman relationships—Missouri—Kansas City—Case studies. 6. Contract
bridge—Social aspects—Missouri—Kansas City—History—20th century. 7. Bennett,
Myrtle, d. 1992—Trials, litigation, etc. 8. Trials (Murder)—Missouri—Kansas City.
9. Kansas City (Mo.)—Biography. 10. United States—Social life and customs—
1918–1945. I. Title.

HV6534.K2P66 2008
364.152'3092—dc22

2008051185

ISBN 978-1-4000-5163-2
eISBN 978-0-307-46036-3

Printed in the United States

Book design by Leonard W. Henderson
Cover design by Whitney Cookman
Cover photograph by AP Images

10 9 8 7 6 5 4 3 2 1

First Paperback Edition

For Mom

"Don't forget that man is a vain creature. Let him suspect that it is he that rules the roost. Manage him without letting him suspect it."
— JOSEPHINE CULBERTSON

"We played perfectly—except Jo."
— ELY CULBERTSON
ABOUT HIS BRIDGE-PARTNER/WIFE

CONTENTS

AUTHOR'S NOTE

Bridge mavens who enter here, I beg your indulgence. For while this is a story about the great game, it is not the great game's story. As you enter a bygone era and follow the glamour and drama of the Culbertsons and Bennetts, you won't need to know the finer points of bridge. For those coming late to the game with their curiosity roused, I offer a brief bridge primer and a glossary of terms, beginning on page 247. I hurry to say that no such primer is called for by this story. It is a tale of husbands and wives. You know the rules by which that game is played.

INTRODUCTION

In the Roaring Twenties, the famous philanderers William Randolph Hearst and Babe Ruth might have thought it, but only Henry Ford said it out loud: Housewives of America should be patient with outbreaks of marital infidelity. "Treat it like the measles," the auto titan said in 1923, the year a shapely young woman gave birth to a son whispered to be his. "Help your husband through it," Ford said, as if what ailed the poor fellow could be fixed with a cool compress against his fevered brow.

One of the period's great thinkers, Henry L. Mencken, so favored blondes, be they starlets or harlots, that a friend, screenwriter Anita Loos, turned the sage's lust into a 1925 comic novel, *Gentlemen Prefer Blondes*. Loos created an archetype, the blond showgirl as gold digger, all giggles and curves, working under a siren's name, Lorelei Lee.

Lorelei is a stenographer in Arkansas. Occasionally, she stops by the boss's apartment. There they engage in extracurricular activities—until the day Lorelei arrives to see she's been preempted by another working girl. For a moment, her mind goes blank. A revolver appears in her hand. Next thing she knows, as she tells the jury at her trial for attempted murder, her cheating boss has been shot.

The jurors and judge alike weep in sympathy for the poor, naïve, wronged, precious young woman. When she is acquitted she rewards each juror with a kiss on the cheek. The judge, too.

Free and on the run from Little Rock to Hollywood, to New York and Europe, Lorelei dances with the Prince of Wales and meets the famous Austrian psychiatrist "Dr. Froyd," to use her spelling. Raising temperatures everywhere, she pursues a man—or, better, men—who will treat her the way to which she dreams of growing accustomed, mainly awash in diamonds and afloat on yachts.

In the way that art and life are reflections, there was about

Myrtle Adkins more than a little of Lorelei Lee. Myrtle came out of Arkansas and became a stenographer. Like Lorelei, she had the look that caused men to take another look. Though a brunette (in this case, a grand exception to the Loos rule), Myrtle stopped conversations by doing no more than entering a room. That, she knew. That, she counted on. And just as Lorelei leaves Arkansas behind, so Myrtle left behind the dusty Arkansas farmland of Tillar.

Unlike Lorelei, Myrtle needed only one man. She even knew the man she wanted. When she spotted him, she moved quickly. With Jack Bennett she would create a life of relative luxury in Kansas City—until one night, as Lorelei does, Myrtle raised a gun against her man.

It happened around a bridge table in 1929, and to this day it is a flashpoint in the history of the card game that in the late twenties became—along with flagpole sitting, marathon dancing, transcontinental foot racing, and swimming pool endurance floating—yet another of America's national crazes.

Of all the mad games that cheered Americans between the world wars, the least likely must have been contract bridge. Descended from whist, the game of English origins that had captivated Napoleon, Talleyrand, and Thomas Jefferson, bridge was as much an intellectual exercise as a game, its language a rigid code that conveyed information to a partner about the 13 cards in his hand, one arrangement of the 635,013,559,600 possibilities.

How quaint that sounds today: bridge as a phenomenon. When Shipwreck Kelly sat atop flagpoles for days, America cheered the sheer lunacy of it. But bridge? Genteel, civil bridge? Four people at a table for hours? Whose idea of fun was that?

It was Ely Culbertson's. An elegant showman, he created on a large scale the milieu in which the Bennetts came to the table on that last night. Born in Romania and raised in Russia, the son of an American father and Cossack mother, Culbertson presented himself as suave and debonair, a tuxedoed boulevardier. He used mystique, brilliance, and a certain madness to transform bridge from a friendly social activity to a national cultural movement that made him rich and famous.

Culbertson sold bridge to anyone who would buy, but especially to housebound wives and mothers. Somehow, as if by some phantasmagorical hypnosis, he persuaded Americans that bridge was—in ways spoken and in ways dared not spoken—about sex.

The intimacy of couples seated together at a small table for hours, the competitive juices afire, the inevitable flirtations, the stimulus of friendly wagers, and the customary defiance of Prohibition were among the game's seductive charms. Millions of American housewives just like Myrtle Bennett would give themselves to Ely Culbertson, and his game.

On his arm as his wife and across the table as his bridge partner was a beautiful American, Josephine, who shared his fame in the sparkle of New York and London. Culbertson knew that when husbands and wives played as bridge partners, the cards were on the table, and so was the marriage. Most couples played bridge together happily, but marriages under stress at home might reach spontaneous combustion when their quirks and eccentricities were exposed at the table. Then gentility might give way to competition, and to the bloodlust feared by Puritans in the New World.

The Puritans were hardly alone in their fear of cards. From the very start—the beginning of playing cards dates to China in or before the thirteenth century—cards and their games have titillated and haunted the imagination. Legend holds that Christopher Columbus's sailors, inveterate gamblers on the high seas, encountered such fearsome weather that they threw their playing cards overboard in hopes of placating the storm gods. Once safe on terra firma, they regretted their rash act, and fashioned new cards. The New England Puritans, always on the lookout for evil, abhorred playing cards, considering them Satanic seeds of laziness, vice, and corruption. They called them *the devil's tickets*.

Bridge can stir devilish passions. It is a game of partnerships, two against two, seated at a table opposite each other. Communication and cooperation, and no small amount of forbearance, are paramount, because, ideally, partners will act as one, thinking alike and waging an intellectual battle totally without ego.

But the ideal can break down with the smallest of misinterpretations of a partner's bids, and the opportunity for error is always there. In a single bridge hand, the number of significant decisions a player makes can reach well into double digits. In poker, a player's failure is his alone (though, naturally, he usually passes it on to the fall of the cards). But bridge is unique in that it gives a player another way to explain his defeat. He can lay blame across the table.

That is petty of him, of course, because whatever glory or despair comes to the partnership is equal property of both. Points, after all, are scored not by individuals, but by the partnerships. Yet missteps, real or perceived, can break a partnership's concentration, egos can rise to the fore, and a sense of betrayal can blow like an icy north wind flowing to the south.

The best partners are personally compatible and roughly equals in ability. A mismatched nonspousal partnership can end with a simple word of regret, but a married partnership is more problematic. Generally, a husband and wife keep slogging through the tribulations, carried along by their personal compatibility. Not every marriage can stand up to the passions of an intense competition, though. Trouble arrives, and is doubled, when partners mismatched at bridge bring to the table the flaws of their married life. Culbertson knew this, and feasted upon it, even as he extolled the game's magnificent virtues.

Anyone intrigued by the intersection of Culbertson's game and the Bennetts' story of passion gone wrong is drawn into the life of Kansas City. Only by understanding that great Midwestern city in the time of Prohibition and the Pendergast political machine is it possible to understand what happened at Myrtle Bennett's trial for murder. Her defense lawyer was James A. Reed, a man who twice campaigned for the presidency, a firebrand orator, former U.S. senator, friend of H. L. Mencken, and discreet practitioner of extramarital romance himself.

The times defined events. At this exhilarating moment in America's media history, talkies were new, radio was in its infancy, and newspapers competed fiercely for an audience. With all this came an insatiable hunger for story, the more sensational the better. Because (as P. T. Barnum once said) no one ever went broke underestimating the taste of the American public, the marketing pitches of the day were skewed toward the breathless and hyperbolic, as seen through the prism of the ruling sex, the male.

Once, the famous movie producer Irving Thalberg told Anita Loos how to write about women in her Hollywood scenarios: "When you write a love scene, think of your heroine as a little puppy dog, cuddling up to her master, wagging an imaginary tail, and gazing at him as if he were God." Thalberg was talking to the wrong woman, of course. From her own marriage, Loos had learned which sex was truly stronger. Once, she found, in her husband's wardrobe drawer, secreted behind socks, a woman's love letter. When her husband tearfully confessed to the affair, Loos allowed him to stay with her.

In those times, Amelia Earhart became "Lady Lindy," Marlene Dietrich dressed in top hat and tails, and Dorothy Parker traded barbs with the men at the Algonquin hotel's "Round Table." All were women of achievement, icons by virtue of their rarity, and yet their work was nearly always judged from a male viewpoint. No matter how individualistic and daring Earhart was in the sky, reporters pigeonholed her as merely a female version of Charles Lindbergh. Beautiful and sultry, even in her men's formal wear, Dietrich played a scene in *Morocco* in which she kisses a woman. The acerbic poet Parker sat with writers Heywood Broun, Alexander Woollcott, Robert Benchley, and George S. Kaufman, tossing off witticisms every bit as cutting as theirs, such as her line on coeds at the Yale prom: "If all the girls in attendance were laid end to end . . . I wouldn't be at all surprised." For such boldness, male critics disparaged Dietrich and Parker as unseemly and scandalous.

For women at home, those housewives whose achievements went unnoticed, a sociable game of bridge offered a place at the table where, by dint of their intelligence and skill, they could prove they were the equals of men, if not their superiors. But many husbands were not ready to follow their wives' lead or to view them in anything but a subordinate role. Culbertson's marketing genius was that he positioned his game as a challenge to women, a dare, really. If a woman truly wanted equality, she had only to buy a deck of cards—and, of course, his books of bridge instruction.

Perhaps as an unintended consequence, though just as likely the shrewdest part of his marketing, Culbertson took advantage of the tension in marriage that is eternal. How much more interesting, he thought, if the game became a war of the sexes.

Myrtle Bennett would be North to Jack's South. The Culbertsons, Ely and Jo, would be the game's king and queen. Spouses, lovers, enemies—these four were all those as the raucous twenties dissolved into the silence of the Depression. Their lives and the game they played became a single story beginning in 1929.

This is that story.

PART 1

♠

The Bridge Storm

1929–1932

Before the Culbertsons made their challenge, the titans of bridge stood shoulder to shoulder on a New York rooftop in 1928 *(from left to right)*: Milton Work, R. F. Foster, E. V. Shepard, Sidney Lenz, Wilbur White-head, Gratz Scott. *American Contract Bridge League, Memphis, TN*

ONE

Ely and Jo

I.

New York City in the twenties was a melting pot of seven million, full of show, big and brawling, an industrial behemoth with enough smoke-stacks and skyscrapers to fill the skylines of a dozen cities. F. Scott Fitzgerald, who wrote of young love and glittery tea dances, as the twenties dawned, suggested New York City had "all the iridescence of the beginning of the world." Its streets swelled with noises of the Old World mixing with the New: gramophones, gangster gunfire, European accents, tinkling champagne glasses, backfiring Model Ts, and tabloid newsboys hawking the sensational. In these high times, New Yorkers could rush to Broadway to see Al Jolson and Eddie Cantor—known to their Eastern European parents as Asa Yoelson and Israel Iskowitz—or thrill to the last acts of the amazing Harry Houdini, born in Hungary as Erik Weisz. They could read a dozen and more local dailies, choose from among thirty thousand speakeasies, marvel as the big-bellied Babe Ruth launched home runs at Yankee Stadium, and see their Democratic governor, the derby-hatted Al Smith, passing through the five boroughs on his way (he hoped) to the White House. Alive and thrumming at street level, the city teemed with gangsters, ad agency pitchmen (selling sex, Sex, SEX!), Wall Street fat cats, socialists and garment district workers, café society personalities and cynical, self-absorbed writers sitting at the Algonquin Round Table thinking up laugh lines. A constellation of celebrities brightened the Prohibition-era night, from the brassy hostess Texas Guinan, who with her pancake makeup and jangling jewelry, greeted nightclub guests with "Hello, sucker!"; to the waiters at Small's Paradise in Harlem, who roller-skated the Charleston across the dance floor with trays overhead; to Jimmy (Beau James) Walker, the dapper mayor of the Tammany Hall machine, who so frequently courted his showgirl all over town that many New Yorkers—not including, of course, Walker's wife—assumed the two were married. In the spirit of the times, Walker later divorced his wife and married the showgirl.

In 1923 Ben Hecht, the writer and playwright, arrived in New York from Chicago and discovered an adventurous city running from the dark memory of war and hedonistically giving itself to the pleasures of the hour, including, he wrote, "the pleasure of not giving a damn." "It was a bold town," Hecht wrote, "indeed, sharp-tongued, and individualistic. Its credo had it that New Yorkers were a master race."

> We busied ourselves putting up the only show possible against doom, which is to seize all the fun there is. Thus people sang louder, drank deeper, danced longer and squandered themselves in every direction. . . . Its finest ladies, including happily married ones, engaged in promiscuous sex as if they were college boys on a spree. . . . New York insisted all its idols wear a grin. It regarded all foreign events, including the first World War, as entertainment. It believed that any war could be won by writing the right songs for it, and not losing your sense of humor. Its patriotism consisted of admiring itself ardently.

In the daily frenzy of New York City, twin journalistic revolutions thundered like elephants down Forty-second Street: the tabloids and Walter Winchell. The New York *Daily News,* America's first tabloid, or half sheet, wailed into existence like a colicky infant in June 1919 with bold headlines and an eye-catching array of photos and illustrations. Within five years, it claimed a readership of nearly one million, easily the largest circulation in the nation. Its success begat another tabloid, the *Daily Mirror,* which arrived in 1922 promising "90 percent entertainment, 10 percent information"; a few years later came the next, the *New York Evening Graphic.* These tabloids took the bygone yellow journalism of Hearst and Pulitzer, Spanish-American War vintage, circa 1898, and ripened it. New York pulsed with a thousand wars in miniature—social, cultural, legal, and, best of all, marital—and the tabloids used them all to their advantage. They reveled in stories of debauchery, extramarital affairs, abortions, murders, union battles along the Bowery, mob violence, heroism, hedonism, mayhem, threats, controversies, and dynamic courtroom trials.

Winchell was an indefatigable, ink-stained gadfly who, as a columnist first for the *Evening Graphic* (a lowbrow daily ridiculed by competitors as the "*Pornographic*") and then for Hearst's *Daily Mirror,* seized upon gossip and turned it into his own high art of ballyhoo. Like the tabloids that launched him, Winchell was abrupt, catty, and always hustling. A night owl, he wrote about Broadway personalities and turned his flashlight upon their tangled, often secretive romances. He challenged the traditional standards of journalistic good taste, maddening competing newspapers and his own editors, who were often unsure whether to publish his latest unverified piece of gossip. Winchell finessed his way around potential libel suits by creating his own "slanguage," a vernacular of the streets, breezy and colloquial. He wrote of secret lovebirds who were "Adam-and-Eveing it" and of a man who felt "that way" about a woman as they awaited "the blessed event." A mention in Winchell's column was greatly coveted, and feared. The column had a chatty cadence, a rapid song-and-dance-man's beat. He dropped names, often of celebrity writers, when possible: "At the opening of a play recently Baird Leonard turned to Dorothy Parker and said, 'Are you Dorothy Parker?' and Dorothy replied, 'Yes—do you mind?' " Winchell reacted physically to gossip, and one observer noted that he "seemed to purr with delight when he had a particularly juicy item . . . He was as fascinated and unself-conscious as a four-year-old making mud-pies." Ben Hecht thought Winchell wrote "like a man honking in a traffic jam." There were other gossip artists at work in New York, but none so widely read, or so intensely despised. The actress Ethel Barrymore, who feuded with Winchell, would say, "It is a sad commentary on American manhood that Walter Winchell is allowed to exist."

Amid this cacophony was the Knickerbocker Whist Club, a noiseless oasis at 26 West Fortieth Street. Here the self-satisfied elites of American auction bridge, the reigning card game of the era, built and burnished their reputations. By requirement, the Knickerbocker's more than 250 members exhibited good temper and a strict adherence to an honor code of card play nearly two centuries old, as attendants, moving with stealth, placed fresh glasses of water at their elbows every half hour or so. Some of the club's older members had been wearing their eyeshades and stroking their chins, deep in thought, since the Cleveland and McKinley administrations. Women were not allowed as members—as bridge players, they were considered conservative and easily intimidated—though club rules permitted them in Thursday night games.

By 1915, auction bridge had forged two world capitals, London and New York, and the most prestigious gentlemen's bridge clubs in both became like fortresses, where wealthy members in evening attire shared stiff drinks with men of their own stature, and tried to take their money at cards. The Portland Club in London was the recognized rule maker of British bridge, a role held in America by the Whist Club of New York, at 38 East Thirty-ninth Street, with its small, exclusive membership (well heeled enough to play auction bridge at fifty cents a point), which included sportsman Harold S. Vanderbilt and club president Charles Schwab, the steel titan who was once Andrew Carnegie's right-hand man.

But for most of the East's leading players, the Knickerbocker was the bridge club of choice. Typically, its members were moneyed men of leisure who, if not natives, had migrated to the city from the Midwest, the South, and Europe. They shared intellectual gifts, competitive intensity, and an unswerving devotion to bridge. Founded in 1891 by twenty enthusiasts of whist, the Knickerbocker started at the

Broadway Central Hotel. It led a nomadic existence over the next three decades, migrating from whist to auction bridge, and moving, after the war, for the seventh time, to the brownstone on West Fortieth. When the New York dailies first devoted columns to card games after the turn of the century, Knickerbocker members became regular contributors, spreading the good name of the club: Robert F. Foster in *The Sun*, George Kling in *The Tribune*, and E. T. Baker in *The Evening Mail*. The club's top players wrote bridge books for posterity and one another, and sought to prove their cognitive superiority at the table. Between games, they gossiped about other members and boasted of success in business and with mistresses.

On the brownstone's fourth floor lived perhaps New York's most influential bridge authority, the Knickerbocker's president, Wilbur Whitehead. One floor below was the inner sanctum of the club's best players, entered by invitation only.

In that inner sanctum, in early 1922, Josephine Dillon made her startling breakthrough. Only twenty-three years old, tall and slender with bright Irish eyes, her reddish gold hair carefully marcelled, her eyebrows expertly penciled, "Jo," as she was known, played bridge with a growing confidence and tenacity. Her table presence and subtle movements were elegant and ladylike, her long, supple fingers dropping the cards softly, her cigarette holder cutting broad arcs, her voice, small as a hummingbird's, passing heartfelt compliments: "Nicely played, Whitey," and "That was magnificent, Sidney." Her women friends called her the Duchess for her regal coolness. Jo Dillon let no one close to her. She shielded her deepest thoughts and feelings. The men liked her immensely, and sought her attention with suggestive comments and furtive glances. Since the war years, she had been a part of their group on Thursday nights. Jo bullied no one at the table. She credited their brilliance, and the experts liked that, too.

Raised in the Bronx, the young Josephine Murphy was graduated from Morris High School (where she played the adolescent game of basketball in steel cages) and later served briefly as secretary to an executive in baseball's Federal League, Pat Powers, who turned to promoting six-day bicycle races. Then she worked as a stenographer for Whitehead. Whitey adored Jo (there were whispers that she had been his mistress) and offered her indoctrination in bridge. Jo admitted to him that she barely knew a heart from a spade, but while working for him she developed a keen interest in auction bridge. Since Whitey was club president, if he wanted Jo on the Knickerbocker's third floor, no one dared challenge him. There, Jo discovered bridge experts pitiless in applying the principles of scientific and practical accuracy in their bidding. They hoped their systems were much like the club's brownstone: built methodically, and solidly, to stand the test of time.

Jo proved a quick study and soon found herself among America's great players: Whitehead, Sidney Lenz, Winfield Liggett, P. Hal Sims, Waldemar von Zedtwitz. Here was a Murderer's Row of American bridge, an eclectic mix of sportsmen and Renaissance men: an amateur magician from Chicago (Lenz); an old soldier/Virginian (Liggett); a banker from Selma, Alabama, who once tried to irrigate the Congo (Sims); and a lexicographer who fought as a baron in the Kaiser's army and whose maternal great-grandfather ran for president of the United States against Abraham Lincoln (von Zedtwitz).

What these men shared was card-playing brilliance.

To them New York City was the center of bridge, the Knickerbocker its pantheon, and they were its gods. They wrote newspaper columns and books about bridge (with modest sales), and believed that every meaningful bridge-bidding system and convention had been conceived in New York. The mention of London would invariably cause one of them to harrumph, "Irrelevant, behind the times!"

These experts saw themselves as a master race, and knew each other by agreed-upon nicknames—Whitey, the Shaggy Giant, Commander, the Baron—monikers earned by amiability, appearance, military service, and birthright.

Of course, the game had long had similarly memorable and celebrated characters, dating to contract's forerunner, whist, and the colorful British writer Henry Jones (whose pen name in his whist writings of the late nineteenth century was Cavendish) and, even ear-

lier, to the famed French gamesman and whist champion Guillaume le
Breton Deschapelles. A brilliant light of his age, and a genius and
braggart of the first order, Deschapelles possessed, according to a
contemporary, "a brain of so perfect an organization for the acquire-
ment of games of skill, that it may be fairly said, the world never, in
this respect, saw his equal." Born to prosperity in 1780, his father
gentleman of the bedchamber to Louis XVI, Deschapelles as a young
man volunteered to march with the spirited youth of Paris in battle
against the Prussians. Trampled by a horse, his skull laid bare by a
saber, another gash traversing his face on a diagonal from brow to
chin, his right hand slashed off at the wrist, Deschapelles, left for
dead, rose. He mastered chess *in four days*, he boasted (which led to
cynical comparisons to the seven days of Moses), and then turned to
whist. He played one-handed, holding and sweeping up his cards
with dexterous elegance. A bold and daring player, he saw his fame
overtake the card clubs of Europe. It was said that backers agreed to
deposit a quarter million francs to support any whist match
Deschapelles undertook. To the Knickerbocker experts, he was
remembered for the Deschapelles Coup, a stratagem of playing the
king, or other high card at the head of a suit, to force out the ace or
other high card held by an opponent, thereby making good a lower
card in his partnership's possession.

Ambling through the Knickerbocker corridors, Wilbur Whitehead usually had a protégé or secretary by his side. Whitey, a hale fellow with a gray mustache, was former president of the Simplex
Automobile Company. A giant of auction bridge, he had invented
conventions of bidding and play: the quick trick table of card values,
the Whitehead system of requirements for original bids and
responses. When he wasn't lecturing (occasionally on the vaudeville
stage) or writing about bridge, Whitey was playing it, or analyzing
his most recent hand. By his fiftieth birthday, in the world of bridge at
least, he had done it all.

Sidney Lenz, a wiry, athletic Chicagoan, was also part of the auction old guard. Lenz would soon become *The New York Times*'s first
bridge writer. His wry sense of humor revealed itself at the table, and

in his columns for *Judge*, a humor magazine. The evolution, beginning in the 1890s, from whist to bridge-whist to auction bridge had hardly troubled Sid Lenz, as the hundreds of auction trophies in his showcase testified. He made his money in the timber business, and retired in 1910 at the age of thirty-seven to devote his life to hobbies and games. A man of many interests, he pursued his hobbies aggressively. He once bowled an average of 240 across 20 consecutive games (a long-standing record), played chess with the famed Cuban champion José Capablanca, and spent a year in India studying magic, becoming a member of the Society of Amateur Magicians, a genius at sleight of hand befriended by Harry Houdini.

P. Hal Sims, from Selma, once represented U.S. banks in foreign nations, and possessed the ultimate bridge table presence. With a thick shock of perpetually mussed-up brown hair, the Shaggy Giant was six foot four and three hundred pounds, the Babe Ruth of bridge, the Knickerbocker's most feared player. Playfully, friends called him Nero. Occasionally Sims brought the Knickerbocker's top players back to his own place so he could play bridge in comfort, wearing his favorite blue bathrobe while settling into a wide armchair.

The jowly Commander, Winfield Liggett, Jr., who limped noticeably from a leg injury suffered during a 1908 baseball game at the Boston Navy Yard, had been an officer on the USS *Montana* during the war, convoying American soldiers to France. A noted carouser who liked his women and drink, "Lig" was known to cavort late at night, sometimes with the irascible New York Giants baseball manager John (Muggsy) McGraw.

Among the Knickerbocker giants, none had a more colorful biography than the soft-spoken Baron Waldemar Konrad Ernst Anton Wilhelm Ferdinand von Zedtwitz, a man of seven names who spoke eight languages. His father, a German baron with estates in Saxony, had died in a yachting accident during the Royal Albert Regatta in 1896 and his title was transferred to his infant son. The boy's mother, Mary Eliza Breckinridge Caldwell, was a Kentuckian and a granddaughter of John Breckinridge, vice president of the United States under James Buchanan, and a presidential candidate in the 1860 campaign won by Lincoln. When Waldemar's mother died in 1910, the Baron came under the guardianship of an uncle in Berlin, who later enlisted him during the war in the Imperial Prussian Army. Von Zedtwitz served as a lieutenant in the cavalry and was awarded the Iron Cross, second class. After the war, he came to New York and began a ten-year battle to claim his late mother's substantial American inheritance, which had been confiscated by the U.S. government during the war on the grounds that von Zedtwitz was an enemy alien. (He later would reach a settlement, agreeing to renounce his German citizenship and title and allow the U.S. government to take a percentage of his mother's estate, which included properties in Kentucky, Newport, and New York, and reportedly was valued at $4 million.) Living at the Plaza Hotel, von Zedtwitz, a bachelor, small and cerebral, his manner every bit the nobleman's, worked by day as a lexicographer, a tedious labor of love that produced dictionaries in Spanish, Russian, and English. At the Knickerbocker, he was known as the slowest bridge player of all, and for nervously twirling thin locks of hair behind his ears as he contemplated his cards. (He had pulled on his earlobes until a physician convinced him to stop.) So deep was his level of concentration that when a waiter once approached the bridge table and spilled water on von Zedtwitz, he didn't look up. He simply said, "Please don't do that again," and continued studying his cards.

To these Knickerbocker elites, bridge was a way of life. As von Zedtwitz explained about the game, "Intellectually, and almost emotionally, it is possible to go through every type of thrill without having to take the risks involved getting the same thrills from life." These elites remembered with precise detail bridge hands played long ago much the way many men remembered long-ago lovers. Their postmortems on bridge hands—and their debates about the merits of the bidding in those hands—lasted deep into the night, fueled by their convictions regarding intensely held strategies and beliefs. A member might arrive from out of town for a game at the club on a Friday night, intending to catch a train Saturday morning, but become so consumed by the bridge that he would not leave until Tuesday.

Most elites did not take women seriously as players. The swaggering Sims advised women playing as his partner in Thursday night games to bid only the unrewarding minor suits, diamonds and clubs, to ensure they would become dummy, and he would play the hand for their partnership.

But Jo Dillon, the cool Duchess, played against the Knickerbocker's best, including Sims, and held her own. Some of the experts felt protective of her. Lenz, a lifelong bachelor, was one of her first instructors. Jo played a shrewd game of bridge, exhibiting flexibility and toughness, and soon became one of New York's leading bridge instructors.

All the while she kept her personal life hidden from the club's experts. Jo and bridge instructor Madeleine Kerwin became inseparable friends during this period, playing bridge, dining out, and attending dance parties in New York. The men of the inner sanctum knew that Jo had married only when she announced herself one day as no longer Jo Murphy, but Mrs. Josephine Dillon. They heard the young couple had eloped, and that her husband was a Princeton boy, a bit on the wild side. Then, in the spring of 1921, Jo no longer was married; she had filed for divorce, and many months later rumors surfaced that her former husband was dead, perhaps by suicide. In the inner sanctum, the experts whispered about this, wishing for more details and noticing how sad and quiet and lonely Jo seemed.

And then one day the Russian showed up.

II.

From the foreign sound of Ely Culbertson's high-pitched voice, his expensive look (European suit, derby hat, wooden cane), and his air of intellectual superiority, the Knickerbocker denizens sized him up quickly: a dandified Russian gambler. Before he arrived among them he had been drifting between the card haunts of Greenwich Village, searching for bigger stakes. He first showed up at the Knickerbocker for a Thursday evening game in spring 1922, accompanied by Mrs. Lucella Shelton, a local bridge teacher. A Russian stranger cloaked in obscurity, partnered with a woman, amounted to easy pickings; several players spotted the two, and offered bets. That night, Ely and Mrs. Shelton won top score, and pocketed their wagered winnings. Ely joined the club a week later and quickly ascended from its penny tables to its five-cent tables. He dazzled members with his sophisticated, if odd, bidding and repartee. Within a few months, his reputation sizzling, he was playing regularly against the club's masters on the third floor.

In the inner sanctum, the experts agreed: such an unusual man, this Culbertson. He was thin, pale, and oddly frenetic. Between deals, he pulled from his coat pocket a gold cigarette case, and tapped it twice. In a moment, swirling smoke from a Melachrino Egyptian-style cigarette clouded his face, obscuring his half-grin, half-smirk. He held thirteen cards in his left hand, the Melachrino in his right, between his index and middle finger, a cosmopolite with a gold ring on his right pinky. His receding hairline and slumping shoulders made him look older than thirty-one, his stated age. He said he avoided physical exercise scrupulously: rather than walk three New York City blocks, he would hail a taxi. At the table, the experts noticed how Culbertson would develop red splotches on his cheeks, how his thinning hair mussed and his eyes shone with excitement.

They knew this Russian only by what he told them about himself. His name, he said, was not pronounced "E-lye," but "E-lee," short for Ilya. He said he had played cards in the clubs of Paris and London, and in other capitals on the Continent. He said his younger brother, Sasha Culbertson, was the noted concert violinist who owned the famed 1732 Guarneri del Gesù violin once played by Paganini and said to be worth more than $50,000. The bridge experts could not be certain about Ely's occupation—once, he mentioned oil. He told them the October Revolution in Russia had cost his family everything: $4 million. The Bolsheviks had brought down the

Romanov empire, he said, and the Culbertson empire, too. He had been to Washington to put in a claim for that lost fortune. All that was left from the spoils of his American father's mining of the oil-rich Caucasus, Ely said, was Sasha's violin and worthless Russian imperial gold bonds. He said he was glad his Cossack mother, Xenia Rogovnaia, an uncompromising tsarist, had not lived to see the day. Of course, he did not mention to the bridge experts that Almon Culbertson, his proud father, despised cards, considering them a waste of his intellect and time. But the family fortunes were gone, and when Ely told his father that he could earn a good living by gambling at cards, Almon reluctantly agreed, and Ely raised his glass and said, "Well, then, let's drink a toast to the Devil's tickets!" In the inner sanctum, Ely talked about bridge scientifically. He was full of bidding ideas and theories—some of them, the experts admitted, intriguing.

Ely electrified their mix. He was like a cup of strong Russian coffee after three decades of tepid tea. Ely talked about himself—and his bidding system—incessantly. Imagine him informing the gods of American auction bridge in the spring of 1922 about the bidding mistakes they were making and offering a new and superior system—his. To Whitey, Lenz, Liggett, and the others, Ely was an interloper, an irritant, a know-it-all. They had been playing cards since before his birth. He was, they decided, a wandering Narcissus, impertinent, peculiar, mysterious, and without money or occupation, dressed up entirely for show. Intellectual, yes, but toxic. From the first, the club's old guard did not trust Ely Culbertson, or like him.

Even worse was his pursuit of Jo Dillon. From the inner sanctum, the experts watched their courtship blossom. Helpless to stop it, they quietly conferred over drinks, always returning to the same question: What does Jo see in him? Already she had succeeded in becoming one of the Knickerbocker boys in ways Ely never would.

From their first shared moment at a Knickerbocker bridge table (as opponents, not partners), Ely Culbertson was infatuated with Jo Dillon. He noticed small details: her lightly freckled face, the high cheekbones, her slight retroussé nose, the smallness of her voice, and the long narrow hands alive with suppressed feelings. Everything about Jo suggested calmness and restraint. She had finishing-school charm. Her presence at the table was steady, cerebral, refined.

Seeing Jo, Ely remembered a moment eight years before in Italy when he first dreamed of his Galatea, a dream so strong he placed an advertisement in a newspaper. He was looking for a wife. And not just any woman, but one whose shape, intellect, and pedigree met his specifications. He did not describe his motive that candidly in the ad. Instead, he hid behind cleverness. No one at the Knickerbocker knew this story, of course, and if they had, it would only have intensified their concern for Jo.

Ely only told the story many years later. In the summer of 1915, with Europe at war, he was twenty-three years old and living his richly entitled life on tsarist rubles while holed up, for the time being, in a Geneva hotel. Slim and elegant, he was five feet, ten inches tall and weighed not even 140 pounds. He had a handsome wardrobe and a thin face with hooded eyes that a writer later would liken to a "romantically idealized Satan."

Better with numbers than with women, he put his scientific mind to use. If he could not find his ideal woman, he reasoned, he would, with a system, *create* her. He had in mind Galatea, the figure in Greek mythology carved from ivory and so beautiful that her sculptor, Pygmalion, falls in love with her. With Pygmalion's love, and Aphrodite's spark, Galatea springs to life. Ely was determined to find a young woman, beautiful and refined, whose personality was not yet fully formed. He would place her in an environment filled with tutors, books, plays, and ideas. They would live in a cultured setting—Paris or London, perhaps—where he would shape a superior woman, his perfect partner, his Galatea.

Beneath the youthful romanticism and naïveté of his plan was a dark dreamer's distended thinking: Ely as Creator. He took a train to Turin, in northern Italy, where, he believed, the world's most beautiful women lived. If he failed there, he would seek his wife in Greece or the Balkans. In Turin he placed his ad in *La Stampa* and other newspapers, announcing himself as an American painter in search of "an exceptional model":

Must be between 18 and 21 years old. Between 5 feet 4 and 5 feet 6 inches tall; between 24 and 26 inches waist; between 34 and 36 inches bust; between 36 and 38 inches hips, legs perfectly shaped; eyes very large, preferably black with blonde hair, or blue with black hair; features either very symmetrical or, if not classical, of exotic attractiveness. Only truly beautiful types need apply. Undress unnecessary. Write, enclosing photograph.

Hundreds of women answered his advertisement, and he met them all at a busy central piazza, moving from one street corner to the next, their individual appointments spaced fifteen minutes apart, his identifying marker a white rose pinned to his lapel. In his derby and suit, sniffing the summer air, he moved like a Russian prince. In these candidates, he saw age, infirmity, obesity, bad teeth. "No, signorina," he said; and to the next, with a shake of his head, "Sorry. No, signorina." It went on like this for several days. He did not find Galatea. But now, in the brownstone at 26 West Fortieth Street, he knew he had.

Their courtship began over dinner, with Jo saying, "It isn't your ideas or your so-called system that makes you win. It's your knowledge of human nature. You'd win with any system." She noted how Ely drew inferences and information from an opponent's smallest hints: a hesitation, a slight change in voice inflection, an arching of the brow. He also knew how to rile opponents. He would goad or gloat at just the right moment. This was sophisticated gamesmanship, a gambler's high art.

In conversations with Jo, Ely belittled the Knickerbocker experts who glorified their own "rules" of bidding. They would rather score two hundred points by following their own rules, he told her, than three hundred points by abandoning them. He showed Jo a "crime sheet" he'd been keeping, in which he had dissected the others' bids and plays, and his own. He could prove they were throwing away thousands of points for no reason other than stubbornness. He showed her notebook pages covered with graphs, curves, and percentages.

He persuaded Jo to explore his ideas. Together, Ely and Jo dealt hands and bid them according to the ideas of Whitehead and Milton Work, a noted American authority on whist, scoring the results. They then bid according to Ely's methods. For two weeks, Jo bid hands, with Ely or alone, according to the three systems. And she became a convert.

Soon she was seeing Ely every day. He would drop into her bridge teaching studio in late afternoons and, with a group of her friends, the two would share cocktails and dinners at the Beaux Arts restaurant next door, a speakeasy with Texas Guinan as its greeter. Together, Ely and Jo walked at night along Forty-second Street, past the New York Public Library, and sat on the benches in the park behind the library with Jo's Pekingese dog, Chu Chin Chow. They talked about books, people, and life. Ely told her that he thought himself much like Spinoza, the seventeenth-century Dutch philosopher, the great rationalist, who ground lenses by day so that he could philosophize by night. Ely played bridge, he said, but his underlying ambition was to create the Modern Theory of Cards, and he intended to reap the financial rewards for it. He told Jo about Russia, hoping she would love the country, for then she might also love him. He understood that her divorce and the recent death of her former husband weighed upon her. He sensed her reluctance to marry again.

He showed her his diary, reasoning that she was entitled to know the deepest thoughts of the man about to propose marriage to her. She read the diary, and it scared her. She told him, "I need a change." Crestfallen, Ely heard her say, "We can never be happy."

She spoke harshly to him that night: "You could be a revolutionist, a monk or a philanderer, but you never could be a family man. You'd hate it.

"Ely, no woman could ever be happy with you," she said. "To you, a woman will always be a companion, an assistant—not a wife. Sometimes, I'm afraid of you. You're ruthless, Ely, because you are ruled by ideas, not by your heart."

She went away, to Saratoga, and Ely thought that maybe she was not his Galatea, after all. *A foolish American girl*, he decided. *They're all spoiled*. He sat alone one night at the Beaux Arts restaurant with a bottle of champagne and his despair. Guinan happened by his table and noticed Jo's absence: "Why the gloom, Ely? Did someone misplay a hand?"

But he was determined not to give up on Jo Dillon. He went to Saratoga, put an arm around her, and kissed her. She did not resist him, but she said, "Ely, I love you, but I will not marry you." Ely's heart leaped: he was still in the game.

Now it was late summer, 1922. They conceived an idea to become America's best bridge pair, and began a period of intensive training, spending hours each night fine-tuning their partnership. They created a mutual understanding of bids, discussed the imponderables of bridge psychology. Then they tested their theories, and their system, Thursday nights at the Knickerbocker, returning afterward to Jo's apartment and working from memory to re-create the hands dealt and played. They made exhaustive notes, analyzed errors. It was during these times when Ely became his most ruthless. Into the wee hours, Jo's living room filled with cigarette smoke and Ely's savage criticisms, until finally Jo, in tears, pushed her chair from the table and shouted, "You're a bridge monster! I'll never play with you again!"

If Ely's intellect amazed Jo, his intensity frightened her. The memory of such explosive bridge table experiences would melt away, but they would help Ely define early on the imperative of partnership cooperation: "This question of morale is automatically solved for those who realize that partnership is simply a sporting proposition," he wrote. "We are drawn together for better or worse and therefore like true pals should stand by cheerfully and courageously." He also created a standing rule: "Never reproach your partner if there be the slightest thing for which you can reproach yourself." At the table he began to treat Jo with deference, and their courtship deepened.

As time passed, Jo came to believe that, among married couples playing as bridge partners, there were three types: (1) those who quarreled everywhere, including at bridge; (2) those who quarreled nowhere, except at bridge; and (3) those who quarreled everywhere, but never at bridge. She and Ely therefore agreed never to discuss a hand while sitting at the bridge table.

They married the following June. The experts in the Knickerbocker's third-floor inner sanctum were aghast, especially Whitey. (Two years later, he founded the Cavendish Club in New York City and invited Jo to join—as long as she promised to keep her husband out.) On the signed affidavit for a wedding license, Ely, too ashamed to define his occupation as "gambler at cards," instead scrawled, "oil business," borrowing from his father's former profession. Jo cited her occupation as "bridge expert." He was thirty-two, she twenty-five. On the affidavit, Jo also cited her divorce in March 1921. Of her first husband, she wrote simply, "dead 1922." Perhaps to protect her own good name, she added a single word, crammed into the tight space above her signature: *Plaintiff*. Jo wanted it known that she, not her first husband, had filed the divorce papers.

The Culbertsons married at the Holy Cross Church in New York City, with Father Duffy presiding. Jo's mother, Sarah McCarthy Murphy, served as maid of honor, and Ely's father, Almon, as best man. Ely bought a thin platinum wedding ring with tiny diamonds, on the installment plan, and promised Jo an enormous square-cut solitaire. The longer she waited, he assured her, the larger the diamond. (He would deliver an impressive solitaire ten years later.) He also gave Jo a small jewel box. It was empty, of course, but one day he promised it would hold a beautiful honeymoon on the isle of Capri, a lovely country home, an engagement ring, sables, minks, and diamonds. They honeymooned at a motel in nearby Long Beach, an inexpensive seashore resort. They drank champagne and walked along the beach. She encouraged him—as a bridge player, as a writer, as a man: "You're better than you think you are."

"Jo-Jotte, I'll make you the happiest woman in the world," Ilya Culbertson promised his Galatea on their honeymoon. And then he amended, "At least in spots."

By the mid-1920s, auction bridge had solidly established itself as an American parlor game, particularly among the intellectual and the well-to-do. The game even found its way into popular literature. In a 1926 short story for *Red Book* magazine, "The Rich Boy," F. Scott Fitzgerald wrote of a young Yale man playing a casual game with friends at the Everglades Club in Palm Beach; the same year, Hemingway's Jake Barnes, in *The Sun Also Rises*, plays three-handed bridge with friends in Spain en route to watch the bulls run at Pamplona.

As late as 1925, contract bridge was hardly known, and played only experimentally. Its evolution dated back more than two centuries to whist, which rose in Britain during the first half of the eighteenth century from relative obscurity, and from earlier games known as triumph, ruff and honours, and whisk and swabbers. Played at the outset in servants' quarters, or "below stairs," the game soon gained popularity among elites. In 1742, the London barrister turned whist instructor Edmond Hoyle (of the phrase "according to Hoyle") published his seminal *A Short Treatise on the Game of Whist, Containing the Laws of the Game, and Also Some Rules Whereby a Beginner May, with Due Attention to Them, Attain to the Playing It Well.*

In the United States and Europe, auction bridge appealed to Anglophiles and other cosmopolites who might have imagined themselves as knights and ladies keeping alive the grand tradition of a whist-based game; in 1912, four such devotees, passengers aboard the *Titanic*, were playing auction bridge when the ship struck ice.

In 1925, though, the millionaire yachtsman Harold S. Vanderbilt, great-grandson of the famed Commodore, decided on revolution at the bridge table. Enough of auction. Its predictability was second only to its bidding dullness. On a cruise ship voyage through the Panama Canal, Vanderbilt, with time to tinker, smoking his pipe and wearing his pince-nez, energized the scoring table and came up with a sophisticated plan for the evolving game of contract bridge that, in his mind, would cause a competitor's heart to beat faster even as a thinker's mind created solutions to problems never before faced at the table.

Here was the essential difference between auction and contract: In contract bridge, only the tricks bid for, and made, were counted toward winning an all-important game. To earn full rewards, sides now would have to take risks by bidding for higher contracts. In auction bridge, a partnership was rewarded for a grand slam by taking all thirteen tricks even if it had bid only to take eight. Some critics said that, in terms of bidding, auction bridge rewarded conservatism, even cowardice. Contract changed that. Vanderbilt also added "vulnerability" to a side that had won one game in the best-of-three-game rubber, increasing the size of their penalties for failing to make contracts and their rewards for making them. A more complex game than auction, contract bridge moved the focus from the play of the cards to the bidding. It called for superior coordination between partners—and cried out for a bidding system. It would make the expert suddenly indispensable to living-room players across the nation. Vanderbilt prevailed upon his friends in Long Island, Palm Beach, and Newport to try the new game. In 1927, New York's gentlemen's-only whist clubs bought in to it and adopted its official laws. Thus modern contract bridge was born.

Short on cash, Ely took a train west to Los Angeles in the summer of 1927, and set himself up in the Biltmore Hotel. There he taught an auction bridge class with twenty students, predominantly women from Pasadena and Los Angeles. Jo joined him in California, and during a visit to Santa Barbara they heard for the first time about contract bridge, the new rage of New York.

In Santa Barbara, Ely and Jo played Vanderbilt's contract for the first time, and the game's faster pace and enhanced scoring thrilled Ely. "Contract will sweep the country," he told Jo.

He returned to New York convinced that if he could develop a set of rules that would enable a novice to learn an otherwise complex game in a matter of a few weeks, then he could make contract bridge, and its adherents, entirely, and profitably, his. He decided that about 70 percent of his established rules for auction bridge would apply to contract. He would study the rest, and apply his science.

Back in New York, Ely and Jo organized a regular contract bridge game at their apartment on East Sixty-third Street. They sought to sell the game to men of the Knickerbocker inner sanctum, knowing they were hidebound and resistant to any game but auction, their safe haven. At first the men didn't come to the Culbertson apartment. Contract, they insisted, was only a fad, and would be dead in a matter of months. But then von Zedtwitz came, and so did Ted Lightner, one of Knickerbocker's young bright lights. Both became converts. Finally, Ely corralled Sims and another top player, George Reith, and they, too, saw the merits of contract.

Ely had begun to develop his "Approach-Forcing" bidding system. Bridge bidding systems are like Sunday church sermons: derivative and oftentimes merely a careful integration of pieces drawn from other systems and turned slightly in a new direction. In essence, Ely's Approach-Forcing system meant that bidding should be advanced slowly, never recklessly, and that certain bids and responses would force a partner to bid once more, and in some instances to continue bidding until the possibility of making game, or one hundred points, was reached.

Ely still lived a gambler's life, his earnings unsteady. On New Year's Eve 1928, alone in their apartment, he gave a champagne toast to Jo: "Here's to the most wonderful wife on earth!" Two weeks later, Jo delivered their first child, a daughter, Joyce Nadya.

At the Knickerbocker, the auction bridge gods remained secure and complacent. They could not know the magnitude of the coming contract bridge craze. Ely knew, and aimed to crush them. First he would steal their reputations and transform himself into the nation's leading bridge authority. Then he would steal their book sales, their lecture tours, and their radio appearances. Battle lines were drawn.

In the summer of 1928, Ely and Jo spent time at Hal and Dorothy Sims's ten-acre estate, a lush, wide-open space with bridges and lakes, in Deal, New Jersey, about sixty miles from Manhattan. The Sims place had become like a sleepaway camp for the Knickerbocker Whist Club's best players. The big house, with its porches, slept about forty, though hardly anyone there seemed to sleep. Bridge-playing guests showed up at all hours, ready to cut into the two-cent, five-cent, and ten-cent tables. Games lasted through the night. If a player left for a train or to go to bed, another would appear. One night a thunderstorm struck with fury: windows burst open, lamps and knickknacks crashed onto card tables, electricity failed, and rooms went dark. Dorothy Sims rose in terror from her bed and raced downstairs. There, she found her husband and young Johnny Rau of Columbia University playing against von Zedtwitz and Vanderbilt, plodding players who abhorred snap judgments. In the darkness, someone lit a match at the table, and Vanderbilt, barely illuminated, turned from his cards and said, "Whose bid is it?"

Some guests stayed a day; others stayed weeks, prompting the wise-cracking Dorothy Sims to place an ancestral coat of arms above the front door that read GUESTS AND FISH STINK AFTER THE THIRD DAY. The Simses held tournaments every few days. Once, Hal Sims came to the table an hour early, saying he hoped to "get in a little cards" before the tournament began. Sunday nights were especially popular because fried chicken was delivered by a neighboring farmer, typically at the last minute, when twenty bridge-playing guests showed up without warning. "Bridge sharks multiply like rabbits. I prefer rabbits," Dorothy Sims would write. "They're less choosy. They're less sensitive."

TWO

Myrtle and Jack

I.

Even before the war, the boys of Memphis made their way to Myrtle Adkins. Her young cousins would wait on the front porch of her house to bear witness, making their presence a nuisance in hopes that one of the suitors lined up there as if for a formal review, would pay them a nickel to leave so he might speak with Myrtle alone in the moonlight. As a young woman, already Myrtle was a statuesque beauty. She liked to dance and enjoyed good times. She kept a few beaus, though each soon learned about her temper. Her relatives wondered if Myrtle's flashes of anger were simply the impetuosity of youth or a determined young woman's attempt to take control of a life that had begun with such hardship.

Myrtle knew the man she wanted, but feared he didn't exist in Memphis. Her ideal was her father, Henry Franklin Adkins, whom she knew only from a tintype photograph and a handwritten letter, her mother's mementos from a nine-year marriage. Henry Adkins had run a small sawmill in Tillar, Arkansas, near McGehee, in Desha County. He died young, just thirty-six, in the last year of the nineteenth century, when Myrtle was a toddler. He lived on in her mind, though, through the tintype image taken in a Memphis studio. With a thick walrus mustache and close-cropped hair parted in the middle, he resembled a young Theodore Roosevelt. Myrtle inherited her father's resolute chin and lustrous, almond-shaped eyes. Alice Adkins, Myrtle's mother, had kept a letter her husband wrote to her in the summer of 1889, four months after their wedding. She had returned home to Catfish Point, Mississippi, to visit relatives, and he wrote to her at night, in purple ink, with flourish and devotion, professing his love, bemoaning her absence, and calling for her immediate return. He also wrote that he was layering himself with cotton lye to combat pesky mosquitoes. If his spelling and punctuation were lacking, his expression of fidelity was not. Henry Adkins wrote: "i was glad to hear that you enjoyed your trip on the boat and that you was feeling so well and that you stood the trip so well. I felt uneasy about you and so so lonsom so lonsom i can't hardley stand it. . . . It is 5 minuts after 8 and I haft to go to Birks to male this leter to night. . . . May God Bless you and Save you. to get home Safe is my Desir. Yours of a Loving Husband. H. F. Adkins." And then, at page bottom, he added a husband's plaintive cry: "Come home Dear Wife, Come home."

Henry Adkins's death left his widow and daughter destitute. The lawyer Abner McGehee, Jr., whose father founded the town that bore their name, hired Alice as his housekeeper, and brought her to Little Rock, where she and Myrtle lived in his home during the girl's formative years. Myrtle and her mother clung to each other, survivors of a family shipwreck. In 1909 they moved to Memphis, where Myrtle quit school at fifteen to work as a telephone operator. By late 1917, she was a twenty-two-year-old stenographer for a Memphis attorney, living at home with her mother and attending night school. With a friend, she visited St. Louis and there, in a private home, she noticed a photograph of a young man. His likeness impressed her: striking eyes, wavy hair, a boyish smile, and a physique that filled out his soldier's uniform in a way that would make any army infantryman proud. *Who was he?* His name was Jack Bennett, and he came from God-fearing, church-going people steeped in the Illinois rural tradition. (Illinois? Henry Adkins's home state!) Myrtle laughed that day in St. Louis and, staring at the photograph, promised herself, "That's the man I'm going to marry." It was the sort of promise most women can't keep.

She approached him on a train.

In a club car on the Illinois Central, bound from Memphis to Chicago during wartime in 1918, Myrtle spotted a young, handsome man in an army uniform. She knew him, but how? Then she remembered: the photograph in St. Louis! Across the train car, she saw that photograph brought to life. The man in uniform was, in fact, the man in the photograph, John G. "Jack" Bennett.

She introduced herself with an extended hand: "Miss Myrtle Adkins, how d'ya do?" She mentioned St. Louis and the coincidence of the photograph.

The attraction was immediate, and mutual. At twenty-five, Bennett was a charmer, well spoken, with high energy. His photograph had failed to convey his swagger, which Myrtle found especially becoming. Bennett told her he had just completed his infantry work at the Fourth Officers' Training School at Camp Grant, in Rockford, Illinois. A pharmacist attached to a medical division, he would be commissioned as a second lieutenant in the 342nd Infantry. The war news from Europe was increasingly favorable. A large number of German troops shipped from the Eastern Front to the Western Front were deserting transport trains. The Allied counteroffensives on the Somme had the German army in retreat.

Jack hailed from a big farm family in southeastern Illinois, near the Indiana border. But there would be no more plowshares for rural-born Jack Bennett, no more dirt beneath his fingernails. Before the war, he had worked as a clerk at the W. A. Ball drugstore in downtown Carmi. Then he spent time in Chicago, and reveled in its big-city thrum. He heard the hullabaloo about Sandburg's just-released poem about Chicago: "a tall bold slugger set vivid against the little soft cities"—that was how Jack saw himself matched against other men—" . . . under the terrible burden of destiny laughing as a young man laughs . . . Bragging and laughing that under his wrist is the pulse, and under his ribs the heart of the people." Chicago and Jack Bennett had much in common.

Only recently H. L. Mencken, master debunker and critic of manners and morals in America, had published a series of ironic essays, *In Defense of Women*. Mencken might have been thinking of Myrtle and Jack, rather than of generic courtship, when he wrote:

[A woman] searches out his weaknesses with the utmost delicacy and accuracy, and plays upon them with all her superior resources. He carries a handicap from the start. His sentimental and unintelligent belief in theories that she knows quite well are not true—e.g. the theory that she shrinks from him, and is modestly appalled by the banal carnalities of marriage itself—gives her a weapon against him which she drives home with instinctive and compelling art . . . The moment his oafish smirks and eye-rollings signify that he has achieved the intellectual disaster that is called falling in love—he is hers to do with as she will. Save for acts of God, he is forthwith as good as married.

The courtship was as brief and intense as Mencken could have imagined. Jack Bennett was going places, and Myrtle was going with him. *So long, Tillar! So long, Memphis!* They talked of a shared future. After the war was won, Jack would be discharged, they would marry, start a family, and live in a beautiful home—and of course Jack would thrive in business. They became engaged after only three dates.

They married in a Memphis church on Armistice Day, Jack in Uncle Sam's uniform. Friends and family would say the selection of their wedding date must have been the work of angels. Nothing else could explain how at eleven o'clock on the eleventh day of the eleventh month of 1918—their wedding day—Germany and the Allies signed an armistice, ending Woodrow Wilson's "war to end all wars." An Associated Press telegraph operator first received the armistice news in the *Memphis News-Scimitar* editorial room: "FLASH: The Armistice Has Been Signed. OFFICIAL." The *News-Scimitar*'s extra editions hit the streets, with newsboys hawking the headlines: "HUNS MADE POWERLESS. Yank Big Guns Crash Out End of War." Celebration moved across most of the Western world. In Memphis, automobile horns blared, strangers kissed, and the streets were filled with the Shrine Band, the Boy Scout Drum Corps, the Ladies of the American Red Cross, and a rolling tank known as a "Hun Crusher." That day the Roaring Twenties began in spirit, and in the Memphis church, everyone agreed that this harmonious convergence of events was surely a sign of blessing on the marriage of Myrtle Adkins and Jack Bennett.

Money was tight in the Bennetts' early years, and they moved often. South Dakota came first, with Jack working in Sioux Falls for the pharmaceutical company Parke-Davis. In 1920, with a nice bump in salary, Jack took Myrtle to Houston and then to San Antonio as a salesman for Richard Hudnut, Inc., maker of French-style perfumes and cosmetics. Jack Bennett was, in the business term of the day, "a producer."

During these years, Myrtle worked as a stenographer for a tire company, a doctor, and the Katy Railroad. The jobs gave her the satisfaction that their marriage was a true partnership.

When Jack invited Myrtle's mother, Alice, to live with them in San Antonio in 1924, it thrilled Myrtle. Jack was earning $6,000 a year. He could afford a larger place, and besides, Myrtle's mother was getting older. Jack treated her with kindness and called her "Mother." He knew Alice Adkins had lived a hard life, raised in poverty on the Mississippi Delta, widowed as a young mother. She sewed as well as any woman Jack had ever met, stitching his trousers and lounging pajamas, and she didn't offer her opinion unless asked for it. She also provided companionship for Myrtle when Jack was away.

Occasionally, Myrtle traveled with Jack on long drives through the open spaces of the Southwest. They stopped in small towns for Jack's business calls, now and then diverting to rivers and lakes. Myrtle had loved fishing since her pigtail days in Arkansas. On the riverbank, she talked about having children, and Jack beamed. The family life was for him. A youthful bliss carried Myrtle through every day as Jack just went on being Jack, his smile bedazzling, his conversations running on about business. He told Myrtle that, yes, business was good, and he emphasized that business was about to get much better.

II.

We see them now in the gloaming of an affluent age, late summer 1929, Jack and Myrtle Bennett, a handsome couple, married nearly eleven years, a hard-driving perfume salesman and his glamorous wife, on the rise in Kansas City socially and financially, their marriage marked by the trappings of the nouveau riche and the sweet attar of perfume. By all appearances deeply in love, they displayed affection, holding hands, embracing, with Myrtle laughing girlishly as Jack conveyed a playful animal heat that made other women in the room blush. Jack was a snappy dresser, handkerchief neatly folded in his breast pocket, his cheeks smacked shiny with cologne, the consummate traveling salesman. He drove from town to town across the Southwest with his car trunk full of accounting ledgers, order forms, and perfume samples. Across his territory, a crew of perfume salesmen answered to him as he answered only to New York.

Jack took in $18,000 a year, nearly eightfold what the average American made in 1929, and his earning potential, like his confidence, seemed limitless. In rural Carmi, the hometown folks thought Jack Bennett was unassailable, and virtually a Vanderbilt. He and Myrtle were now country-clubbers. They lived the American Dream in a city calling itself the Heart of America. They attended parties and hosted their own, at home and at their clubs. The glossy magazine advertisements of New York admen pictured couples who looked just like the Bennetts. Theirs was a buoyant look that celebrated youth, determination, triumph, and the prosperity of the Coolidge years—("The business of America is business!")—a winning look that sold soap and dishwashers and lawnmowers and automobiles. Kicking up clouds of dust beneath an azure sky, we see Jack and Myrtle motoring—a fashionable hobby for showoffs—through the open verdant space north of Kansas City, in Clay County, in their Hupmobile Cabriolet Roadster, a handsome convertible with a rumble seat ("A brook that babbles and a pretty girl who doesn't . . . and a Hupp on the river bank . . . try that some sunny Sunday!"). In a halcyon age of high speeds and good times, Jack sat tall in the driver's seat as Myrtle's chestnut hair blew wildly.

A New York adman might have put them in a bigger car, a four-seat sedan, with a freckle-faced boy and his lil' sis in the backseat, finishing the perfect American family portrait. But Jack and Myrtle, now thirty-six and thirty-four, had no children. Myrtle had twice lost babies through miscarriage in the mid-1920s, defeats from which she had not recovered. Jack tried to ease her pain, buying her diamonds, trinkets, expensive new dresses in New York, a LaSalle, the latest modern appliances. But certain things about a woman—the melancholia, the sobbing spells—a busy man like Jack Bennett could not understand.

Whereas Ely and Jo lived in an uncertain house of cards, struggling to pay the monthly rent, Myrtle and Jack rocketed upward in the belief that a true salesman's luck never turned. Ely and Jack shared certain traits, however; each was an outsize dreamer with an inner conceit, a gift of gab, and an unshakable trust in his finely tuned intuition. Ely, the card sharp at the table, knew how to read men and their tendencies. Jack, the salesman on the road, knew how to read women and their vulnerabilities.

With Jack on the road, Myrtle had plenty of free time and, increasingly, contract bridge filled it.

Bridge in the summertime conjured one magazine's grand images of the game played at "broad-verandahed country places, remote mountain lodges . . . luxurious Dude ranches," perhaps with a Fourth of July motif, invitations placed inside of hollow miniature firecrackers and pictures of famous Americans cut from magazines or rotogravures and mounted on red, white, and blue art paper for patriotic place cards. Each guest might be required to sing verses of "The Star Spangled Banner," with bonus points given for singing the correct lyrics.

Vanderbilt's modern game seduced millions of American women, among them Myrtle Bennett. Much like marriage, contract bridge required a partnership based on understanding and trust. Myrtle studied bridge, read about it in newspapers, and played it with friends in homes and clubs several afternoons a week. Sometimes they gambled a tenth of a cent per point, just to spice things up. Still, Myrtle played with a competitive edge because that was her nature.

Jack loved to see his home swell with guests and laughter, and he and Myrtle frequently hosted small dinner parties and bridge games, inviting other couples—the attorney J. Francis O'Sullivan and his wife, or perhaps their upstairs neighbors, Charles and Mayme Hofman—with Jack hoping to be perceived as a lavish host. Jack had spent a fortune on home furnishings and did not mind if his friends gossiped about them. The conversation at the Bennetts' bridge table, set up in the center of the living room, was breezy, the play relaxed, though Myrtle typically sat at the edge of her chair, an indication of her intensity and level of engagement, a bridge-playing posture more common to men.

During breaks in the game, music poured from the Bennetts' radio, filling the room with the sounds of an orchestra, or Rudy Vallée crooning "Vagabond Lover," or, from local station KMBC, broadcasting live from the El Torreon Ballroom, the jazz of Bennie Moten and his Kansas City Orchestra, a powerhouse on the black side of town, recently joined by a Harlem pianist, William Basie, soon to be known as Count.

As soon as the bidding recommenced, though, the music was turned off.

The noted New York bridge teacher Madeleine Kerwin believed that women lacked imagination at bridge, but studied harder than men to improve their game. Kerwin wrote: "Men have more psychology, both in bidding and in play. As they make better poker players, so they apply their knowledge of human nature in sizing up the weak points of an adversary's game. Intelligent women players accept constructive criticism and are pathetically eager to perfect their game. They do not attempt to dominate every situation and they consider their partner's judgment both in bidding and play.

"The weakness of the average man's game," Kerwin added, "lies in his colossal conceit."

In 1925, Jack and Myrtle arrived near the great bend where the muddy Missouri accepts the waters of the Kaw. Only five years before, the Kansas poet C. L. Edson had put to verse Kansas City's epic rise:

> *Ships made Carthage, gold made Nome,*
> *Grain built Babylon, the wars built Rome;*
> *Hogs made Chicago with their dying squeal,*
> *Up popped Pittsburgh at the birth of steel.*
> *Come Kansas City, make your story brief:*
> *Here stands a city built o' bread and beef.*

Caught up in the hurly-burly of the modern, mechanized nation, Kansas City in the 1920s thrived as a Middle American crossroads where the products of the East met the produce of the West. Automobiles filled its newly paved streets. Its downtown skyline took impressive shape with some of Missouri's tallest buildings, twenty-five stories and more. Up went shopping districts, movie palaces (the Midland, the Plaza, and the Pantages), and Muehlebach Field, where the minor league baseball champion Kansas City Blues held sway. (Segregation aside, the more talented local baseball team was the Kansas City Monarchs of the Negro League, with stars such as Wilber "Bullet Joe" Rogan and Dobie "Black Cat" Moore.) Kansas City's industries multiplied and diversified. Now, beyond the famed stockyards and packing houses and a continuing dominance as a regional grain market, the city developed as a communications leader, forged iron, milled flour, turned corn into sugar, refined and stored oil from the Southwest, assembled motorcars, and built plows and harvesters.

North of the city nearly seven hundred acres of cornfield had been remade into an airfield from which planes rose each morning and dropped off passengers each night in Hollywood or on Broadway.

Chicago suddenly was only four hours away!

At Union Station, meanwhile, 250 trains passed each day beneath the cathedral-like mass of marble and Bedford stone. One writer took in the scene at the train station and remarked on the merging of the disparate social castes: "In a waiting room a block long, farmers with coach tickets brush against millionaires with private cars." Suddenly, Kansas City ranked as the nation's number two railroad center, behind only Chicago.

Civic boosters proudly rattled off the city's nicknames, of which there was no shortage: Paris of the Plains, City of Fountains, the Most American City (its population only 6 percent foreign-born). Once a rugged Western town defined by cattle drives, gambling, and the appearances of the Clay County outlaw Jesse James, Kansas City still saw the wide-open frontier as central to its spirit.

That, and a good stiff drink. When Dr. Georges Valot, secretary of France's Bureau for the Study of the Liquor Problem, would come to America in the early 1930s, he would judge Kansas City, above Reno and New Orleans, as America's wettest town, comparable only, he said, to Juarez, Mexico. "I have seen the streets of Paris at their worst, or best, but they are nothing like Kansas City," Valot would say. "If you want to have a good time, go to Kansas City."

Famous Americans dropped in during the twenties, announcing themselves in curious ways. The novelist Sinclair Lewis, a disturber of the peace, spent six weeks in Kansas City in spring 1926 holed up downtown in an Ambassador Hotel suite, researching a "preacher novel" that became *Elmer Gantry*. During his visit, Lewis stood at the lectern of one local church and challenged God to strike him dead in fifteen minutes. He took off his watch and waited; he survived. In his hotel suite each Wednesday, Lewis held "Sunday school classes" over lunch for eighteen local clergy. They liked Lewis, and admired his zeal for his subject. The perpetual skeptic, he prodded them and probed deeply into theological issues, once asking, "What the hell right has the church to exist anyway?" At another turn, Lewis pointed a finger at a minister and challenged his belief in God; a Catholic priest calmed the novelist, saying, "Sit down, my son, and don't blaspheme." Lewis paused, and replied, "Will you have a drink, Father?" The priest said, "I will." The local clergy should have known what was coming. The fictional Elmer Gantry proved a scoundrel and hypocrite with a lust for power. He drank alcohol to excess, engaged in sex with church secretaries and congregants, and trampled choir girls in escaping a burning tabernacle. As *Gantry* hit the bestseller lists, a few Kansas City ministers shouted betrayal, though others rushed to Lewis's defense. Myrtle and Jack Bennett wouldn't have minded the furor—they no longer spent their Sundays in church; they were on the golf course. Sinclair Lewis, meanwhile, enjoyed Kansas City. "I've had huge and delightful reglimpses of the Midwest and Babbittry," he wrote to his wife. He told one local reporter, "It is a good booster town and I like it. As yet it has not become Europeanized; it still retains the American ideal which the Eastern cities have lost."

The following winter, another luminary of the twenties showed up, the famed flagpole sitter Alvin "Shipwreck" Kelly. Small and tightly muscled, with a sun-weathered face, forever the seaman high on a ship's mast, Kelly was nearly forty, a former navy sailor and Hollywood stunt actor, now a genuine faddist for hire. He sat on flagpoles for a living, the latest curious fad to sweep the country. In Kansas City, Shipwreck sat on an inverted motorcar brake drum high atop a flagpole fixed on the roof of the Westgate Hotel at Ninth and Main streets, more than 125 feet above downtown, for 6 days—or, to be precise, 146 consecutive hours. Crouched low, knees raised, deep in thought, he made a self-styled rendition of Rodin's *Thinker*. In the falling snow and rain, Shipwreck looked utterly ridiculous. He waved at times to tiny specks on the street below, and watched individuals with upturned heads collide with each other. Hundreds gathered. A thousand.

City to city, the reaction was always the same: "How's business?" came a shouted call. "Looking up!" Shipwreck deadpanned.

He was a spectacle, a human fly, an artifact of the age, a self-promoter of the highest caliber. He told newspapermen he had walked barefoot in Siberia, climbed the smokestack of the SS

Leviathan, fasted twenty-six days and nights atop flagpoles in five cities, fur-traded in Russia, handled more than one hundred thousand wounded or dead soldiers on European battlefields without contracting illness, manned the first American transport to run through the German submarine blockade, doubled as a stunt man for twenty-one Hollywood film stars, escaped seven severe diseases and epidemics, survived shipwrecks (ergo, his nickname), and could whip any man in the world, including heavyweight Jack Dempsey. And the newspapers wrote it up just like he said it. So it must have been true. Now there were flagpole sitters everywhere. Shipwreck traveled the country sitting on flagpoles, trolling for dough.

In Kansas City he earned $1,100 for his act, sponsored by Orbit chewing gum. He had perfected a way to make certain he never fell asleep. He placed his thumbs inside holes in the flagpole's shaft— about the same size as finger holes in a bowling ball. If he dozed and began to sway, the twinge of pain in his thumbs would awaken him, keeping him from a fatal mistake. Staring through the windows of Kansas City's office buildings, Shipwreck said he saw men in one room who looked high powered as they conferred in earnest. In another office he saw a bootlegger deliver four bottles to a man. Through another window he saw a young woman slap a man's face. Watching the entrance to a nearby cabaret one night, he saw five fights among patrons, and patrolmen raiding the place for illegal alcohol. He said he saw life in Kansas City as it was.

Tom (T.J.) Pendergast did not have the time or patience to look skyward at Shipwreck's silliness. He was too immersed in conducting the business of invisible government. Soon Pendergast would move into the two-story yellow brick storefront at 1908 Main Street. There, in his upstairs office, sitting behind his rolltop desk, a powerful man, bulbous and jowly, with a massive head seemingly cut from a quarry, he would rule as boss of the city's municipal machine. As lord of the so-called Goat faction of the Democratic Party, he was a mighty man in Kansas City, self-satisfied, and a good husband and father (or so his ward captains said). As a sign of his growing pros-

perity, he and his wife would move with their three children into a
newly built mansion in the Country Club District, choosing as an
interior motif the French gilt and glitter of the Louis XV period.

Pendergast's office at the Jackson County Democratic Club on
Main Street had the ambience of a fraternal lodge: spare, wooden,
with creaky floors and two photos, one of U.S. senator James A.
Reed of Missouri, oratorical star of the Pendergast machine, the
other of former president Woodrow Wilson. (The Reed-Wilson
match was odd given that they hated each other.) There was also a
painting of the Boss, Pendergast, and a framed cartoon from *The
Kansas City Star* showing his late brother, Jim, with a ballot box in
his hands.

Boss Pendergast moved through political shadows in Kansas
City. But three mornings a week, locals lined up outside his office in
the predawn hours for an opportunity to see him, if only for a few
moments. They waited in a line that extended from an anteroom,
down the stairs, and out to the sidewalk in front of the Southwest
Linen Company, and waited to be called by the Boss's secretary, an
old steamboat pilot named Captain Elijah Matheus. In these brief
meetings, the Boss's language, rough-hewn and ungrammatical, came
straight from his working-class origins in the West Bottoms; his sen-
tences often began "They was" or "I seen." Over the years, a steady
parade of mayors and senators, aldermen, down-and-outers, and
wives with deadbeat husbands arrived to see Pendergast. Much as in
the fictional Oz, where the Cowardly Lion and Tin Man go to the
Wizard to ask for courage and a heart, Kansas Citians went to
the Boss in search of patronage and hope. More often than not, he
delivered.

One day, sitting at his desk pushing papers, the Boss ripped into
a steak sandwich—two steaks, actually, no bone or fat, no salt or
pepper, dry as could be—and opened another letter from Senator
Reed in Washington, whom he had known for more than thirty years.
Reed sought a job for a local man named Cromwell, who had lost
employment after thirty-three years in the Waterworks Department.

"When we had the controversy with Longwell it was Mr. Cromwell who gave us the inside facts. I have never forgotten that service," Reed wrote. "He is old and must have some kind of employment." The Boss admired Reed, whom he had first launched as prosecutor in 1898, and then as Kansas City's mayor. He vowed privately to make Jim Reed the next president of the United States. "Please do what you can for Mr. Cromwell, and I know you will. Cordially Yours, Jas. A. Reed." Chomping on his sandwich, shreds of beef sticking between his teeth, the Boss put Mr. Cromwell on his to-do list.

Pendergast's enemies charged that he bought loyalty for elections with such dealings, but the Boss had a ready answer: "What's government for if it isn't to help people?"

Myrtle Bennett was a devout Democrat, and once worked in Texas for the local Democratic Committee. She never saw a Republican worthy of her vote. She had heard of T. J. Pendergast, of course—was there anyone in Jackson County who hadn't?—as well as the whispers of his illegal operations. But there had been a time in her own young life, in Arkansas, when a local man of political instinct, later elected judge, had rescued her and her mother, offering nothing more than kindness. That man was Abner McGehee, Jr., a Democrat. Myrtle understood Pendergast. There was nothing wrong with helping people in need.

But Pendergast's legions of critics called Kansas City "Tom's Town," and the statehouse, "Uncle Tom's Cabin." The Boss had placed his machine men in all the right political places: his man Reed in the U.S. Senate; his man Henry McElroy, under the reworked municipal government charter, as Kansas City's new city manager; his man Jim Page as Jackson County prosecutor; his man from Independence, Harry S. Truman, as a Jackson County administrative judge; plus enough Kansas City aldermen to keep his ward loyalists happy. The city's police force also answered to the Boss's touch. His organization profited from bawdy houses and liquor and gambling interests, bought votes, stuffed ballot boxes, and stole elections. For the Boss, it was all in a day's work. In such prosperous times, he wore felt hats and new three-piece suits with a gold watch dangling from the vest pockets. In Kansas City, T. J. Pendergast was above everything, and above nothing.

This was Jack and Myrtle's Kansas City in the twenties: liquor flowed. Ministers sparred. Trains rumbled. The Boss ruled. Swine squealed in bloody slaughterhouses. Bluesmen swung deep into the night. Civic boosters called out to tourists, "Come to Kansas City!"

In 1927, Jack and Myrtle found their way to the city's handsome new residential section known as the Country Club District. Developer J. C. Nichols's vision of upscale living had become a locus for Kansas City's well-to-do, with fine homes, elegant new apartment buildings, parks, fountains, babbling brooks, and a stylish shopping area of Spanish architecture known as The Plaza. Sinclair Lewis, for one, called it an "incomparable development."

When Jack Bennett bought into Park Manor, a four-story Italianate brick structure with red-tile roof at 902 Ward Parkway in the district, neither he nor Myrtle had ever lived anywhere so elegant. Their first-floor apartment had six rooms, polished wood floors, archways, two luxury bathrooms with built-in tubs and pedestal lavatories, a place for Murphy rollaway beds, and all the modern conveniences, including incinerators and mechanical Frigidaire refrigeration. The building's interior hallways and front foyer set a stylish tone with wrought-iron stairrails and ornate rope molding with gold lace. The basement, light and airy, had ample space for six lockers, a Kewanee steam heating plant, laundry tubs, and separate rooms that would serve as living quarters for the black help.

Out front, Brush Creek whispered its way through a park of cottonwoods, pines, and gnarled oaks along Ward Parkway.

"It gives you the comfort and convenience of apartment life, makes you an owner instead of a tenant and you acquire definite property value," a Park Manor advertisement explained. "Those buyers who have the courage to buy good property in the right location on today's low market will surely realize a great benefit in the future, for Kansas City will have a program of expansion and rapid growth in the next few years which will not be exceeded by any of her sister cities that compete with her now."

Jack Bennett put down $4,890, agreed to a monthly cooperative payment of $117.36, and began introducing himself to his new neighbors, the William Reids, the Stuart Boyntons, the James Mayalls, and up on the fourth floor, the Hofmans. His neighbors worked as managers for companies that sold telephones, clay products, life insurance, and automobile radios. He liked nearly everything about Park Manor; unfortunately, so did petty thieves and prowlers. When the neighborhood suffered a spate of break-ins and robberies, Jack reacted honorably. Typically he brought his .32 Colt automatic pistol on business trips; but now, when Myrtle accompanied him, he left the gun with her mother. Alice Adkins thanked him, hid it in her bedroom, and hoped never to use it.

Jack might've aspired to become a great man of business in Kansas City, the next Armour or Kemper. But he had his eyes on a bigger town, New York. Once there, he would advance up the Hudnut perfume company ladder and then, who knew? Maybe Paris?

For now, a Kansas City social climber, Jack joined the Chamber of Commerce, and the Indian Hills Country Club, where he golfed with friends and business associates, and sometimes played with Myrtle, dressed in her smart two-piece sport dress. Jack joined the downtown Kansas City Athletic Club, too, just the place to defuse a traveling salesman's tensions. The athletic club featured a gymnasium, handball courts, swimming pool, a cigar stand, card rooms, a barber shop, steam room and heat cabinet, and a Turkish bath department with salt rubs and oil rubs. On summer evenings, Jack and Myrtle took to the club's rooftop garden for supper and dancing. Together they stood at the open casement, serenaded by an orchestra, staring out at the twinkling lights of Kansas City.

When Jack drove off on another trip, Myrtle became, like her father in 1889, "so so lonsom so lonsom i can't hardley stand it." Jack was essential to her daily life. When he was gone, she worried about him, missed him. She spent days and nights alone, or with her mother, wondering where Jack was at that moment.

It created a housewife's lonely discontent. A survey in a Midwestern city found that 85 percent of housewives were, like Myrtle, unhappy. The writer Doris Blake chastised them: "They simply let themselves be clouded mentally by the fictitious glamour of work outside the home. That glamour, so far as the great percentage of working women is concerned, is just plain apple-sauce." But this was not Myrtle's problem. She had worked during the early years of her marriage and she had no desire to work again. Another story on the women's page of *The Kansas City Star* in autumn 1929 came closer to addressing Myrtle's problem: "We have the vote, we have all the liberty that it is possible to obtain, and yet, the great majority of the well-to-do young women of our time are restless, frantic almost in their search for self-expression."

For Myrtle, and for many American housewives, bridge increasingly filled that void, creating an outlet for their self-expression. The game exercised their intellect, and their emotions. The intensity of each hand, the ego of players, and the expectations between partners stirred their competitive impulses. Twice a week, Myrtle played with other women at club luncheons; she also arranged games at her apartment. She read about bridge in *The Blue Diamond*, the monthly newsletter from the Kansas City Athletic Club, and there were always new books on instruction, the most popular by New York experts such as Milton Work, Wilbur Whitehead, and Sidney Lenz.

Jack did not study bridge; no time for that. He played cards the way he conducted his business, with bravado and a glint in his eye. On the golf course and at parties, Jack showed his affection for Myrtle, freely and often, reaching for her hand or throwing his arm around her waist. It was his way, showy and physical, an alpha male establishing his territory. For her part, Myrtle gave up bridge at night when Jack was in town. She wanted to be home for him.

THREE

Ely's Grand Scheme

Every human being floats, so to speak, in an invisible sea of mental complexes—be they that of inferiority or superiority. An inferiority complex is like a delicate wound that never heals completely, and at the Bridge table, it is especially apt to be irritated because other social beings are present.

—ELY CULBERTSON
in *Contract Bridge Blue Book*

Ely was consumed by contract bridge. To refine his bidding system, he reconsidered the game's mathematical probabilities and created rules: "Whenever a hand contains a biddable suit (be it even a four-card minor) the suit and not the no-trump should be preferred." In the Culbertson System, a player would value high-card combinations in his hand as "honor tricks" (an ace was one honor trick, an ace-queen combination one and a half honor tricks, an ace-king two, etc.) and then bid according to established rules based on that number and the length of the suits. In his system, all opening bids would require at least two and a half honor tricks. Ely read the old guard's newest books (*How's Your Bridge?* by Sidney Lenz; *Contract Bridge: Bidding and the Club Convention* by Harold Vanderbilt). He had a keen sense of the inner rhythms of cards, and a fine-tuned radar for cheating. He had observed cheaters using secret signals: long puffs on a cigarette demanded a lead in spades, and two short puffs to suggest strength elsewhere. Ely saw hidden meanings in the way a cheating player held his cards, separating his fingers, and in the time that player took to make a play or bid. Even so, his gambler's bank account was virtually depleted, and now, with the birth of a son, Bruce, in spring 1929, he had to provide for a family with two small children. Jo urged him to write his bridge book, but Ely shook his head, tapped his gold cigarette case twice, removed a Melachrino, and, through its smoke, replied, "Not yet." He said no one would buy a book written by a bridge unknown. But he would spread his name by creating his own bridge magazine. Then he and Jo would win key tournaments. His bidding system would carry his name: The Culbertson System. He would use sex—suggestively—through terminology ("Approach-Forcing") and expressions ("Going to bed with the king," and "You've got strength but you haven't got length," and "Lay down, let's see what you've got"), and in the way he described the husband-wife bridge union, as if peeping through a bedroom keyhole. His attack would be multifaceted, and he would pursue it relentlessly. Like a pirate about to board a ship, Ely plotted his takeover of the bridge industry. It would happen. It was only a matter of how soon.

Two men came to see Ely in the summer of 1929. They wanted to profit from the surging interest in contract bridge by publishing a correspondence course on the game. They needed a writer and couldn't afford the sage royals Wilbur Whitehead or Milton Work, whose annual earnings from bridge lectures, writings, and teachings matched those of corporation executives. Publisher Lewis Copeland and Herbert DeBower, founder of the Alexander Hamilton Institute, came to Ely and Jo's apartment on East Sixty-third Street to see if Ely might be their man. But they offered Ely only a few hundred dollars plus a nominal royalty.

Sensing a bigger opportunity, Ely invited Copeland and DeBower to a follow-up lunch at the Ritz, where he dressed fashionably, laughed easily, smoked constantly, and, as was his custom, spoke to the waiters in French. Ely was selling himself with charm and élan. He impressed his listeners, who also came for dinner the following night at a summer home Ely and Jo had rented in Westhampton, not to be confused with the more glamorous hamlet that four years earlier had served as the basis for F. Scott Fitzgerald's West Egg in *The Great Gatsby*. There, Jay Gatsby lives and throws his grand parties, fifty yards from the Long Island Sound, between big houses that rent for $12,000 to $15,000 a season. The house Ely and Jo rented was an architectural eyesore, eminently available, that featured an overgrown garden with stucco monsters and gargoyles sitting, standing, and straining to fly. The bootlegger Jay Gatsby wouldn't have spent a minute in the place.

After dinner, as Jo tended to the children, Ely got down to business. What he wanted, he said, was not a correspondence course deal. He wanted financial backing on a grand scale.

He explained that interest in contract bridge was building across America and that, each day, thousands of players were leaving auction for contract. He wanted to ride the crest of this cultural wave. Women were the driving force, he said. Whereas hidebound men stuck with auction, women were more venturesome and open-minded toward the new game. But, Ely insisted, they were nonetheless coaxing and dragging their sneering, howling husbands to contract in unprecedented numbers. There was big money to be made.

Ely believed the game needed a standardized system of bidding so that it could be learned quickly. He had collected a thousand bridge "test hands" that reflected the experience of millions of players, and had classified them by suit length, freakish or balanced distributions, and honor-trick strength. He had developed his Approach-Forcing system. At the moment, he said, there were too many books—Whitehead, Work, Reith, Vanderbilt, Lenz— promoting systems too complicated for everyday players. But if one man with a system easily understood by social players across America could break through this noise . . .

Ely vowed to be that man.

He would outwork, outthink, and out-advertise all the other experts. Now, for his two listeners, he laid out his plans to build a bridge empire. First, he and Jo would capture the American Bridge League championship and the prized Vanderbilt Cup, emblematic of national team-of-four supremacy. In so doing, he would build credibility for the Culbertson name. He would also create a nationwide network of instructors teaching the Culbertson System. His planned October launch of *The Bridge World* magazine would allow him to spread the Culbertson brand. With his trophies, monthly magazine, and network of teachers, his mastery of contract bridge would be inarguable. Then, and only then, would he write his bridge book. It would sell hundreds of thousands of copies, and he would leverage those sales in columns in newspapers and national magazines, on the lecture circuit, and on radio. He might even put his name on a brand of bridge supplies.

Ely proposed the formation of a partnership: 51 percent for him and Jo, and 49 percent divided between Copeland and DeBower. This partnership would share in the revenues generated by a newly created "public idol"—a witty, charming man with the pedigreed manners of the royal court, a man whom millions of American housewives and bridge enthusiasts would admire as their teacher and mentor—the tuxedoed, spotlessly manicured Ely Culbertson.

To the two men on the Culbertsons' davenport that night, the question was not whether this idea was presumptuous or preposterous—it was both—but rather, was Ely Culbertson serious?

As evidence of his sincerity, Ely produced a memorandum emphasizing the importance of publicity, propaganda, and advertising. Nations and churches had taken shape through the manipulation of the masses, he explained. He would do the same—first with women. He would make three basic appeals: to the ego, to fear, and to sex. He would show how, at the bridge table, women and men would be on an equal intellectual footing. He would use fear to suggest that women who did not play bridge would be left behind in their own communities, uninvited to luncheons, afternoon teas, and dinner parties. He would use the sex angle by promoting husband and wives playing as partners. He would heartily recommend bigger spats and arguments between husbands and wives at the bridge table as a way to defuse the petty inhibitions and tensions of daily married life.

In projecting on the screen of *the mass mind*, he said he would fictionalize himself. Ely the Celebrity, an artificial creation, would be tough, cocky, comically conceited, sophisticated, if eccentric—very much like the man sitting before them now. He would project himself as flawed, because flaws made a man seem more authentic. He would glorify his brilliant coups at the bridge table but also publicize and magnify his mistakes, which would humanize him and double his publicity. His public character would be projected through newspapers, radio, motion pictures, and word of mouth. Ely said he understood the mass mind from having watched revolutionary crowds in Russia, and from studying the master orators who had held those crowds spellbound.

Copeland and DeBower asked about the practical issues of his plan.

Wait, Ely said, there was more.

A second character would be required, he said. That would be Jo. Her character traits would also be fictionalized. More than merely the greatest woman bridge player, Jo would become, Ely said, *my favorite partner*. Yes, he said with cunning, women would love that: a husband who saw his wife as his intellectual equal, or his superior. Jo would be projected as calm, steady, a lover of peace, the perfect foil for Ely—and she would be pitched as a better bridge player than Ely, too. Ely and Josephine Culbertson would become the First Couple of American Bridge, a husband-and-wife team in complete harmony.

No, gentlemen, Ely said, he would not write a bridge correspondence course. But when the moment was right—not now—he would write his bridge book. In fact, he would write several books. The first would be the *Contract Bridge Blue Book*, a title with an impressive official sound. (And a familiar sound, though Ely's listeners no doubt were unaware that in 1906, still the age of bridge-whist, Paul F. Mottelay had written *The Bridge Blue Book*.) This book, Ely said, would be followed by the *Red Book* and the *Gold Book*. Then he would produce summary handbooks for each that could be carried easily in a woman's purse or a gentleman's pocket. (The idea of pocket books for games was a familiar one, too: in 1802, an adaptation of Hoyle appeared under the title *The New Pocket Hoyle*, and was frequently reprinted.) In these six books, Ely would strategize on bidding and play.

In a nation of 120 million, there were perhaps only 20 public idols. Ely admitted that no one had heard of the Culbertsons. But soon, if all went according to plan, the Culbertson name would be on the lips of millions of bridge lovers.

The two men asked Ely how much money he needed.

Ely said he would need to rent an office for his magazine. There was also his teachers' organization, and the need to promote his personal appearances.

Fifty thousand dollars, he said.

Silence filled the room.

Or, Ely said, $25,000.

Silence.

Or perhaps $15,000. His inevitable success, he said, would simply take longer to materialize.

DeBower and Copeland wished him well and left to find another bridge writer on the cheap. They laughed at him then, but less than three years later, Ely and Jo Culbertson were millionaires, the First Family of a full-blown American bridge craze, and it had happened nearly as Ely had plotted it.

Late in September 1929, Ely was a bridge magazine editor at long last. *The Bridge World*, his creation, would list on its masthead a business department, an editorial department, a circulation department, an executive office, and the headquarters of the Culbertson National Bridge Studios. This sounded impressive, except all of it was crammed into a dingy three-room office with tattered furnishings at 45 West Forty-fifth Street. The "staff" amounted to two frazzled young women unsure if their next paycheck was coming. Ely played

the Knickerbocker and other clubs on weekends, and when his winnings surged his magazine staff got paid, sometimes with raises.
When the cards did not fall, no one got paid.

In a stroke of fortunate timing, *The Auction Bridge Magazine*
founded by Work and Whitehead fell into bankruptcy earlier that
month, clearing the field for *The Bridge World*. Ely would claim a
first printing of twenty thousand, though more likely it was considerably less than that. He dedicated his magazine to the elites and near
elites, "a relatively small community of Bridge players equal to a fair
sized city," a readership that would influence the social bridge
masses. His first issue, nearly completed, spread across forty-eight
pages and was every bit as elegant as its editor, especially the cover,
with a medallion that bore an eighteenth-century male image and the
name of Edmond Hoyle (though no true portrait of Hoyle was
known to exist). Inside, above the table of contents, the masthead
read, "THE BRIDGE WORLD, Ely Culbertson, Editor." Articles by Lenz
and Whitehead (a reprint, "Reading Concealed Hands") helped
establish the magazine's credibility. There was a cartoon by H. T.
Webster of *The New York World*, a diagrammed Bridge Hand of the
Month, reviews of the latest books, and a column titled "Pro Et Con-
tra," ostensibly edited by Jo. There was a full-page sketch of Jo, looking askance, above the fray, and quoted as saying, "Contract today is
in swaddling clothes." There was the gratuitous condolence extended
to the defunct *Auction Bridge Magazine*, and Ely's even more gratuitous rave of Harold Vanderbilt's new book for its "vigorous thinking
of a high intellectual order." (Ely craved the support of Vanderbilt,
who had conceived the modern game.) *The Bridge World* masthead
listed foreign editors, A. E. Manning-Foster, in London; Pierre Bel-
langer, in Paris; and Guido Branca, in Rome; plus eleven contributing
editors, including Jo, Lenz, Whitehead, Lightner, and the Baron von
Zedtwitz. Bridge teacher Madeleine Kerwin lit a fire with a controversial article about the arrogance of men who refused to accord
some women their rightful position among elites. "From the heights
of his masculine egotism the average man Bridge player refers with a
pitying smile to 'women players' and 'women's afternoon Bridge

game,'" Kerwin wrote. "Any woman teacher knows of the difficulties in giving instruction to men. They cannot submit to a woman's judgment and they will obstinately persist in a bad system of bidding, or in out-of-date leads even when paying for correction. . . . Intelligent women players accept constructive criticism and are pathetically eager to perfect their game. They do not attempt to dominate every situation and they consider their partner's judgment both in bidding and play."

That fall, the New York Whist Club won the Vanderbilt Cup for Teams-of-Four, with Ely and Jo (plus Lightner and von Zedtwitz) finishing a disappointing third. A week later at the American Bridge League championships at the Drake Hotel in Chicago, Ely and P. Hal Sims won the Men's Auction Pair title, while Jo and Olga Hilliard partnered to win the women's competition. Some of the elites did not show at Chicago, though. Sidney Lenz, feeling the ill effects of arthritis, remained at home. Whitey was detained in Manhattan on business. Milton Work didn't attend, either. Then again, Work rarely risked his whist reputation in bridge tournaments. In Chicago, Ely's contract team-of-four again failed to win, though he took solace in the increased press coverage of the ABL event. The Hearst Newspaper Syndicate sponsored a radio broadcast of one contract hand between the winners and runners-up in the team-of-four competition: the Knickerbocker Whist Club (Sims, Liggett, Reith, and Derrick Wernher) versus the Chicago Auction Bridge Club.

His tournament victories would come (and soon), and *The Bridge World* would record every aspect of Culbertson's genius. In his inaugural issue, Ely emphasized that his magazine would work only for the greater good of contract bridge:

> THE BRIDGE WORLD will fill, we confidently believe, an important place in the American home. As the only magazine devoted to Bridge, the favorite intellectual recreation of the majority in all walks of life, it will afford a medium for the exchange of free thought on subjects of common interest to Bridge players, and a place where the news of

the Bridge world and its fascinating doings has been especially gathered for the information of the lover of the game.

As is well known, the Editor of THE BRIDGE
WORLD has certain well defined views on questions of
bidding and play. This does not mean that those holding
opposite views will be excluded from the presentation of
them in the magazine.

Quite the contrary is true. It is in the crucible of conflict that truth is proven.

He knew how to manipulate people, ideas, and situations. From
the beginning, Jo had it right. Ely played people better than cards. It
was an unteachable skill shaped either by a sixth sense or a gambler's
instincts. He could change his personality to fit the setting. At home,
he treated Jo in much the way Jack treated Myrtle, as a utilitarian
accessory who, characteristic of the age, was expected to sublimate
her own desires to those of her husband. Dark, truculent, and imperious at the office, where he drove his workers as hard as he drove himself, Ely walked into a lecture hall and became, suddenly, incandescent.
In lectures he was witty, urbane, and considerate, a personality unrec-
ognizable to his magazine staffers. How he transformed himself in
this way they did not know. But it worked so well they wondered:
Who is he, really?

Like his magazine, Ely was colorful, gossipy, and intellectual. He
mocked other bridge experts, even some who served as his contributing editors. He built his reputation in part by tearing down the reputations of others. He barely hid his self-promotion. In a single
forty-eight-page issue of *The Bridge World*, the self-absorbed Culbertson had his name appear 164 times.

No bridge development or anecdote went unnoticed by the new
editor. In New York, a doctor sued for separation from his wife,
charging she had violently slapped him during a bridge game. "Marion, behave yourself," the doctor said after being slapped, and the
game, though strained, continued. In December 1928, a similar story

out of Chicago had hit the national wires: Mrs. Ruth Kelso Wood had doubled a four-diamond bid. When her opponent took ten tricks and fulfilled his contract, Mrs. Wood's husband, Gerald, playing as her partner, erupted in a rage. He struck her in the face. A few months later it happened again, this time in a progressive bridge game, with rotating partners, the Woods suddenly a partnership again: Mrs. Wood trumped her husband's ace, a fumble on her part, but Gerald Wood didn't wait for her explanation. He stood and, in a familiar rage, struck her in the face. The couple separated, and then, after a cooling-off period, reconciled. They agreed never to play again as bridge partners, until, at a friend's home, the host pulled out a bridge table. Partners again, the Woods saw a new disaster bring the same result: He struck her again. Mrs. Wood sued for a divorce, which was granted by Judge William N. Gemmill. The judge, a bridge player himself, seemed confused as to why the wife had trumped her husband's ace. "How did you come to do that?" the judge asked. Her attorney interceded: "Your honor, it is permissible to trump an ace." From the bench, the judge nodded, and said, "More married couples should hear your story. If husbands and wives didn't play partners in bridge maybe there would be fewer failures in matrimonial partnerships. I'm hearing too much lately about spouses who failed to recognize an indicative bid."

Most readers undoubtedly laughed. Not Ely. Marital spats at the bridge table gave life to his sales pitch. They dramatized the game, carried it from the sepia-tone age of auction into the louder, more sensational modern age. These marital spats made real the battle of the sexes. They made headlines. They got people talking. And Ely would use them to his advantage.

FOUR

Four Spades She Bid

I

Early on a Sunday morning, September 29, 1929, a familiar knock at the Bennetts' front door: Charles Hofman, their fourth-floor neighbor, a portly, practical man, had arrived at the appointed hour, dressed for the links. Well rested from vacation, Hofman had come for Jack. Together they drove to the Indian Hills golf course, exemplars of the modern Kansas City gentry. They left their wives and spent the next four hours on the rolling green space of Mission Hills, Kansas. They knew many of their fellow club members, chatted and slapped backs with them in the clubhouse, gathered two boy caddies and two friends, and played a leisurely round.

They returned to the Bennetts' apartment in early afternoon famished. Their wives whipped up supper. Mayme Hofman, just twenty-eight, a decade younger than her husband, was among Myrtle's closest friends, and a part of her regular bridge circle. No one would mistake Mayme Hofman for middle class. On a night out she put on her airs and her big-city look, swaddled in mink or ermine, with long evening gloves, each piece of her ensemble well considered. Finishing supper now, Myrtle and Mayme said they wanted to golf, too. The couples had played the day before, a happy affair on a brisk afternoon that ended with Jack strutting off the course with his arm around Myrtle. The husbands needed little convincing to play again, and the timing was right: club rules allowed women to play only late in the day.

And so at midafternoon they drove back to Indian Hills, soaking in the last of an autumn Sunday. Myrtle looked smashing in her two-piece gray woolen sport suit with vest and skirt. Jack, in a clean, classic look, wore slacks and a long-sleeve white polo shirt. The Bennetts and Hofmans played twelve holes before dusk intervened. At the finish Jack phoned his aunt Nellie to beg off their scheduled dinner. He and Myrtle would spend the evening with the Hofmans. The four shared a round of drinks. On a cool night, alcohol warmed their spirits, and once back at the Bennett apartment, their spirits would get warmer still.

Since the Hofmans had given their maid the night off, Myrtle invited Mayme and Charles to join her and Jack for icebox leftovers. The couples made sandwiches, and as the wives cleared the dishes, the husbands took to the living room.

Myrtle and Mayme joined them, while Alice Adkins sat on the davenport sewing. The girls suggested a night out, a moving picture perhaps. But thirty holes of golf had left their husbands fatigued. They didn't want to shower and change; too much bother. Besides, it had started to rain, and Jack planned to rise early for a two-day business trip to St. Joseph and Atchison. *Yes, yes,* Jack reassured Myrtle, he would be back in time for the Tuesday night party they would host at the athletic club. But then he would leave again, for ten days out west, riding in his Hupp, selling the sensual smells of Paris. Myrtle planned to take advantage of his absence by redecorating their apartment.

The night was fast getting away from the couples. Sitting in the living room, they discussed the latest dispatches in *The Kansas City Star*. It seemed the girls at Wellesley were abandoning their short bobs, with more than half wearing their tresses long again. Kansas City's police chief insisted that at no time since Prohibition began, in 1920, had the city been freer from bootleg joints and commercial gambling than now—(Ha! Not that the Bennetts or Hofmans believed any of that.) The former senator Jim Reed had addressed the state bar, colorfully, as always. In New York, the stock market quaked: sensational fluctuations, selling flurries causing hundreds of millions of dollars in value to disappear. Jack watched his stocks quiver. Even the usual bedrock, the so-called Morgan stocks (United States Steel common, Johns-Manville, New York Central), revealed startling weakness. The decline of radio stocks worried Charles Hofman, a sales representative for six concerns, automobile radios among them. The industry buzz centered on the soon-to-be released "Roamio" automobile radio from Crosley and the Galvin Corporation's "Motorola" model 5T71. Optimists on Wall Street urged calm. October 1929, they said, would be much better for the stock market.

Myrtle suggested a game of contract bridge. Sometime after 9:30 P.M., Jack brought out the square fold-up card table. They would play Vanderbilt's game at one tenth of a cent per point. Still wearing their golf clothes, and teamed as couples, it was the Bennetts versus the Hofmans. Myrtle sat directly across from Jack, and Mayme faced her husband. Jack, with his cavalier approach to bridge, looked at Mayme, an inviting smile in his eyes. Alice Adkins watched the game with sleepy eyes from the davenport.

Soon, the Bennett apartment would become the most widely discussed living quarters in Kansas City. Its interior layout, the dimensions of each room, its pricey accoutrements, would be fodder for conversation all over town. A diagram used as a courtroom exhibit would feature childlike scribbling with arrows and dotted lines to denote the movements of Myrtle and Charles Hofman beside boldly drawn identifications: MOTHER'S CHAMBER and MR. AND MRS. BENNETT'S BED ROOM. The diagram made the apartment seem small and misshapen, though one attorney would all but announce that the Bennett place was as big as a prairie.

The fold-up bridge table sat in the center of a living room that measured eleven by eighteen feet, and only a few strides from the arched front door. The table was surrounded by four armchairs, and two small side tables. Near it, an overstuffed davenport was pushed against the front wall. Across the way, a table.

The second bedroom, for Myrtle's mother, was at the far end of the apartment, farthest from the bridge table. To get there, one passed through another archway, down a hall, past the dining room and kitchen: roughly forty-five feet from the bridge table.

Behind the living room was an enclosed porch, perfect on late summer nights, and a few feet away, a door led to a master bedroom that measured fifteen by eleven feet. Next to Jack's dresser was a small master bathroom, eight by five, offset one on either side by two doors. The far door led to a small den with a desk and chair.

Atop Jack's dresser stood two photographs in frames: Jack dressed for the evening, in a felt hat with a black band, bow tie, and overcoat, his expression suggesting self-assurance; and Myrtle, her hair bobbed, eyes almond-shaped and alive, wearing lipstick and a fur collar, her expression intense.

Bridge was the day's rage all across Kansas City. Card parties were held at country clubs, at the Ladies' Altar Society of St. Peter's Catholic Church, and at Lodge No. 26 of the Benevolent and Protective Order of Elks. The Kansas City Athletic Club's newsletter reported, "The club is proud of the way its members are showing their interest in the bridge lessons, and it congratulates itself on the choice of a teacher. Mrs. Ann Wesson, who is teaching the classes, is an expert player as well as a splendid teacher. Not a person who started with the class has dropped out. This speaks wonders for the teacher and for the interest she has developed among her 'pupils.'" In *The Kansas City Star*, bridge games illuminated the week's social calendar: "**Monday:** Mrs. William Henry McLaughlin, bridge tea. **Tuesday:** Bridge luncheon at the Kansas City Country Club. **Wednesday:** Miss M. B. McDonald, bridge tea; Women of Meadow Lake Country Club, luncheon and bridge party. **Friday:** Miss Margaret Burke, bridge supper. **Saturday:** Wood Hill Country Club, dinner bridge; Mrs. Ralph Christie, bridge luncheon; Mrs. Karl Koerner, bridge luncheon."

The Bennetts' living room blazed with light, floor lamps brightly illuminated, additional light thrown in from the bedroom, the bathroom, through the hall archway. The light danced on Myrtle's diamond wedding ring and her gold necklace.

Outside, a cool breeze blew through the cottonwoods and gnarled oaks along Brush Creek. At the card table, the bidding began, time passed quickly. Done with her needlework, Alice Adkins turned in for the night.

II

In the mid-1920s, Jack Bennett, with his can-do spirit, blew into the towns of his western territory, his roadster at high roar. He carried sample cases of the Richard Hudnut company's elegant perfumes. To St. Joseph and Atchison, Joplin and Hot Springs, he brought the mystique of Gay Paree, and its illusive *odeurs*. To Main Streets in Hannibal, Topeka, and Springfield, he brought perfumes fashioned as the four "loveliest of feminine moods"—Romance, Gaiety, Sophistication and Adventure—each in a colored flacon suggestive of a mood *particulière*. His arrival in smaller towns produced a mixture of curiosity and awe. He was a well-heeled, big-city man with stories about his far-flung travels, like an explorer arrived from a distant land. He came in a fine suit, New York–bought, his white shirt stiffly starched, handkerchief folded neatly in his lapel pocket, his wavy light brown hair slicked down beneath a stylish felt hat, its brim turned up slightly. Just in case, he typically kept his .32 Colt automatic pistol in his car's glove box. With perfumes and suggestions of money, he drew the attention of women along the way.

No mere peddler, he was an essential cog in the wheel of modern American business, the commercial traveler. He sold directly to store managers. He studied his target sales numbers, and nearly always exceeded them. His view of himself was neatly encapsulated by Sinclair Lewis's fictional real estate man George Babbitt, who in a civic speech says, "Here's the new generation of Americans: fellows with hair on their chests and smiles in their eyes and adding machines in their offices. We're not doing any boasting, but we like ourselves first-rate, and if you don't like us, look out—better get under cover before the cyclone hits town!"

Jack Bennett was such a cyclone. He closed deals, winked at

salesladies, filed reports to the home office in New York, and blew off for the next town. He carried loose-leaf binders, advertising circulars, and expense account reports. He embraced the modern principles of scientific salesmanship and efficient management. He trained new salesmen, showing them the tricks of the trade, and pushing them hard, because their success was *his* success.

He counted Kansas City as part of his territory. But Jack's hard-sell manner did not work at the downtown National Bella Hess Company. General manager E. L. Olrich refused to purchase Hudnut perfumes because Jack insisted they be sold at prices Olrich thought inflated. More than once, Jack left in a huff, after slamming his brief-case shut on the general manager's desk.

To make amends, Jack often invited Olrich to lunch. Once, they played golf at Indian Hills. There, he intended to build a relationship that might open Bella Hess's doors to his perfumes. But at the thir-teenth hole, Jack's sweet talk ended. He drove two balls into a lake, and in anger heaved his golf bag, clubs and all, over a fence. He stalked off to the clubhouse, alone.

Olrich had witnessed tantrums on a golf course before, but never anything approaching this. He retrieved Jack's bag and carried it, and his own, to the clubhouse in what he considered an act of friendship. It was only later that Olrich decided Jack Bennett had *expected* him to fetch the bag.

In *Death of a Salesman,* playwright Arthur Miller writes of traveling men who "lived like artists, like actors whose product is first of all themselves, forever imagining triumphs in a world that either ignores them or denies them altogether." Miller's salesman, Willy Loman, is "way out there in the blue, riding on a smile and a shoeshine."

Jack Bennett would be neither ignored nor denied. His employer, Richard Hudnut, Inc., was a success story nearly half a century old. In 1880, in a small drugstore at the corner of Broadway and Ann Street in New York City, Alexander Hudnut established the nation's first beauty salon. His son Richard, fresh from Princeton University, noticed the more fashionable women buying the few simple facial preparations the store offered. He developed the concept of compounding toilet preparations, and sailed to Paris to learn more about it. A half century later, living in retirement in a French château near Nice, Hudnut watched as the cosmetics industry blossomed in ways he could not have imagined as a young man. Elsie McCormick, women's page columnist of the *St. Louis Post-Dispatch*, noting the cosmetics industry's rapid expansion during the late twenties, wrote, "Many a woman has looked at the long array of bottles on her dresser and wished that she was back in the Middle Ages again. All a lady did then for her complexion was to wash it in dew on May Day every year . . . The cold cream era was followed by an age of specialization. The face was suddenly divided into as many areas as the Western front, with special preparations for each sector."

In its advertisements, the Hudnut company evoked a Paris of silver, crystal, and lace, and tantalizing fragrances. One ad showed Hudnut's new salon at 20 Rue de la Paix in Paris, a baroque setting with chandeliers, mirrors, elaborate ornamentation, and "an almost fairy-like loveliness." About its face powder Poudre le Debut, Hudnut proclaimed, "The moment you take the cover off the box (it is one of the most strikingly modern boxes you've ever seen on a dressing table), you'll know its subtle fragrance could be nothing but Parisian." Hudnut sold face powders of Pearl, Pearl With Glow, Naturelle, and Sun-Tint, and lipstick in "gay little *compactes*, topped with genuine cloisonné enamel, that come in the four colors of the mode—blue, black, jade green, ivory white—and are as valuable to the ensemble as a bit of costume jewelry."

By the late twenties, advertising in America had reached a zenith, with $1.5 billion spent in 1927 alone. Near the top of the profession was Bruce Barton of the New York advertising agency Batten, Barton, Durstine and Osborne. Facile with words, Barton brought General Electric to familiarity, writing the first ad that carried GE's logo, two letters within a curlicue circle—"The initials of a friend." In 1926, Barton's award-winning GE advertisement in *The Saturday Evening Post* called out to housewives, "Any woman who does anything which a little electric motor can do is working for three cents an hour." In his 1925 bestseller, *The Man Nobody Knows*, Barton went so far as to portray Jesus Christ as a manly businessman who "picked up twelve men from the bottom ranks of business and forged them into an organization that conquered the world." Barton's astonishing success occasionally put him on the defensive about advertising. He would liken admen to surgeons, teachers, architects, and ministers, since all were *called* to their high-minded professions. Barton said, "We build of imperishable materials, we who work with words." To make his point, he emphasized that the words of the Gettysburg Address would last long after the Lincoln Memorial had crumbled.

Even as Jack Bennett blazed his Roadster through the back roads of Missouri, Kansas, Arkansas, and Oklahoma during times of high prosperity, his profession was becoming anachronistic. Advertising was altering the business paradigm. It reduced the need for face-to-face selling and, with it, the importance of the commercial traveler. Sears and Montgomery Ward sold by mail order, eradicating the need for middlemen. In his study of traveling salesmen in American culture, *100 Years on the Road*, Timothy B. Spears noted that such "drummers" became a part of an irretrievable past: "As influential factors in the creation of consumer desire, their glory days were over."

Jack was too busy making fistfuls of money to worry about the future. That wasn't his nature. Besides, he was an optimist. Neither did he worry about the sorry reputation of traveling salesmen. When Henry James returned to America in 1904 after an absence of two decades, he bemoaned how traveling salesmen "loomed" in dining cars and hotels with their "primal rawness of speech" and "air of commercial truculence." James pitied them as "victims and martyrs, creatures touchingly, tragically doomed." Such salesmen were famous for their loud suits, smutty jokes, and sexual indiscretions. The humor magazine *Captain Billy's Whiz Bang*, in 1921 published "A Drummer's Prayer," in which the supplicant asked God to "curb our tendency to flirt with the married women; the single ones don't count, and they expect it."

Myrtle understood the essential loneliness of the commercial traveler's existence—alone in motel rooms, in a different town each night. She knew the design of Jack's life on the road. After all, she had seen it firsthand during their many trips together. She knew Jack worked hard, and often late at night. She knew some of his salesmen, and liked them.

But she also knew Jack. She noticed the way young women looked at him, and the way he looked at them. He had his charms, as all great salesmen did. Jack also had a short fuse, even with Myrtle, *especially with Myrtle*, who had a short fuse of her own.

Every time she opened their bedroom closet, Myrtle saw and smelled the Hudnut perfumes. In each colored flacon she saw Jack. In each of those seductive Hudnut ads she heard Jack's voice: "Today, romance may beckon. Tomorrow, adventure. The afternoon may bring a blithe mood of gaiety and evening find you, indeed, *la belle femme sophisticate*."

It was all about sex. That's what Hudnut sold. That's what Jack sold.

Inevitably, when Jack was on the road, Myrtle wondered if he slept alone.

Living in the basement, the maids at Park Manor gathered during off-hours by the lockers and laundry tubs to swap stories about their employers. Naughty gossip is what it was, mocking the Boss Man and his wily wife. The maids whispered about intimate scenes, loud arguments, secrets they knew. They laughed about the curious ways of their white employers in the fancy apartments. But the Bennetts' maid had an admission to make: Myrtle and Jack were genuine lovebirds. "They coo and bill around," she said, "like a couple of doves."

But the maid had not seen a lover's letters to Jack.

Soon after their 1925 arrival in Kansas City, even before the move to Park Manor, a deep fissure had formed in Myrtle and Jack's marriage. In a moment unseen by their maid, Myrtle discovered letters in the pockets of Jack's trousers. In the letters a woman in St. Joseph, fifty-five miles upriver from Kansas City, professed her devotion to Jack, and luxuriated in the affections they had shared.

It was happening all over America. A 1928 survey revealed that one quarter of married American men and women had engaged in at least one affair. Sex became a national topic of conversation, and a release, physically and intellectually, from the war years and the Victorians. Hollywood censors limited an on-screen kiss to seven seconds, and ministers across the nation decried the crumbling social mores as the devil's advance. In 1927, two million rubber condoms were used daily, with a failure rate of 50 percent. To please their lovers, some young flappers shaved their pubic hair in the shape of a heart or a derby hat, the emblem of Democrat Al Smith. Dorothy Dix, the noted advice columnist, worried about these modern young women who thought nothing at all "of kissing every Tom, Dick and Harry who comes along and in indulging in petting parties and 'necking.'" Advertisers shaped their pitches seductively ("CAMAY: For the fresh *natural* skin men admire"), and newspapers, too. Silas Bent, assessing the salesmanship and showmanship of American newspapers during the late twenties, wrote, "Psychologists assert that sex should occupy the centre of attention only during adolescence. If that is so, the preoccupation of the American newspaper with this topic accounts in part for a sort of perpetual adolescence found characteristic of its readers."

The discovery of the St. Joseph letters added to the despair Myrtle was feeling over two miscarriages, the second in 1926. Jack consoled her in his way, but his expensive gifts could not brighten her darkness. Their friend attorney J. Francis O'Sullivan sensed Myrtle's melancholy. He had seen Myrtle rise from a dinner table, walk across the room, and sit alone, dabbing a handkerchief to her eyes.

Myrtle told friends she was losing her husband. He lusted for the prestige and attention that came with money, she said, and she knew his pursuit of wealth would put him in the company of women who would find him irresistible—as she once had.

Now each time Myrtle heard Jack's Roadster drive off, even if only for a game of golf at Indian Hills (he said) or for a smoke at the athletic club (he said), she wondered: Was Jack about to cheat on her again?

III

Charles Hofman caught Mayme's eye. From across the table, he read Mayme's stern expression: *This is not good. What do we do?* A fine day together had been a fine evening together, at least when Myrtle and Jack were ahead on points. But now the cards turned, with the Hofmans pulling in front. The ill winds of marital strife blew north and south. With digs and icy stares, Myrtle and Jack had taken to sniping at each other.

At bridge, Myrtle was tough and competitive—and Jack's superior. Everyone knew that, except Jack.

Jack was Jack, an alpha male. He won on his own terms. He answered only to New York, not to his wife. Then again, Myrtle did not cower, especially at the bridge table. Their problem was communication, subtle misreads. The Bennetts were not synchronized. They did not *listen* to their partner's bids. In the center of Myrtle and Jack's bridge partnership was a hole of uncertainty and mistrust. Myrtle felt alone in the partnership, as if, at the table, the game was three against one. And in her stinging criticisms of his play, Jack heard a wife's insubordination.

For much of this night, Myrtle had seemed like a jack-in-the-box, popping up from the table each time she'd laid down her hand as dummy. As Jack played for the partnership, Myrtle held her breath, hoped for the best, and disappeared into the kitchen to prepare his breakfast, still six hours away. She filled a percolator with coffee and water. On the skillet she laid strips of bacon. From their bedroom closet she removed Jack's business clothes. She would rise early, too, to see him off. She was dutiful that way, a helpmate, the wife Jack wanted.

In the best case, every hand in bridge is a new moment. Nothing else exists: no past, no future, and no emotion. Strategic breakdowns and miscommunications between partners sometimes lead to feelings of resentment, or worse. Then the largest question rises over the partnership like an evil moon: "Who is in charge?"

♣   ♣   ♣

Now, in the Bennett living room, the bidding began on the ultimate hand.

Jack opened: "One spade."

Charles studied his cards: "Two diamonds."

Myrtle didn't waver, going straight for game and the bonus for winning the rubber: "Four spades."

Mayme: "Pass."

Jack, confident the hand was his to play (and win): "Pass."

Charles liked his holdings. Thinking penalty points, he turned the screws on his friend: "Double."

Jack played the hand, needing ten tricks to make a four-spades contract. He did not succeed. He came up two tricks short. Myrtle unloaded on him. Jack replied that she had no reason to raise his bid. Myrtle said, "I laid down a beautiful hand, we had the cards." Jealousy and alcohol and competition tore at the seams of a marriage coming apart, stitch by stitch.

Charles heard Myrtle call Jack "a bum bridge player," and Jack's reply that maybe he wasn't the only one. Charles thought it uncalled for, all of it. It was only bridge; what the hell did it matter? And where was this argument heading, anyway?

Jack stood, leaned across the table, and grabbed Myrtle's wrist, twisting it slightly. He slapped her face, hard, several times. The table nearly toppled. Charles grabbed a metal leg, steadying the table.

A moment passed. Stunned silence. Jack loomed over Myrtle, still seated in her chair.

Charles Hofman looked at Myrtle, at Jack, at Mayme. Myrtle's face was contorted, white with rage: "No man will strike me," she said. She asked the Hofmans to excuse themselves so that she and Jack could resolve their dispute. But her determination faded in seconds. Moving to the davenport, holding a hand to her cheek, she broke into a sob. Mayme sat beside her and embraced her. Jack folded the card table, slammed it against a wall, and announced, "I'm leaving." Charles heard him mention St. Joseph, a motel for the night. Myrtle, rising up, said, "Then go."

Jack walked away, to a living room closet, and removed a small traveling bag. Charles joined the wives on the davenport, Myrtle sandwiched between him and Mayme. He heard Myrtle say, "Only a cur would strike a woman in front of guests." Jack stomped between rooms, jeering at her from a distance, their argument recurring.

Charles Hofman's passing thought: *Has Jack gone mad?*

From the living room to the bedroom and back, Jack smiled malevolently, belittling Myrtle. Mayme wrapped Myrtle in her arms and gave Charles a look. He understood its meaning: the diplomat's role was now his. Charles approached Jack and told him, gently, that slapping Myrtle was wrong and that he should apologize.

Jack snapped at him. "Let her alone," he said. "Myrtle has these brainstorms."

Charles tried again: "But . . . "

"The hell with you, leave me alone," Jack snapped. "We'll settle our own difficulties." Then he said to the Hofmans, "Maybe you'd better go upstairs."

And Myrtle, between sobs, agreed: "Yes, I guess we had better call it an evening."

Jack told Myrtle to get his pistol. If the petty thieves and prowlers vandalizing the neighborhood came while he was gone, Myrtle and her mother were on their own. Jack would take his .32 Colt automatic to St. Joe.

As peacemakers, the Hofmans made no headway. Mayme said to her husband, "Let's get our wraps."

Myrtle went up to Jack, at the living room closet, her manner conciliatory.

Mayme retrieved her coat from the bedroom, leaving her husband's cap on the bed. She walked to the front door of the apartment.

As Jack reentered the master bedroom, Charles tried to play peacemaker once more, throwing his arm around Jack's shoulder, walking with him around the bed, past an ornately framed photo of Myrtle as a young girl, on a settee, her chestnut hair flowing down her back, beautiful. He asked Jack not to leave. He urged him to settle the argument with Myrtle, to do the right thing. He told Jack he was making a mistake telling Myrtle he was going to leave her tonight.

Jack did not answer, his thoughts far away. He paced between the bed and the dresser, snapping out clothes for his trip to St. Joe.

Charles Hofman stepped into the small master bathroom, a door on either side.

Across the apartment a door slammed.

Now Charles Hofman saw, through the bathroom's far door, Myrtle, sobbing still, moving toward him, and toward Jack, her right elbow slightly bent, and in her hand, held slightly below waist level, a gun, Jack's pistol, pointed obliquely at the floor. In the next fifteen seconds the shape of Myrtle's life would be determined—and in Kansas City, the Roaring Twenties would come to an explosive end.

Charles said, "My God, Myrtle, what are you going to do?"

What she did, a jury would decide.

FIVE

Myrtle's Blur

In the holding cell at police headquarters, night became morning. Myrtle's shrieks became elongated echoes. Standing beside her was Mrs. Evelyn Helms, who in June, after years of neglect and cruel treatment, had gunned down her husband. The flash of headlines that followed reported that the Helmses were down-on-their-luck vaude-villians, singers, and acrobats. Evelyn Helms had known hunger, dep-rivation. Her husband had threatened to leave her. She shot him during a chase in which he had run from their house and fallen in the yard. She stood over him, gun in hand, and was heard to say, "You will leave me, will you?" She fired once, repeated her question, and fired again. She tried to turn the gun on herself, but there were no bullets left. Myrtle had read about her in the newspapers. Now, it was just the two of them: Evelyn waiting and watching to see if Myrtle might try to kill herself.

The doctor's hypodermic injection blurred sights, sounds, time. As Myrtle's central nervous system slowed, so did her ability to make sense of her world. Police detectives asked over and over, "A bridge game, yes, Mrs. Bennett, but after your husband failed to make the contract, what happened next?" In Myrtle's confusion, the order of the night's events altered and merged into a black nightmare. A finesse of the queen of diamonds, her laying cold fatty strips of bacon on the skillet for Jack, the raw sting of his hand upon her face, the pistol's rubber grip, the intruding newshound from *The Kansas City Star* arriving to the apartment with police, riding in a patrol car as the Country Club District lights flickered past. *Where is Mother?* Myrtle smiled lazily now, her tongue clumsy from the sedative, as she peeked through the bars and asked Patrolman T. B. Ruth, "Won't you give me your revolver? I want to shoot myself, too." No reply, and then Myrtle asked Patrolman G. R. Woodman, "Won't you give me *your* revolver?" They looked at her: she was tall, lovely, out of her mind.

Sleepiness billowed like heavy fog. Images came and faded: her golf shoes, two-piece dress, a putt, a chip, Jack's arm around her waist. Myrtle seeking expiation now, explaining to a policewoman: "I shot him. I went into mother's bedroom and got the gun. I went into the den and he was packing his grip. He said he was going to leave me. I shot him." Then came sleep, though fitful, with a husband-murderer staring at her. *Can you forgive me, Jack?* So handsome. Such high times together, they danced, made love. But there were the nights apart, the arguments, their two babies dead.

Two hours later, Myrtle awakened. Her mother appeared and brought a change of clothes. Myrtle's blouse had a small rip near the shoulder, a tear in the sleeve. Charles Hofman showed up, too: tense, smoking, fearful. *Yes, the bridge game, four spades bid, and with those cards how could Jack have failed?* Hofman brought J. Francis O'Sullivan, Myrtle's friend, Jack's friend. O'Sullivan and his wife played bridge with Myrtle and Jack, though now he spoke as the attorney he was: "Myrtle, do not talk to anyone about anything, *do you understand?*"

Newspapers loved the sensation of the bridge game gone wrong. Myrtle's friends often saw their names in the society pages connected to mentions of a bridge luncheon or a daughter back from a summer motoring trip. This was different. This was shocking. *The Kansas City Star*'s front-page headline screamed: DEATH AFTER 4 BID. Gossip became headlines: UNHAPPY FOR YEARS and "She Is in the Death Cell," the latter a reference to the holding area for those who had threatened to kill themselves and would be closely watched. The *Journal-Post* decided, "That her husband should strike her before guests, that was a blow of stunning force to the wife. She saw in her husband's act confirmation of her suspicions that he was growing less affectionate . . ."

The Bennett story made front pages across the nation, and warned of the dangers of America's bridge fever. *The Chicago Daily Tribune* headline put it simply: "Slaps Wife in Bridge Game; She Kills Him."

Acting as Myrtle's attorney, O'Sullivan told the judge at the preliminary hearing that Myrtle required medical care in a sanitarium. Jim Page, the brawling Jackson County prosecutor, balked. She must be held without bail, Page contended, and tried for first-degree murder. Page talked big: he would aim for the death penalty.

Myrtle insisted on one last look at Jack's body before his aunt Nellie Scyster took it by train to his boyhood home in Illinois. Jack would be buried in the Bennett family plot in Union Ridge beside his mother. Accompanied by a sheriff, Myrtle and her mother spent an hour at the undertaker's office. She called Jack's name. She asked for his forgiveness. She touched his face. She wept. "He and mother were all I had," she said. "And now I have taken him away." She remarked that Jack fell dead at the same age as her father, thirty-six, a comment that prompted Alice Adkins to cry with her. Myrtle wondered why Jack's funeral couldn't be held in Kansas City. Adkins said that was a bad idea. Too many curious people would attend. "I understand," Myrtle said. "It is all right."

Myrtle asked the undertaker to find a different suit for Jack. He hated the brown one he was now wearing. Neither did he like the tie his relatives had selected. Soon after he bought that tie, Myrtle said, Jack knew it was a mistake.

And the undertaker had neglected to place a neatly folded handkerchief in Jack's breast pocket. Myrtle knew her perfume salesman husband would not want to go through eternity without one.

Soon after closing the first issue of *The Bridge World*, Ely read in the New York newspapers the shocking story from Kansas City. When Myrtle shot Jack, it was, for the Bennetts, a family tragedy. But for Ely, it was the answer to a new editor's dream: a bridge story with marital strife, hints of infidelity, a mindless bidding system, a botched contract, and, best of all, gunfire. *The Bridge World*'s next issue would tell that story.

Because contract bridge lived in the mind, it was difficult to dramatize on paper or in lectures. Even Ely's imagination and dramatist's flair could not have created the Bennett story. Husband-wife tumult was an accepted truth in bridge. But this was unthinkable. At the Knickerbocker Whist Club, and at bridge tables across the nation, conversation about the killing and Myrtle's upcoming murder trial brought as many chuckles as shivers of fear.

Ely exploited the Bennett story. "Perhaps from the tragedy, which happened recently in Kansas City, when Mrs. John G. Bennett shot and killed her husband, following a technical discussion about the way in which the husband had bid a hand at Bridge, a lesson of the importance of precise bidding valuation will finally be realized," Ely wrote in his magazine. After Myrtle called Jack a "bum bridge player," Ely noted, "He bravely controlled himself under this supreme provocation.

"But the argument waxed acrimonious. Evidently, it was a clash between male and female Bridge inferiority complexes.

"We shudder at the thought of what would happen if a wily lawyer for defense (well versed in all the fractional distinctions between a Jack and a ten) shall by implication lay the murder at the feet of some of our international Bridge idols!"

Ely hired one of those international bridge idols, Sidney Lenz, to analyze the Bennett-Hofman hand. In *The Bridge World* of December 1929, the magazine's third issue, published eight weeks after Jack's killing, Lenz wrote, "Tragedies, comedies, and the broadest farce have stalked in the wake of many a Bridge game ever since the vogue became far-flung. It is doubtful if any of these cases have equaled the Bennett disaster in intensity and intricacy."

Lenz dissected the bidding and play of the last hand. He decided that Jack's initial bid of one spade was unsound. Jack should have passed, Lenz wrote.

Lenz's story was accompanied by a diagram of the hand featuring each player's card holdings: "This innocuous-looking deal at the Bridge table resulted in the killing of John Bennett by his wife," Lenz wrote, adding, "There unquestionably was a good chance to win the contract if Bennett had played just a bit better."

Titillated bridge aficionados sought to know every detail about the hand. An accurate reconstruction of card distribution, and the bidding sequence, not only provided fodder for bridge-table discussion, but allowed for a technical assessment of whether Myrtle or Jack had botched the contract.

Typical of social players, though, neither the Hofmans nor Myrtle remembered the distribution of cards in that hand, only the bidding. Therefore, what Sidney Lenz analyzed in his usual academic manner—and what would be reproduced in magazines, newspapers, and bridge anthologies as *the fatal hand* for the next seventy-five years—was like so much in salesmanship during the age of ballyhoo. A complete fabrication, no more, no less.

With $50,000 posted as bail, Myrtle was released to O'Sullivan. Among the sureties guaranteeing the bond were Charles and Mayme Hofman, who had left Kansas City for a time to escape the newspapermen and the prosecutor's office. Her nerves shot, Mayme required rest. Myrtle, meanwhile, spent a month in the local sanitarium of Dr. Wilse Robinson, suffering from a nervous breakdown.

Meanwhile, her friends discussed how they might help. They knew what Jack Bennett was—a sleep-around, a cad. Soon the whispers began: "Get Jim Reed!" In Kansas City there was no more famous attorney, no more famous man, and if any lawyer could make a jury see the truth deep within that bridge game, it was former Senator Reed. Obtaining Reed's legal representation was a long shot, certainly. Reed represented the rich and famous, and they paid him well. But Myrtle's friends, prosperous enough, were accustomed to getting their way. What about the senator's idealism, they wondered, his sense of decency? Wouldn't Reed want to rescue a good woman driven to righteous rage?

In the months of judicial maneuverings and delays that followed, the cry of "Get Jim Reed!" grew, until, as spring perennials bloomed across the Country Club District, the idea became reality.

SIX

Senator Reed Comes Home

Jim Reed was bigger than Kansas City. He smoked cigars with H. L. Mencken. William Randolph Hearst and Clarence Darrow were among his friends. As an attorney he represented Henry Ford, and oil companies. His political oratory had rained fire on Woodrow Wilson's League of Nations. At the moment, he was eyeing the White House.

If such a famously celebrated and controversial Kansas Citian were asked to serve as criminal defense attorney for the Boss's wife, Caroline Pendergast, or for the local millionaire businesswoman Nell Donnelly, the request would be understood. There would be political considerations, and chits repaid.

But Myrtle Bennett was an obscure housewife of a Ward Parkway perfume salesman. The simultaneous sensations of the bridge craze and the killing had drawn the nation's attention and maybe that of Reed, who didn't play bridge (he preferred a hearty game of Red Dog), though always craved attention. Reed was a maverick. But even so, why on earth would he take Myrtle Bennett's case?

The Old Roman came home by train in March 1929. A loving multitude six thousand strong awaited his arrival. Filling Kansas City's Union Station was a brass band (he loved brass bands!), Pendergast loyalists (Attendance: Mandatory!), the Boss himself (fedora, suspenders), red-white-and-blue bunting (the colors of Washington, Jefferson!), a wealthy, married businesswoman (awaiting her next secret rendezvous with the Old Roman), and hand-painted banners that proclaimed JIM'S HOME, HURRAH, JACKSON COUNTY DEMOCRATIC

CLUB, and FAITHFUL JIM. This was Senator Jim Reed's favored milieu, richly American, the haze of cigar smoke and heartwarming huzzahs, reminiscent of stump speeches he had made in Missouri pastures filled with calls of "Give it to 'em, Jim!"

The scene roared vividly to life. It was all syrup, smiles, and exploding flashbulbs. Boss T. J. Pendergast, choreographer of this event (and of a "Jim Reed for President in 1932" movement), had missed no detail. Reed's wife, Lura, received roses, snapdragons, and forget-me-nots. Even Jackson County's administrative judge, bespectacled Harry S. Truman, smiled broadly for the cameras, and Truman *hated* Jim Reed for his party disloyalty and for what he had done to Woodrow Wilson.

Virile at sixty-seven, with a chiseled profile, ruddy complexion, and hair the color of morning frost, Jim Reed, a nineteenth-century man with nineteenth-century sensibilities, and a self-styled Jeffersonian, was now, as a venerable elder, the living portrait of a Roman senator. Thirty years in politics, the last eighteen as U.S. senator from Missouri, Reed knew these gathered people, and they knew him. They remembered how his oratorical sword had cut through big government, foreign entanglements, Prohibition, woman suffrage, and, most famously, the League of Nations. In each instance, he filled the Senate chamber with oratory influenced by the old masters that soared even in the next day's newspapers. Missouri was the Show Me State, and no one doubted that Jim Reed in Washington had *shown them*. Other senators treaded lightly around him, fearing his invective. Pennsylvania senator George Wharton Pepper described Reed's verbal assaults as "chemical." "It was," Pepper noted, "as if he had thrown acid upon his victim." Reed had mastered the art of senatorial repartee. With his satire and willingness to strike below the belt, he inspired fear. Because of his personal attacks and his practice of talking to the gallery, his colleagues often invoked a rule regulating senatorial conduct during debate. A senator once asked Reed to suspend a lengthy address to allow for a vote on a routine matter, to which Reed, with no small hubris, replied, "We will vote on the resolution in ample time, and you can also hear me. You will thus revel in a double pleasure." He said he opposed woman suffrage because wives would merely vote the same as their husbands (therefore not changing the vote, but *doubling* it), and besides, he added, the women of Missouri opposed the amendment. He spoke of "nature's law of love and life," which he viewed straightforwardly: "That man will remain master in external conflicts, including politics, and that woman will continue mistress of the home, the mother and guardian of the generations yet to be." From the Senate floor in September 1918, Reed attacked colleagues who had caved to the suffrage lobby, his voice rising in righteous indignation: "Now we find a petticoat brigade awaits outside, and Senate leaders, like little boys, *like pages*, trek back and forth for orders. If you accept that office, Senators, then put on a cap and bells and paint your cheeks like clowns, as did the court fools of the middle centuries, and do your truckling in a proper garb." According to the old-fashioned doctrine embraced by Reed, men should bare their bosoms to the iron hail of battle while their women, with the divine spark, would stand behind them, protected, and ready to bind their wounds.

Reed made the suffragists' blood boil. Women in Missouri rose up to create "Rid Us of Reed" clubs and banded together with Wilson loyalists to lock Reed out of the 1920 Democratic National Convention in San Francisco, an embarrassing moment for the Old Roman. But Fighting Jim fought his way back, and in his final speech in the Senate, begun on a Saturday and concluded on a Monday, he railed against the Volstead Act, which enabled federal enforcement of Prohibition. In that speech he spoke of the 1928 Republican National Convention in Kansas City, when "some of the leading 'political prohibitionists' were paying the bellboys $7, $8, $9 and $10 for a pint of class whiskey that no Missourian would ever think of drinking." Reed threatened to make public the names of those Republicans "who vote dry and drink wet." After a worrisome two nights in the nation's capital, Reed returned on Monday and put the minds of his Republican colleagues at ease: "I am not going to do it!" They could not wait to rid him from their chamber.

He possessed what one writer called a "magnificent bellicosity."

Like a gargoyle by the gate, he stood sentinel protecting the Constitution and individual liberties. These were his political anchors. He never tired of paying tribute to the Constitution and the men who had framed it. Among his oratorical devices, he used repetition, analogy, sarcasm, florid language. He made few gestures with his hands. Rather, he used his eyes—they transformed from a deep watery blue to gunmetal gray—and his famous sneer. He made emotional appeals to patriotism and mother love, drawing huge crowds in courtrooms and in the Senate's public galleries. Even without modern amplification devices, he never struggled to be heard, speaking in a high baritone, and sometimes, for effect, whispering. Oswald Garrison Villard, writing in *The Nation*, suggested in 1928, "Like [Daniel] Webster it is impossible for Mr. Reed 'to be as great as he looks or sounds.' "

Reed stated his positions with such force and eloquence that no one ever forgot where he stood. This puzzled members of the Capitol press corps, for there seemed little political sense to it. Reed's orations seemed reckless and stated without concern for personal backlash. His attacks from the Senate floor were often personal, bitter. Newspapermen considered him enigmatic and wrote off his presidential prospects, even as the public requested his office to mail out 750,000 copies of his speeches on Prohibition, and more than a million copies of his speeches on the League of Nations, "the most monstrous doctrine ever proposed in this Republic." His admirers considered him an oppositional force without equal, but his detractors, noting that he had written not a single important piece of legislation in eighteen years, viewed him as destructive, an obstructionist. As senators crafted legislation, one question seemed essential: Can this get past Reed?

Now Reed climbed atop an information booth counter at Union Station, the band and the throng quieting. Later on this night, he would be fêted at a banquet with five hundred guests at the Muehlebach Hotel, featuring special whole stuffed poulet, Reed-style, and wax busts of Senator Reed at the speaker's table. Atop the counter, Reed said, "I prefer to come back here to live with my friends and neighbors than be king of any country on the face of the earth. It is the finest thing a man can have: neighbors and friends who stand by him."

It was folksy, homespun. He told the crowd he was done with politics, but how could anyone believe that? "He may talk of retiring, but nobody can associate him with the idea of repose," *The Kansas City Journal-Post* said. "He was a born fighter and will remain so, with the last faint exhalation of his fleeting breath. Otherwise he would not be our Jim." Even as Reed spoke, the presidency was in his head, and the Boss was holding meetings and making phone calls on his behalf.

For several years, Jim and Lura Reed had lived in the Muehlebach, but in 1927 they moved into a fine brick home, with a basement library, a sprawling sun porch with high-backed rocking chairs decorated whimsically with the original cartoons of Reed's caricaturists, and a yard in which to romp with Jeff, their German shepherd. The house sat on Cherry Street, in the Country Club District, not far from the Pendergast mansion, and only a few miles from Myrtle and Jack Bennett's apartment on Ward Parkway. The Reeds would have a good life now, with a maid, a chauffeur, and Tom, their longtime cook, who had returned with them from Washington, where he had mastered the Southern breakfast of hot corn bread, fried chicken, baked ham, and waffles.

At Union Station, Reed was moved to tears and dabbed a handkerchief to his eyes. He made one comment to the crowd that had the ring of complete truth: "I shall resume my law practice. I'm going to keep busy."

Reed was, without challenge, the most famous man in Kansas City. There were others whom Kansas Citians embraced as their own, but they had only a limited local connection. Joan Crawford, the Hollywood starlet, once lived in Kansas City under the name of Billie Cassen. But an old Kansas City friend approached Crawford and pleasantly brought up the old days, only to hear Crawford say, "I'm sure you are mistaken. I never remember meeting you at all." A young writer briefly worked as a reporter for *The Kansas City*

Star before his 1926 novel, *The Sun Also Rises*, attracted warm reviews—his name, Ernest Hemingway. And a one-time paperboy for *The Star*, who left Kansas City for California in 1923, created the first sound animated cartoon, *Steamboat Willie* (1928), featuring Mickey Mouse. "We thought of a tiny bit of a mouse," the artist would say, "that would have something of the wistfulness of Chaplin—a little fellow trying to do the best he could." The artist was Walt Disney.

Even Jim Reed did not belong entirely to Kansas City. Born in rural Ohio, near Mansfield, during the first year of the Civil War, Reed and his family drove a covered wagon and five thousand sheep to a farm in east-central Iowa (or, as he pronounced it, *Eye-oh-way*), just over the river from present-day Cedar Rapids. His father died soon after, and Jim Reed worked the fields, the family's heavily mortgaged farm hovering near bankruptcy. His older brother was said to have died out west at the hands of horse thieves. Neighbors considered his mother Nancy cold, "vinegary," and suspicious of change. She raised her children with the teachings of the Presbyterian Church. In 1877, at sixteen, Reed won a state oratorical contest. Friday debates were customary at the high school, and townspeople came to hear the boy orator talk about the Constitution and the Bill of Rights. He attended Coe College briefly, read law in a local office, and began a private practice in Cedar Rapids. Along the way, he ran for alderman (and lost) and then fell in love with a married woman. Their love affair prompted the woman's husband to file for divorce. In an early sign of his boldness, the bachelor Reed swept in and married the woman, Lura Olmstead, even though, at the time, she was forty-two and he just twenty-five. Running from the storm they had created in Iowa, they moved to Kansas City.

Jim and Lura Reed arrived in 1887, a time when four-mule teams drove through mud to the axles in the boomtown's streets. Reed rented a corner in a downtown room filled with desks, and hung out his shingle. His ambition and his oratorical skills, most notably stumping for the Great Commoner, William Jennings Bryan, in 1896, captured the attention of alderman Jim Pendergast. Elected Jackson

County prosecutor in 1898, Reed would win all but two of his 287 cases (one of his defeats: Jesse James, Jr., acquitted on robbery charges), and then twice was elected as a reform mayor of Kansas City. As mayor, he delivered an eloquent welcome address at the 1900 Democratic Convention in Kansas City. That year, even *The Kansas City Star*, his most implacable foe, suggested, "It would hardly be possible for Mr. Reed to order a beefsteak and a dish of hash brown potatoes without impressing his rare declamatory gifts on the waiter." Reed also paid his political debt to the Pendergast brothers, naming younger brother, Tom, to a two-year term as Kansas City's superintendent of streets, a plum patronage job, and allowing Tom's older brother, alderman Jim, to appoint the majority of the 173 men on the police force. Reed took on the local utility interests, and became known for courage and toughness. "There is no more compromise in Jim Reed," *The Star* wrote in 1902, "than in a crowbar." Even so, one adversary in Kansas City called him the Saw-Voiced Raven of the Kaw, and another, Bridlewise Jim, to be led like a horse in the Pendergast stable.

The defining moment of Jim Reed's political career as an oppositional force occurred ten years before his return home to Union Station. For some Democrats (including the one in the White House at the time), the moment forever marked Reed as a party traitor.

September 22, 1919. The subject at hand was a proposed peace treaty with Germany. Senator Jim Reed rose from his front-row desk in the Senate chamber. Senators poured from the cloakroom. The public gallery became energized. Now the floor was his. *The North American Review*, in assessing Reed's speeches, wrote, "We find him nearly always occupying one of two roles. Either he is Nemesis, hunting down his prey inexorably, or he is Leonidas, dying at the pass. One moment discovers him ruthlessly pressing his adversary; the next reveals him waving a splintered sword above a bloody but unbowed head and defying the hosts of hell to come."

As part of the proposed Treaty of Versailles, a League of Nations would be created to prevent wars through disarmament and collective security. It would have no army, and so, if a military crisis arose, League member states would provide guns and troops. A group of Republicans—the "Irreconcilables"—firmly opposed the treaty. "Mild reservationists" sought minor changes. "Strong reservationists" would vote for the League only if American sovereignty were assured. Of course, Reed would suggest that joining the League of Nations *with reservations* would be like marrying with reservations: "What would they amount to, once married?" Reed aligned with the Irreconcilables led by the Republican Senator Henry Cabot Lodge, President Wilson's most voluble enemy.

For four hours, Jim Reed presented his evidence. Reed despised Wilson for what he viewed as a pretentious man's desire to make himself president of the world. More than one hundred thousand people had gathered in Washington to cheer Wilson's return from the Paris negotiations. "Dare we reject it," Wilson warned the Senate about the impending vote on the treaty, "and break the heart of the world?" But Reed invoked George Washington, who, in his Farewell Address, said, "It is our true policy to steer clear of permanent alliances with any portion of the foreign world." Reed added, with a sneer, "So spoke the creator of this republic. Who will be its destroyer?"

Now, from the Senate floor, Reed appealed to prejudice by offering race equality as an evil. He pointed out that Britain, with its voting protectorates, would have six votes to the United States' one, and that League membership would be composed of three dark-skinned men to each white man. He spoke of "barbarism" and "voodooism." Reed worried that "a single spark struck even in a remote and barbarous country may start a conflagration which will blaze around the world."

"The trouble with you gentlemen who want to overturn the world," Reed said, "is that you set up a proposition of a great power and you forget . . . it may be used for our assassination."

A senator asked Reed if the United States would need a much larger army and navy if it opted not to join the League. "Not at all, sir. Let me puncture that balloon," Reed replied, as laughter filled the public gallery.

Let me tell you something, there was a time when a lot of the people in the world—and I believe that is the reason why we got into this war—believed that the Yankee, as they call us, was a fat, sleek, overfed lounge lizard; that he would not fight; that he could not fight; that he was chasing dollars, and had no spirit in him that made it possible for him to go out and die. And so Germany threw the glove in our face. But that mistake will not be made again for a century of time. [Applause erupted in the gallery.] They found you can take a boy off an American farm and land him in France, and in two weeks' time he could go over the top with the best of them. They found out these soldiers did not need the discipline of camp and of military establishment. They already had the discipline of American citizenship. They found out that these men could laugh in the face of death, and that they could go down into the shadows with a smile upon their lips. They found out that we can raise ten million men, if we have to, and that all the powers of earth and hell can not whip us on our own soil. [The gallery again erupted in applause.]

Reed finished in a patriotic fervor: "I decline to help set up any government greater than that established by the fathers, baptized in the blood of patriots from the lanes of Lexington to the forests of the Argonne, sanctified by the tears of all the mothers whose heroic sons went down to death to sustain its glory and independence—the Government of the United States of America."

A thunder of applause came from the public gallery. Senators rushed to congratulate Reed. Soldiers clanged their helmets. A crippled young soldier slammed down his crutch on the rail in front of him with such force that the crutch broke in half, with one half falling to the floor below, and he shouted, "By God, you are right, Senator!" When the call came for quiet, the audience hissed in disapproval.

In early September, Woodrow Wilson boarded a train and delivered forty speeches in three weeks to cheering throngs. The president sought to save the Treaty of Versailles in the name of peace and humanity.

But he suffered headaches, sleeplessness, coughing fits. On September 25, in Pueblo, Colorado, Wilson gave his final public speech. At two o'clock the following morning, his physician found the president gasping as a facial muscle twitched. Wilson told him that he wanted to carry on, but admitted, "I just feel as if I am going to pieces." The remainder of his tour canceled, the president returned to Washington.

Six days later, Wilson suffered a massive stroke at the White House. He never again functioned effectively. His most vocal critics, including James A. Reed, were blamed.

On that night in March 1920, when the Senate voted against the United States joining the League of Nations (the United States would sign treaties with Germany, Austria, and Hungary), Wilson told his physician, "Doctor, the devil is a busy man."

A reporter rushed to Reed in the Senate lobby. "Senator, what does this vote mean?" the reporter asked. "Mean?" Reed replied. "It means this is the greatest day in American history since Cornwallis hauled down his flag at Yorktown."

Reed would pay a price for his stance. In 1922, he fought for his political life in the Senate race against Breckinridge Long, a former Wilson official whom Reed termed an "administration valet." Among those opposing Reed were the Wilsonians, the Ku Klux Klan, the anti-alcohol "Drys," the statewide press (at least, much of it), women, and blacks who had not forgotten Reed's fear-mongering about a "colored"-dominated League. In rural towns, Reed's advance troupe set up a tent big enough for five thousand listeners, and Reed, in a blue silk suit and white shoes and with a Panama hat on his head, stood inside the big top and gave two-hour speeches. He spoke from the backs of trains, and once from a pine platform in an oak grove, the rows of faces lit by kerosene flares. From his deathbed, former president Wilson described Reed as a subversive meddler, a "marplot." He called the senator "incapable of any sustained allegiance to any person or any cause." But Reed, in a startling victory, narrowly defeated Long in the primary and then, with help from the Pendergast machine and crossover Republicans in St. Louis, including those of German ancestry who enjoyed beer more than Woodrow Wilson, defeated Republican R. R. Brewster to win reelection to a third six-year term.

His presidential run in 1924 withered, and at the 1928 Democratic Convention in Houston, Reed delivered a speech for Governor Al Smith of New York, even as he suffered from disappointment that Smith's nomination wasn't his. Later, Reed reportedly was offered the vice-presidential position on the Smith ticket, but turned it down, saying, "Gentlemen, I appreciate the compliment but I do not care for a back seat on a hearse."

Reed desperately wanted to become president. In *The American Mercury* magazine in 1929, though, H. L. Mencken wrote, "[Reed] would laugh himself to death in the White House. Worse, he would come to despise himself. It is not a place for realists."

To Mencken, Reed was

> an anachronistic and disquieting reminder of the days when a Senator of the United States stood on his own legs and was his own man. . . . The stature of such a man as Reed is not to be counted by his successes. The important thing is that he fights. . . . The forensic talents of the man are really almost unparalleled. He is, for our time, the supreme artist in assault. There are subtleties in the art he practices, as in any other, and he is the master of all of them. The stone ax is not his weapon, but the rapier; and he knows how to make it go through stone and steel.

In spring 1930, J. Francis O'Sullivan approached Reed to seek his help, and to gauge his interest in representing the widow Bennett.

Though Jack Bennett earned an enviable living, his widow was not an automobile titan or an oil company. Jack had purchased $32,500 in life insurance polices. The payment to Myrtle of $2,500 from his war-risk insurance went uncontested. But a dozen members of the extended Bennett family contended that they—and not Myrtle—were Jack's rightful heirs. If a jury convicted Myrtle of murdering Jack, they stood to collect the three remaining $10,000 policies. It was clear that Myrtle could not afford to pay Jim Reed's usual rates.

Reed met with Myrtle and listened to her story. He asked if Jack had ever struck her before that last fateful night. He agreed to take Myrtle's case.

He would, by damn, tell that jury what to decide.

SEVEN

Ely and Jo: Stars on the Rise

Adaptability is a basic law of the survival of the fittest in bridge and no player, however perfect technically, can claim to be an expert or indeed even be a winning player, unless he learns how to play bad partners as well as he can play bad cards. Players who bemoan bad partners are certainly less justified than those who bemoan bad cards. Partners (and opponents) can be largely controlled and guided by superior skill.

—ELY CULBERTSON,
in *Contract Bridge Blue Book*

At the Knickerbocker Whist Club, the bridge masters smiled tightly at Ely Culbertson as he walked past. Then came the whispered innuendo. They called him devious, deceitful, a crackpot, a womanizer, a fraud. They heard him refer to Jo as Sweetka, and Jo speak of Illiusha, and they knew that Culbertson was, like Lenin and Trotsky, dangerous. The word spread: *Culbertson's a Red! Another Vladimir Ilyich!* For years these bridge experts had been individualistic competitors, but now they became a collective with a shared disdain for the Russian. Ely was struck by the irony of his life: growing up in Russia, he was considered an American; and now in America, he was called a Russian.

His fate: always to be an outsider. He pondered the gossip, and then made his play. His rivals had forgotten his family's paternal roots, the Culbertsons of Titusville, Pennsylvania. Slyly, he joined the Sons of the American Revolution, and touted his membership.

For every card his enemies played, the elegant man of mystery had a trump.

Contract bridge proved a splendid populist game during hard times. It was respectable and social, and a deck of cards could be had for thirty cents or less. That bridge was a partnership game for four made it an ideal fit for two couples looking to spend a quiet social evening together, and helped spur its ascendancy during these years. By the middle 1930s, other parlor games would also experience widespread popularity. Board games such as Movie Mart (based on films) and Finance (about banking) presaged the rage of 1935, Monopoly, the real-estate game that swept the nation. In November 1935, *The New York Times* explained the inescapable lure of such games against the backdrop of the Depression: "Instead of carrying the person away from daily affairs, they in effect bring daily affairs to him in a new guise, on a small scale, with 'the world to win.' "

Even so, none rivaled the parlor-room supremacy of bridge. Bridge had become "the supreme hostess technique, supplying the best inexpensive guarantee our culture has discovered against a 'dull evening' when friends 'drop in,' " according to Robert S. Lynd and Helen Merrell Lynd. In 1935 the Lynds returned to Muncie, Indiana, with their team of cultural anthropologists to produce a sequel to their seminal 1925 study of a small Midwestern city (later identified as Muncie, population thirty-eight thousand), *Middletown: A Study of Modern American Culture*. In Muncie, they found women leading a bridge surge that seeped down even to sixth graders. Leaders of girls' groups in Muncie complained that bridge had distracted girls from other activities. Bridge allowed couples to socialize without having to discuss life. "Social talking presents far more risks to the hostess, as it is a much more personal type of relationship liable to run on the rocks of monotony, vacuousness, gossip, or outright antagonisms," the Lynds wrote. "[Contract bridge] is an unparalleled device for an urban world that wants to avoid issues, to keep things impersonal, to enjoy people without laying oneself open or committing oneself to them, and to have fun in the process."

But widespread troubles emerged at the table: cheating, a lack of decorum, tensions. Was it the hardship born of the Depression, the bloodlust inherent in a competitive game, or the base instincts in the American character?

Lt. Col. Walter Buller, the British bridge savant, defined four categories among the world's players: (1) first class; (2) good; (3) average; and (4) bad 'uns. By Buller's computations, first-class players represented only a "fraction infinitesimal," good players comprised 4 percent, and all others the remaining 95 percent.

Social players—Buller's 95 percent—committed the most egregious acts. In Seattle, a wife threw an alarm clock at her partner/husband, knocking out one of his teeth. In Chicago, a husband watched his partner/wife fail to make a contract and struck her with a cutglass bowl.

The elites, angling for supremacy, were guilty of more subtle infractions: stealing glances at opponents' hands; hesitating for effect before playing a singleton, the only remaining card of a suit in a player's hand; using secret signals to pass information to partners.

The bridge old guard rose up to defend their game. In summer 1930, Wilbur Whitehead wrote, "Personally, I have always deplored playing the game too seriously. Bridge, after all, is only a game and a social one at that. Its primary purpose is to entertain."

Milton Work longed for the gentlemanly days of whist, reminding readers that bridge "is a game in which superiority in play, not superiority in cunning, is the desideratum." Work offered a method to end the cheating that dated to the days of whist: "Ostracize the offender . . . Unless that is done, the ethical player will decline to participate in contests in which such practices are winked at."

The Saturday Evening Post summed up the state of American bridge in 1930: "Now and then a wife does throw the cards in her husband's face, and one did shoot and kill her partner one night . . . Unpleasantness is now general, for every player has developed a genius for argumentative protectiveness toward his or her pet convention. Insults are no longer kept for the intimate friend or relation." The real hardship, the magazine suggested, was endured by the bridge hostess: "Likely as not, at twelve o'clock she stands alone in her living room, looking gloomily down at the neat tray of sandwiches, peanuts and potato chips which have not been touched. From the elevator shaft the noise of battle wafts into the room, and later rebounds, from the street below, through the window. If the game is not broken up violently, the players are, as a rule, too nervous and excited to eat."

The only remedy, *The Saturday Evening Post* said, was to standardize the convention and bidding methods—that is, create one system to satisfy the world: "If Germany and England and America and the other powers of the world can get together and agree, it seems little enough to ask of men and women who have only cards, instead of battleships, to play with."

Ely's task was to make certain that the universally accepted system was his.

Ely's grandiosity was much like Jim Reed's. He saw himself as an emperor of his realm, fortified by his intellectual superiority, and the rightness of his ways. Ely had his own magnificent bellicosity. As Reed had trampled Wilson and the party traditionalists, so Ely would trample the existing authorities of bridge. As Reed now laid plans to gain the highest office in the land, so, too, did Ely plot his ascension.

What he needed most, Ely knew, was a good controversy. People rushed to controversy. Controversy sold magazines. He created small controversies when he could. In April 1930, he took on Dr. Alfred Adler, the famed Viennese psychologist, who reportedly told an audience at Columbia University, "Bridge players are usually suffering from an inferiority complex and find in the game an easy way to satisfy their striving for superiority." Adler also said, "Most people play cards to waste time." Ely viewed Adler's comments, "like his books, but half truth." He accused Adler of jealousy that "the world is more interested in Bridge sects than the 'isms' of Psychology. . . . In these times of intense struggle for material and mental felicity what would the dear professor want us to do in order to feed the worm of inferiority which is gnawing our vitals?" Ely's circulation grew to more than eight thousand, and then fifteen thousand, as the magazine itself grew from thirty-two to forty-eight to sixty-four pages.

Still, to launch his name on a national scale Ely needed more. He needed to put himself at the center of a controversy. In London, he found the trump card that would change everything.

The blustery Lt. Col. Buller, bridge writer for *The Star* of London, seemingly chimed with his lofty opinions about bridge with the frequency of Big Ben. Attached to the War Office as a staff captain during the war, Buller was well known in London social circles. In his book *Reflections of a Bridge Player*, published in November 1929, Buller criticizes American experts for their boastfulness: "Mr. Wilbur C. Whitehead describes himself, or permits himself to be described, as 'The World's Greatest Authority.' Mr. Milton Work is also described as 'The World's Greatest Authority.' Then Mr. Sidney S. Lenz is advertised as 'The World's Champion Bridge Player' and 'The International Champion.' It is all very confusing. None of these gentlemen has ever played with first-class players in this country . . . I feel sure that a good four could be got together to take on the Americans, and that, while not necessarily the best available, they would beat them 'sky-high.' "

In *The Bridge World* of April 1930, Ely used those words to his own advantage, issuing a "friendly challenge" to Buller. An unspecified American team-of-four (clearly, Ely had his own team in mind) would travel to England in the summer of 1930 to play a British team selected by Buller in a duplicate match of at least three hundred deals for any stakes *within reason*, and in accordance with the rules of London's Portland Club. Ely called for "a show down," and did so knowing Britain had not yet fully embraced contract bridge (most Brits still played auction), and that its top players had little experience with *duplicate* play. In the proposed duplicate match, two tables would be arranged in separate rooms. In one, the Americans would occupy the north–south positions, and in the other east–west. Each hand dealt in the first room would be reproduced in the second room. On each deal, then, a team with the better cards in one room would receive the worse cards in the other. This would eliminate the luck of the cards. The outcome would be determined by skill.

Buller bit. He accepted the challenge immediately. The match would be played in September in London at New Almack's, at No. 19 Upper Grosvenor Street, Park Lane, a historic club founded in 1765, during the age of Hoyle, by a former valet of the Duke of Hamilton.

The Bridge World crowed that, except for chess, this Culbertson-Buller match would be "the first purely intellectual competition between England and America in history, arousing widespread interest on both sides of the ocean."

Already, the spinmaster was spinning. Ely admitted in the magazine that his team-of-four (Lightner, von Zedtwitz, Ely, and Jo) was perhaps not America's best—it had finished third in the Vanderbilt Cup the previous fall—though certainly it ranked among the best. "The overwhelming majority of America's advanced players," Ely wrote, "will abide by the victory or defeat of this team."

At the Knickerbocker Whist Club, though, eyes rolled and bile rose. *Who does Ely Culbertson think he is?* He held no claim to being America's top bridge player. His team-of-four was not America's best.

By the design of this match, though, Ely would wrap himself in an American flag. He was representing the country and traveling to a foreign land to do so. Americans would cheer for him and Jo against Buller just as surely as they would cheer for Harold Vanderbilt and his yacht *Enterprise* in his defense of the America's Cup against Britain's Sir Thomas Lipton and his *Shamrock V*. That yachting competition would be held near Newport, Rhode Island, at virtually the same moment Ely and Jo cut cards with Buller in London.

Ely had outmaneuvered the bridge old guard, and not for the last time. He had put himself in a position to be noticed on a broad scale. When Jo learned of Buller's acceptance, she said to Ely, with exasperation, "How could you do such a thing!" Ely's honest answer might have been, "How could I not?" He was desperate for money and attention. Ely told Jo they would need $5,000: $2,000 for travel expenses, $2,000 for betting, and $1,000 to leave behind for their magazine and the children. As for von Zedtwitz and Lightner, he reassured her, "Waldy and Teddy will pay their own way."

Jo demanded to know how Ely would get this money.

"From the *Blue Book*," he replied.

"Suppose you don't write it?" Jo said.

He would. Ely said bridge teachers had been asking for a book on the Culbertson System. He would self-publish (through his magazine's printer), and sell his new book for two dollars. To collect the money required for the trip to Britain, he said he would announce in *The Bridge World*'s next issue that a special autographed edition of his book could be purchased now for only $1.50 and delivered considerably in advance of regular trade channels.

And so he did just that. The full-page advertisement read: "At last!! A book by Ely Culbertson 'the man behind the big guns of Bridge.' . . . Simple enough for a child, Deep enough for a master player . . . CONTRACT BRIDGE BLUE BOOK By ELY CULBERTSON, Editor-In-Chief, the Bridge World." Ely said four thousand orders had arrived in the mail. He told Jo they had their money, plus a little extra for tipping English butlers.

The pieces began to fall into place. In July 1930, Ely's team-of-four captured the championship of the American Bridge League Summer Tournament. *The Bridge World* teammates posed together beside their trophy on a lawn in Asbury Park, New Jersey: Ely (hunched over, exhausted), Jo (in a dress, at ease, her hand on the trophy), the bookish Lightner, and the wiry von Zedtwitz, dapper in his white knickers and two-tone shoes. As the ocean breezes blew through the convention hall, Ely's team-of-four had defeated a Columbia University team by nearly 1,500 points and then, in a hard-fought final, fought off a Knickerbocker team captained by Hal Sims by only 415 points. The magazine trumpeted that twelve of the sixteen teams in the tournament had played the Culbertson Approach-Forcing system, including all four semifinalists. According to the conditions of this

ABL trophy, the winners could be challenged at thirty- to ninety-day intervals. Sims filed his challenge at once. The caption in *The Bridge World* beneath the photograph of the champions read, " . . . And now to England!"

But there was still the matter of writing the *Contract Bridge Blue Book*. Ely had not written a word. The liner SS *Île de France* would sail for Southampton, England, on September 5. In early August, Ely finally began dictating to three secretaries for hours at a time. "The book," he offered, "is arranged to fit the needs of all classes of players from the veriest tyro to the super-expert." Tense, surly, ill-tempered, gaunt from fatigue and weight loss, he worked deep into each night.

In his magazine, he turned up the hyperbole about the Buller match, which, suddenly, amounted to "the world's championship." Over Labor Day, with their departure for England days away, Ely and his teammates made their mandatory defense of the Asbury Park title at the Knickerbocker Whist Club, and won again, this time defeating Sims's team-of-four by 2,840 points. Ely and Lightner played east–west in one room against Sims's teammates Lee Langdon and Michael Gottlieb, and netted 1,635 points. Playing the same hands in the other room, Jo and the Baron von Zedtwitz finished 1,205 points ahead of Sims and Willard Karn. *The New York Times* praised Jo and von Zedtwitz for "the absence of errors in their defensive play." In *The Bridge World*, Ely couldn't resist the temptation to crow about his team's second consecutive victory over the Shaggy Giant: "When a team-of-four is defeated on both North–South and East–West hands by 2,840 points the results though not 'official' are, to say the least, significant."

In this same September issue, *The Bridge World* celebrated the completion of its first year of existence, with Ely editorializing, "Some altruistic souls accuse us, rightly, of 'self-promotion.' In this we have our artistic, not commercial, temperament to blame. We love Bridge passionately and frequently cannot distinguish between Bridge and self-promotion. We have inaugurated this magazine with the object of promoting Bridge and, through service, ourselves. In a measure we have done both."

According to a story he told later, Ely dictated the final chapter of the *Contract Bridge Blue Book* in a taxi en route to the ship bound for England. Then, as the SS *Île de France* pulled from shore and Jo waved to her toddlers Joyce and Bruce on the pier, Ely's publisher shouted, "What about the dedication?" Without hesitation, Ely shouted back, "*To my wife and favorite partner*. And don't forget to make it all caps."

In dinner jackets and evening gowns, British society turned out for the Americans. Among those moving through the thickly carpeted card rooms at New Almack's were Sir George Milne, chief of the Imperial General Staff, and Sir George Montague Critchett, 2nd Baronet, of Lord Chamberlain's office, and Emmanuel Lasker, world champion of chess, covering the match for German newspapers.

At a welcome luncheon at the Ritz, Ely deadpanned that 325,000 bridge experts in America thought they should have been playing the match in his place. One British writer mentioned how fortunate the American team was that brawn and muscle would not determine the outcome since the four Americans weighed a combined 520 pounds (only a slight underestimate). The newspapers marveled at Jo's glamour. The London *Star*: "She is a very beautiful woman and her photos are treasured by bridge fans in America, just as film lovers keep the pictures of their favorite 'stars.'" The broad-shouldered Lt. Col. Buller posed for photographs with his teammates: the physician Dr. Nelson Wood-Hill, navy lieutenant Cedric Kehoe, and the silver-haired former stage actress Mrs. Gordon Evers, who had lived for twelve years in America and toured the country with the actor and stage manager Sir Herbert Tree.

In room one, a correspondent for the London *Evening Standard* watched Jo and von Zedtwitz play against Buller and Mrs. Evers, a crimson cord separating spectators from the table. The correspondent noted Mrs. Evers's quiet voice and *miraculously* delicate hands; the twinkle in Buller's eyes; Jo's youthful prettiness, her tortoiseshell eyeglasses, and her most delightful American accent; and von Zedtwitz's thin, inscrutable face and his nervous habit of brushing away imagined dust specks from the sleeve of his black dinner jacket. Jo lit an occasional cigarette and, between hands, sat in silence. Buller smiled at a friend in the gallery. A. E. Manning-Foster, dean of British bridge writers, thought the play maddeningly slow even when bids seemed obvious. It was, he decided, all part of the methods.

The Brits assumed a lead of 960 points after the first afternoon session. That night, though, just past midnight, as the twenty-eighth hand was dealt, with England leading by 595 points, the referee announced the final hand of the evening. In room one, Buller faced a bid of four hearts. He held six clubs to the ace and nine, and his partner, Mrs. Evers, had twice passed. Buller bid five clubs. Von Zedtwitz, holding five clubs to the king, queen, and jack, confidently doubled. Buller failed to make his contract, set four tricks. An unmitigated disaster, the hand cost his team 1,400 points. In room two, playing the identical hand, Ely faced the same decision as Buller: whether to overcall a four-hearts bid with five clubs. Ely considered his options for three minutes and more, and then passed. Kehoe played the hand at four hearts and failed by one trick. The Brits lost only 100 points in the proposition. Even so, the Brits' combined loss on the hand of 1,500 points sent the Americans into a lead they would never relinquish.

Some in the British press referred to the session as "Black Tuesday." Buller bristled from criticism that "when in difficulties, he sucks his thumb." He said he never was in difficulties and never sucked his thumb.

Two days later, when the Americans' lead exceeded four thousand points, Hubert Peters of *The Manchester Guardian* noted how the Culbertson team's "machine-guns were working with deadly precision, and Buller's storm troops were mown down as they advanced." Peters added, " 'Card sense,' on which Colonel Buller relies, is an admirable foundation for match play, but in itself is not enough. It must be supplemented by method. . . . The 'forcing' system is justifying all that is claimed for it. It is a logical system, void of artificial conventions, and it is a sheer delight to the spectators to see it in action."

The onslaught of criticism from the British press infuriated Buller. "Disloyalty," he called it. "In the middle of this match everything that can be done to dishearten the players has been done in a section of the British press."

Ely's team-of-four won by 4,845 points. To prove the value of the Culbertson forcing system, the Americans rotated partners throughout the seven-day match. (The Brits did not.) Buller said he would make no excuses. Later, though, he prattled on, reminding readers that, after early match breakdowns, his team won the last five days of competition. Further, since his team had now gained experience playing under duplicate conditions, he felt certain that, were his team-of-four to meet the Americans again, it would win "hands down."

No one in Britain was listening.

In the London *Evening Standard*, Frank England doubted that any British team-of-four could defeat Culbertson's four, whose bidding was "more informative, more certain and more exact. Their bidding is standardized, each player knowing within certain clearly defined limits what any particular bid means."

During a closing banquet at New Almack's, the British audience rose to its feet and serenaded the Americans with "For they are jolly good fellows." Jo, who had trembled over the very idea of the Buller match, beamed.

Two more British challenges came, from Crockford's, an elite bridge club in London. Ely accepted both, and his team-of-four won the first by nearly five thousand points, and the second by six thousand. The consensus among the British press was that the Americans had triumphed because of superior teamwork and their scientific system of bidding, the Culbertson System. It was enough to prompt A. E. Manning-Foster to write, "The matches at Almack's and Crockfords have taught us all a lot. Those who have not learnt from them or taken the lessons to heart are unteachable."

Ely basked in his newfound glory. His fame was spreading, across the Atlantic and across America. The first printing of the *Contract Bridge Blue Book* (six thousand copies) had sold out, and so had the second and third printings. By November, *The Bridge World* was calling Ely's book "The New Best Seller of All Bridge Books . . . 4th Edition Now

Ready." The advertisement boasted, "Now you may have for your own use the ideas and methods of the Culbertson System, which today is synonymous with *Winning Contract* ... Learn at first hand—direct from the master player himself. With the Culbertson System *you will win regardless of the system used by partner or opponents*." His book would soon be published in London, as well.

The Buller match became the rock that triggered the Culbertson avalanche. Back home, Ely announced a nationwide lecture tour. On tour, he would talk about the Buller victory, the Bennett murder trial, and the Culbertson System. Jo planned to write two bridge books of her own. The first Culbertson Teachers' Convention (sixty dollars per person covering three days of instruction) would be held in New York in November. More quickly than Ely imagined, he had created a phenomenon in his name. His enemies insisted that nearly every theory in his book had been stolen. Their personal attacks only spurred sales. C. C. Nicolet, bridge writer for the *New York World-Telegram*, would write, "Nowhere else in the modern world, except possibly backstage at the Metropolitan Opera House, can one find so many persons so anxious to shout scandal and accusations at so many colleagues. Few bridge experts have kind words for any others. They criticize even their favorite partners bitterly." In February 1931, the twenty-fourth edition of the *Blue Book* rolled off the presses.

EIGHT

The Senator and Mrs. Donnelly

At home on Cherry Street, the senator was a man of habit and creature comforts. After dinner, a smoker's hour, he reminded his elderly wife, Lura, that he didn't want his cigar to bother her, so he would slip outside. Then, disappearing into the evening darkness and his cloud of smoke, Jim Reed would stroll across his lawn toward the neighbors' mansion. He told friends the two houses shared a dog run, which was true, but the connection ran deeper, especially after nightfall, when the man of the house next door was out on Boss Pendergast's town. Reed had arranged for the prominent couple to live next door, and sometimes, at his instruction, after dinner, their back door was unlocked. Unnoticed, the senator would snuff out his cigar and step inside. Then he'd climb the back stairs to the master bedroom and walk into the arms of Mrs. Nell Donnelly.

When they first met, the attraction between the senator and Nell was immediate, mutual, and seemingly inevitable. They were two of the biggest celebrities in Kansas City, and in their own marriages, emotional and physical needs were going unmet. Reed was handsome, dashing, and charismatic. Even in his seventh decade, he remained vibrant and virile, and he carried big ambitions: the White House, for one. Nell was perhaps the most successful businesswoman in America, richer than even the senator. She was stylish, determined, and twenty-eight years younger than he—and nearly half a century younger than his wife. A brunette, small, with glittering eyes, Nell dressed with elegance and carried herself in style. She was impressive and imposing, and every bit as unlikely to take a subservient role as the man she loved. Nell had asked her garment company's attorney, James Taylor, if he might introduce her to his famous law partner, James A. Reed. So Taylor escorted her down the hall on the nineteenth floor of the Telephone Building and made the introduction. When Nell sued to protect patent rights on the Handy-Dandy Apron—a suit critically important to her company's future—she hired Reed. In 1927, he won the case.

If the senator had built his legend on words, Nell had built hers on house frocks and aprons. In 1916, Peck's Dry Goods Store in Kansas City sold its original order of more than two hundred of Nell's pink gingham-check frocks in the blink of an eye, and demanded more. By 1929, the Donnelly Garment Company was employing a thousand workers, nearly all women, and producing five thousand signature "Nelly Don" dresses daily. Nell was steaming to Paris and Vienna to study the latest dress styles of the Continent.

The differences between Lura and Nell were striking. Born in 1844, the year James Polk became president, Lura Reed was now eighty-six years old. Decades before she had settled into a traditional wife's quiet life at home. She participated in charity work, joined a garden club, played in a weekly bridge game with friends. When her husband was first elected senator, Lura told friends, before leaving for the nation's capital, "Honestly, I would be happier here in Kansas City with my dogs, cats and horses." In Washington she counted President Taft and his wife, Helen, as friends, but mostly the capital's social scene left her cold. No woman should want her husband in politics, Lura once said. The wife, she said, never sees him, and added, "The game is not worth the candle."

Nell Quinlan Donnelly, for her part, was a modern-age woman, barely forty, energized by national politics and an assertive business engine of the twenties. Nell once told a national magazine, "People often express surprise that this company of which my husband is the head was founded on one of *my* ideas. What surprised me is that more husbands' businesses are not the outgrowth, at least in some measure, of their wives' ideas. It takes two to make a marriage, and both are endowed with brains. Why should only one of the contracting parties put his brains to use, considering that the profit is mutual?"

What Nell did not say to the magazine—but in private moments told the senator—was that her marriage was in ruins.

Paul Donnelly once threw an ashtray at Nell at dinner—a symptom of a deeper problem: intense depression. At forty-six Paul had seen his hair turn prematurely white, his physique soft. His wife's growing fame made him feel diminished. He sought comfort in alcohol and women. He often showed up late to the office, hung over. Only blocks from the bawdy houses that lined Twelfth and Fourteenth streets, he tried to sweat out his late-night carousing in the steam baths at the Kansas City Club. He warned Nell repeatedly that he did not want children. He swore that if she ever became pregnant he would kill himself. To show he meant business, he pulled a pistol from his desk drawer and held it to his head. His dramatic performances initially terrified Nell, but over time grew pathetic. Typically, Nell would wait until Paul had left for lunch before sneaking into his office to remove his pistol. Then she would walk to the top of their offices in the Coca-Cola building, and drop the gun down an elevator shaft, the distant clank putting her at ease. Years later she would estimate that she dropped thirty of Paul's guns down that shaft.

And to think, Paul Donnelly had once been her emotional ballast. Raised on a farm in Parsons in southeastern Kansas, the twelfth child in the family, Nell had escaped her father's stern rule in 1905, at the age of sixteen, when she moved to a Kansas City boarding house. At seventeen she shocked her family by marrying a man in the boarding house across the street, Paul Donnelly, who was twenty-three. Though born poor, Nell said she did not intend to remain poor. Paul put up the money to fund his young wife's schooling in domestic science at Lindenwood College in St. Charles, and later paid for her initial order of pink gingham-check frocks. Nell showed a flair for design and production technique. Upon returning from war in 1919, Paul became the president of the newly formed Donnelly Garment Company.

But his fondness for night life intensified during the twenties, and he was hardly discreet. There was little that could be done about his philandering, Nell would say later. She just did not want to *see* it.

Then, one night, she did. She arrived home to find Paul sharing intimacies with a woman. It was not right, Nell said, for another woman to be in *her* bed with *her* husband, but she emphasized how it was especially wrong for this woman to be wearing *her* pajamas.

At that moment, Nell determined to find a replacement—for her pajamas, and her husband.

There was a public Reed and a private Reed. In 1925, the former senator reflected on the social changes in the five years since the passage of the woman suffrage amendment, writing in *The American Mercury* magazine, "The dresses are a little shorter, the flapper is a little flappier, the hair-bobber becomes more opulent, and the cigarette vendor enjoys a boom. These fortuitous conditions may be the result of the new freedom, or mere coincidence. I venture not to say."

But privately, with Nell—no lion, this Reed—he explained his opposition to woman suffrage with a caveat: "That was *before* I met you, Nell."

Few in Kansas City knew that Reed's romance with Lura had started with an extramarital affair, or that Lura informed him in the early years of their marriage that she no longer was interested in having sex. At least that was the story Reed told Nell, and the same story that, upon his arrival in the nation's capital in 1911, he had told Roy Roberts, Washington correspondent for *The Kansas City Star*. Privately, Reed explained to Roberts that he had married Lura in 1887 to make her a respectable woman again. But Lura no longer wanted to bother with sex, and so it was understood between husband and wife that Reed would seek his physical comforts elsewhere. The senator told all of this to Roberts, and insisted he could not serve the people of Missouri effectively if the Kansas City newspapers, or any other newspaper, pried into his personal affairs. His conversation with Roberts was risky, given the contempt Reed held for the journalist's newspaper, and vice versa. *The Star*'s publisher, William Rockhill Nelson, a Republican stalwart, had opposed Reed in every election. Reed, in turn, had attacked *The Star*, no matter the issue. One writer even surmised that "if Nelson ever supported James A. Reed, the support would've ruined Reed's career." Reed once cracked, "Down at Eleventh and Grand there is a newspaper that calls itself the Star. Old Bill Nelson is its mammy, Old Bill Nelson is its pappy, and Old Bill Nelson is its wet nurse. God created the heavens and the earth, and from the ooze of the earth He created the slimy reptiles that crawl the face of the earth, and from the residue thereof He created Old Bill Nelson." Despite such vitriol, an understanding with Roberts was reached, and Reed roamed free.

Nell loved and admired Reed. As a man of strength and honor, she thought James A. Reed loomed over Paul Donnelly like the Lincoln Memorial loomed over the Reflecting Pool. She thrilled to Reed's 1928 campaign for the Democratic presidential nomination, during which he gave speeches in thirteen states and pounded away at the corruption of the Coolidge administration, borrowing his slogan from Andrew Jackson ("Throw the rascals out!"). One day, Nell appeared at the Reed-for-President campaign office in Washington and startled staffers by making a $1,000 contribution—more than anyone except William Randolph Hearst. She was with Reed at the Democratic National Convention in Houston when New York governor Al Smith, and the Tammany machine, crushed him on the first ballot: Smith got 849⅔ votes, Reed 52. Even so, Nell thought her senator one of the greatest men who ever lived.

There is a photograph of the senator and Lura aboard an ocean liner on their Atlantic crossing in late autumn 1930. They are seated in deck chairs, Lura in a cloche hat, a fur boa draped around her shoulders, the senator sitting stiffly at her side, his expression quizzical. He looks uncomfortable and unhappy, as if he would rather be anywhere else.

By December, back in his law office, Reed returned to his preferred habits. Nell's handsome Lincoln convertible sedan would pull in front of the Telephone Building. As her chauffeur, George Blair, waited dutifully, Nell would enter the senator's office high above Kansas City.

A fine and spacious office, it had a view—and a divan.

During such visits, the senator's standing order to his secretary was that he and Nell were not to be interrupted *for any reason*.

Their visits usually lasted an hour and more.

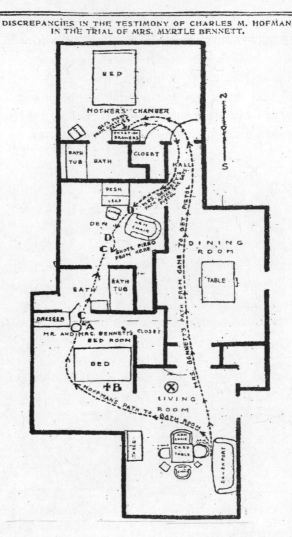

At Myrtle's 1931 murder trial, this diagram of the Bennett apartment was used as an exhibit. The dotted lines show the movements of Myrtle and Charles Hofman on the night Jack was killed. The "A" denotes where Hofman, in testimony at the preliminary hearing, said he saw Jack standing near a dresser – this spot would have put Jack in plain view of Myrtle approaching from the den at "D." But at Myrtle's murder trial, Hofman placed Jack in a different spot, across the bedroom at "B." Hofman at "C" moved through the bathroom to meet Myrtle at "D." The "X" in the living room shows where Jack Bennett fell.

Missouri Valley Special Collections, Kansas City Public Library, Kansas City, MO

NINE

Myrtle's Murder Trial, Part 1

February, 1931: Fifty Communists marched to Kansas City's city hall from their spare third-floor office on Eighth Street, placards in hand, demonstrating against unemployment. A young woman, nimble, angry, smart—an effective Communist—led with the rallying cry: "Comrades, don't starve—FIGHT!" She made her appeal in the name of forty thousand unemployed workers in Kansas City, each as hopeless as Hoover. As she demanded an emergency relief fund for destitute families, her voice echoed between tall buildings . . . The motion pictures rolled: At the Uptown, Edward G. Robinson starred in a gangster picture, *Widow from Chicago,* while the Warwick featured Walter Huston's latest, *The Criminal Code* ("He defied the criminal code . . . and paid . . . She defied the moral code . . . and suffered.") . . . The Wickersham Committee in the United States Senate portrayed Kansas City as the center of far-reaching operations in the sale of bootlegged liquor. One report described enforcement of state liquor laws in the city as "a joke or a farce" . . . *The Kansas City Star*'s religion editor visited H. L. Mencken at his home in Baltimore and, during an interview, watched him smoke three large cigars and a corncob pipe. *The Star*'s man asked Mencken: "You're a'gin everything—the Bible, religion, the church, the clergy, pedagogy, oratory, prohibition, preachments of all kinds, uplift, and the cherished ideals of most of us. Is

there anything good you're in favor of?" The Sage of Baltimore gave the question considerable thought. Then he
replied, "Yes, I'm in favor of Anheuser-Busch" . . . The
Depression deepened, and the funnyman Eddie Cantor
joked, "The situation is so terrible that when a man goes
into a smart hotel these nights and asks for a room on the
17th floor, the clerk says, 'For sleeping or jumping?' "

Outside the old brick Criminal Courts Building in Kansas City, in the
shadow of the turreted Jackson County Courthouse, a few blocks
from the Missouri River, dozens of fine automobiles crowded the
streets: Buick Roadsters, Austin Coupes, Ford Phaetons. The Myrtle
Bennett murder trial opened on February 23 and brought out a high-
hat crowd, society women in their furs and pumps. These women
arrived early and shivered in the winter cold outside the padlocked
front gate, knowing the courtroom's ninety-nine seats would be
awarded on a first-come, first-served basis.

When Myrtle Bennett and her lead defense attorney, Senator
James A. Reed, mounted the building's front steps, the crowd parted
and stared, chattering in their wake.

"Do you think the senator can get her off?"

"Lucky for her she has the money. *She'll get all the breaks.*"

No one could be certain why the senator had taken this case. Jim
Reed wasn't saying. He told Nell that as an attorney he was, in effect,
a hired gun. He said no client called him unless something had gone
dramatically wrong. It then became his job to represent the client's
interest and to make order out of chaos in that person's life (as
defense attorney, though, Reed typically tried to create chaos to dis-
rupt the order that suggested his client's guilt). His friends insisted
Reed sought only to defend the honor of a woman wronged by her
husband and by public opinion. One rumor said Reed was defending
the liberty of Mrs. Bennett at no cost. Cynical reporters wondered if
Reed had taken this case only to feed his ego. Privately, Nell might
have prevailed upon Reed to aid Myrtle Bennett. She surely identified
with the sufferings of a childless wife at odds with a philandering

husband who was trying to control her. The trial also offered an opportunity for a former senator who had famously opposed woman suffrage to strengthen his bona fides with women voters for the 1932 Democratic presidential nomination.

The newspapers assumed Reed had not taken the case for money. Henry Ford had paid Reed $100,000 when charged with libel and anti-Semitism in a 1927 case in Detroit. Another Reed client, the Universal Oil Company—awarded $25 million in a patent infringement suit against the Standard and Shell Oil companies—reportedly had poured $750,000 into Reed's pockets recently for more than a decade's work. What the newspapers did not know was that Reed's personal investment expert had borrowed heavily and lost nearly everything in the stock market crash. Neither did the newspapers know that Reed was contesting his fee from the Universal Oil Company, demanding more, and that to date he had received nothing. He needed money.

Reed had gotten a trial continuance to allow him and Lura to make their earlier scheduled crossing to Europe in the fall of 1930. Later, Myrtle underwent an emergency appendectomy, and then peritonitis set in. She went to Memphis to recover, and, once there suffered from influenza. Some in Kansas City wondered if her murder trial might ever happen.

Locally there were signs of a deepening interest in contract bridge. *The Kansas City Star* now published regularly on its women's page a frivolous fictional feature, "After the Bridge Party" ("Mrs. Waterstradt just insisted that I drop by to see her new poodle. Such a cunning little thing . . . "), as well as a regular column, "Correct Contract Bridge," by Mrs. Clyde A. Bissett. She kept her eye on the national bridge scene, informing her readers, "Ely Culbertson, now world champion and a leading authority on contract bridge . . . advocates the use of what he calls 'honor tricks.' "

The night before the trial, Reed paced in his law offices. Messengers delivered telegraphs from the East and Southwest. A boy showed up with a large photographic chart, diagrams and drawings of the Bennett apartment.

Prosecutor Jim Page had deep concerns. The stakes for him were enormous. All of Kansas City would be watching. Page aspired to a judgeship, so he needed a conviction in this case, but he worried about the presiding judge, Ralph S. Latshaw. Page had attacked Latshaw and other circuit court judges for their work on the county's board of paroles. As a tough-on-crime politician, Page thought judges doled out paroles too freely. He also worried about Latshaw's long friendship with Reed. All three were Pendergast loyalists, but Jim Reed was, after all, Jim Reed. Twenty years before, Latshaw had been on the bench—in the very same courtroom as this Bennett trial—for the 1910 trial of Dr. B. Clark Hyde, accused in the poisoning death of the eccentric octogenarian philanthropist Col. Thomas Swope. It had been the most sensational murder case in Kansas City history. Reed served as special prosecutor in the case, and his closing argument had launched his senatorial career. In that argument, he described Latshaw as "a man who loves fairness as the sun loves to shed its light," and then he called out to jurors, "I am asking, gentlemen, that poisoners shall not escape, that great wealth shall not be sufficient to hold back the lash of justice and that because a man is rich and can get shrewd and cunning lawyers to defend him, he shall escape while the poor man's son is punished."

Page worried, too, about Charles and Mayme Hofman. They were his key witnesses, but they had remained devoted friends to the defendant. What if the Hofmans altered their earlier sworn statements from the preliminary hearing? Would Page be permitted to impeach his own witnesses?

The Jackson County criminal courtroom was ancient, wooden, and rickety, its floor-to-ceiling windows on one side battered by winter rains and sleet. Faded paintings of bearded politicians from Missouri's lustrous past hung from the walls along with an old clock and a calendar from the Des Moines Life and Annuity Company. Wire netting had been attached to the ceiling to aid the acoustics. A simple wooden witness chair was placed beside a court reporter's desk illuminated by a small lamp; Latshaw's bench was a few feet away. The defendant faced Latshaw while sitting at the far end of a thin table shared with attorneys for the prosecution (to Myrtle's left) and the defense (to her right). The twelve jurors sat in armless swivel chairs in two rows of six. There was a table for newspapermen, a desk for the bailiff, and a wooden railing that separated the public from the trial participants. Windows nearly always remained open in Latshaw's courtroom. Reed worried that everyone in the crowded room would catch cold. This was, after all, winter.

As the trial opened, cuspidors were pushed beneath tables, out of sight, so as not to offend the sensibilities of fashionable women. The chief deputy sheriff arrived in a pea-green suit, his trousers stiffly pressed and his shoes, as one newspaperman noted, "polished like apples of the unemployed." Moments before the bailiff's "Oyez! Oyez!" prompted those assembled in the courtroom to rise, Charles and Mayme Hofman, warm and snug in their camel's hair and mink coats, took their seats. So did Alice Adkins, who sat in the gallery beside Arkansas judge Abner McGehee, Jr., for whom she had worked so long ago and who had come as a character witness for Myrtle. Sitting just behind Jim Page were several of Jack's siblings, newly arrived from St. Louis and rural Illinois.

Myrtle entered with Reed and co-counsel O'Sullivan. Nearly as tall as the senator, she wore a buttoned long black woolen coat, neatly tailored, over a simple frock of black crêpe unseen by anyone in the courtroom. A matching beret covered her hair. She wore black kid gloves, black pumps of alligator leather, and pewter-gray hose. Without makeup, her face was pallid, with dark circles beneath her eyes. She seemed a picture of haggard, quiet desperation. She had been eating little, and drinking too much coffee. Her life was about to be laid bare. In the courtroom, Reed treated her deferentially.

Jury selection took three days. It unnerved Myrtle to hear would-be jurors admit that they had discussed her case in a business office, a packinghouse plant, at home, in a small-town corner store. For the jury selection Reed had activated the Pendergast machine, instructing block captains to learn every biographical fact and known prejudice of prospective jurors. (Even as Page complained loudly about the hidden work for the defense by the machine men, O'Sullivan admitted with a wink, "A few boys have been earning some honest dollars.") Reed studied prospective jurors' occupations, associations, and living habits. Probing back two generations, he asked one would-be juror, "Are you any relative of the man by the same name who is a banker in Independence?"

The senator studied a photograph of the forty-seven men impaneled, and penned brief notations by some.

"Looks like a skinned cat."

"This is a weak man."

"Easily influenced."

"Never had a thought in his life."

Myrtle would not be judged by *a jury of her peers*. Eleven years after the Nineteenth Amendment gave women the right to vote, twenty-six states, including Missouri, still categorically excluded women from juries. Some states insisted that while voting was a *right*, jury service was a *privilege*. (Missouri would change its law in 1945.)

Both the prosecution and defense sought a jury of married men. Of the twelve selected, nine were married, three single, and only one knew how to play bridge. The jury that would determine Myrtle's fate included a night watchman, railroad conductor, factory foreman, insurance salesman, storekeeper, telegraph operator, and retired railroad agent. During the trial, jurors would be kept under guard at the Gladstone Hotel.

Page announced in court he would not seek the death penalty, prompting Myrtle to smile, if weakly, while Jack's sisters glared. Jim Reed said only, "My client is innocent."

Reed would appeal to the jurors' chivalry. He would demonstrate that Myrtle, a chaste and honorable woman, had periodically suffered violence at the hands of her husband. Jack had struck and humiliated her. Reed would ask jurors, in effect, to protect Myrtle, as they might their own wife, mother, or daughter. He knew how jurors, particularly married ones, thought and felt. He knew about the shifting values, and verdicts, among juries in murder trials of wives who had killed their husbands. An old unwritten law allowed a man to murder a libertine who had had sex with his wife. And American courts early in the twentieth century seemed to approve a wife's taking lethal action against a physically abusive husband. Of eighty white women who killed their husbands in Chicago between 1875 and 1920, only two were found guilty and sentenced to prison terms of more than a year. (Black women, who committed a disproportionate number of the husband killings in Chicago, were convicted at nearly five times the rate of white husband killers.) Murdering wives in Chicago during this period often came from wealthy families and were thirty-three years old on average—Myrtle's age, in September 1929, was thirty-four. These women overwhelmingly acted to protect themselves from physical abuse, and typically used a gun. Most of these killings were premeditated, and many wives later expressed not remorse but relief, even joy, over the act. Some knew their legal defense strategies even before killing. One told Chicago police, "I look upon my act as a morally justifiable killing." Another carried to the shooting a newspaper article that detailed the acquittals of fourteen husband killers. Chicago prosecutors blanched. In 1906, one defended the right of a husband to use physical force against his wife: "If this jury sets the precedent [that] any woman who is attacked or is beaten by her husband can shoot him, there won't be many husbands left in Chicago six months from now." In 1917, another prosecutor asked jurors if they planned "to join the great army of boob ex-jurors who have acquitted women of murdering their husbands although they were absolutely guilty." Immediately after killing her husband in 1919, a Chicago woman said: "I will need no attorney—the new unwritten law will save me. I will tell my whole story to the jury and they will free me."

It was instructive to consider the two white husband killers in Chicago convicted of murder. One was an unschooled nineteen-year-old dressmaker from Mississippi, who, the prosecutor said, had accepted the attentions of other men. Therefore, he argued, the husband's physical beatings of her were appropriate, and the killing could not have been in self-defense. In the other conviction, in 1919, a forty-six-year-old Swedish immigrant had stabbed her husband to death after he had attacked her with a knife. Neighbors testified that the wife had been a "husband beater" for years—she was much bigger than he—and that once she poured boiling water on him. A few weeks before the killing, neighbors saw the husband running from home holding a bloody handkerchief to his face, charging, "She tried to kill me." A jury of married men convicted the wife, and she erupted in the courtroom: "I suppose if I had been young and beautiful, I would have been turned loose just as other women who have been tried for killing their husbands."

Reed knew Myrtle's acquittal was not certain. Evelyn Helms, who shared the holding cell with Myrtle on the night Jack was killed, offered a cautionary tale. Jurors heard that Helms's husband had starved and belittled her, and a stream of character witnesses testified to her essential decency. Still, in October 1929, with Jim Page prosecuting the case, Helms was convicted of murder and sentenced to ten years in prison.

Reed would play the card of female virtue. He would show Myrtle as a loving daughter and an obedient wife, caring for her husband's every need, frying his bacon, packing his traveling bag. Even as jurors and spectators heard Reed defend Myrtle's honor, they could not know of the lawyer's own indiscretions with Nell Donnelly. They certainly did not know that Nell was pregnant with Reed's child.

As the trial began, Nell, two months into the pregnancy, was not yet showing. Even so, she and the senator had to devise a course of action. Nell believed she and Reed must obtain divorces and marry. She would buy out Paul Donnelly's half-share of the business. Paul's threats to kill himself if Nell became pregnant were irrelevant now.

But Reed had a different view. For one, he refused to divorce Lura. He could not—and would not—do that. They had been married forty-three years, since even before Nell was born. Further, Reed told Nell that he would never marry an Irishwoman. He said he had endured more than enough from Pendergast machine voters, the shanty Irish working in the guts and grime of the stockyards. Reed knew that Nell's father, as a teenager, had emigrated from County Cork, Ireland, before the Civil War, and that he had married Catherine Fitzgibbons, daughter of Irish immigrants. Jim Reed was saying he did not want to marry Nell. Decades later, Nell demurely looked down at her hands, placed neatly in her lap, and said, "But I talked him out of that one."

With the Bennett trial under way, the senator and Nell agreed they would sit down with Paul Donnelly. They would tell him the child belonged to Reed and that if Paul said a word to anyone, he would risk all their reputations and, worse, the financial well-being of the Donnelly Garment Company.

Nell and Jim Reed agreed there was but one way to extricate themselves from this thicket. Before making any move they would have to wait for Lura to die.

Myrtle, Jo, and Nell all waited on their men. Myrtle had sat at home, waiting endlessly for Jack to come off the road. Nell went about the daily business of her dressmaking waiting for Reed to deliver her from marital hell. Jo suffered two forms of waiting: at the bridge table, as the calculating Ely intentionally took forever to decide on his bids, and at home, as she waited for him to leave his cocoon of self-absorption.

Yet none of these women was particularly submissive. In fact, for their times, they were at the opposite end of the spectrum: Myrtle, the competitive bridge player and one-time stenographer; Nell, the millionaire entrepreneur; and Jo, the trailblazer fearlessly invading male inner sanctums. These three women shared a constitutionally low tolerance for waiting that made their waiting particularly unbearable and that would lead, naturally, to flare-ups and extremes of behavior.

Bulldog was the word often used to describe the combative prosecutor Jim Page. In truth, he looked more like a St. Bernard, sad-faced, with jowls, his girth filling out his dark suits.

Page's opening statement was brief, direct. He described the bridge game at the Bennett apartment and the altercation it prompted. He said Jack had died after being chased through the apartment by Myrtle, and that she had fired four shots, the first two missing, the next two proving fatal. "The evidence will show that this woman, before she shot her husband, traveled 60 or 70 feet to get that gun, opened and closed two doors, turned off and on lights," Page said. And then, he added, "[s]he came up behind and shot her husband in the back. . . . The evidence will show that blood was on both sides of the [front] door as the man was shot going out of his own home. He came back and died on the inside of his own place." Page intended to call Charles Hofman as his first witness. If the Hofmans altered their earlier sworn statements, Page intended to shift course and present much of his case in rebuttal. He told the jury, "It was felonious, malicious, willful and premeditated murder with malice aforethought."

Now it was Reed's turn. The senator could have waited to deliver his opening statement until after the state had presented its case. He opted to weigh in now, though. His thatch of white hair neatly parted, his horn-rimmed glasses far down his nose, Reed began softly, grandfatherly. From the back rows of the courtroom, women spectators leaned forward. From the first row, Jack's siblings eyed the senator warily. Page waited for the senator's theatrics, certain they would come.

"Gentlemen of the jury," Reed began, "after hearing the statement of the state's case as recited by Mr. Page, I can't understand why he signed that information." Twenty years before, as prosecutor in the Swope murder trial, Reed had told jurors, "I have never tried to appeal to your passions. I have not tried to wring a tear. It is the cheapest and easiest thing that a lawyer ever did." But just now, as he led jurors through a detailed history of Myrtle's humble upbringing, telling of how her father's death had left her and Alice Adkins destitute, Reed's lips quivered and his eyes grew moist.

"I object," Page shouted from the prosecutor's chair. "Whether she was destitute has nothing to do with this case."

Reed told Judge Latshaw he only wanted to show his client's life history.

Page exploded: "I don't want him standing there trembling, tears in his eyes, talking about the defendant being destitute."

Reed: "Maybe you would tremble, too, if the facts of this woman's life were—"

Page: "I'll tremble because this defendant shot her husband in the back!"

Latshaw's gavel thundered. "Gentlemen, gentlemen," he said. Reed continued. Hearing the senator tell her life story, Myrtle, sitting at the defendant's table, sobbed and dabbed a handkerchief at her eyes.

Page rose from his chair: "I want to tell this court that if the defense counsel proposes to give the defendant's life history, I'll call enough witnesses to give the life history of the deceased. What's fair to one is fair to the other."

Undeterred, Reed told of his client's years as a telephone operator and a stenographer, and when he mentioned her work in a law office, he turned to Myrtle and asked how long she had held that job.

About three years, Myrtle replied, through broken sobs.

Infuriated by what he was seeing—emotion, tears, *a goddamn stage show*—Page asked Latshaw to pause long enough to give "counsel for the defense and his client a chance to finish their cry."

"Jim, I just can't help it," Reed told the prosecutor. Then Reed said, "I am not trying to be emotional. I wish I could be as cold-blooded about it as some in this courtroom."

In this case, Reed told jurors, he would show Jack as a competent young man with a temper, a character flaw perhaps, and how, when he departed on business trips, he left his .32 Colt automatic pistol with Alice Adkins, his mother-in-law, for her protection. He said Adkins knew about guns, having lived in Mississippi, as he would put it, "among the colored folk." But, he added, "I don't imagine she had seen many of those devilish weapons such as her son-in-law gave her." Reed then described the day of the killing, the golf outing and the bridge game with the Hofmans. Reed said he didn't play much bridge, but he loosely described the bidding of the fatal hand, and said that when Myrtle was dummy she left the table to devotedly prepare Jack's breakfast and to pack his bag, "as she always did, and as a wife should." Upon her return, he said, a bridge table argument broke out between husband and wife, and Jack slapped Myrtle five or six times in the face, "hard." Now Reed emphasized: "He talked to his wife, gentlemen of the jury, of abandoning her." Jack ordered Myrtle to retrieve his gun, Reed said, kept in her mother's bedroom, in a chest of drawers, beneath linens. "Crying, Mrs. Bennett obeyed, as she was in the habit of doing when her husband asked her." He said Myrtle turned on the light in her mother's room, still sobbing, took the gun and walked into the den. There, Reed said, she saw Charles Hofman step from the master bathroom and approach her. Hofman's movement startled her, Reed said, and she stumbled against a chair in the den and the gun discharged twice, accidentally. (A few feet away, Myrtle's sobs grew louder. O'Sullivan patted her hand to comfort her.) "She started into the living room, and Bennett rushed toward her. No doubt he had heard the shots. No doubt he was alarmed. He caught her this way—come here and let me show how it was done."

On cue, O'Sullivan stood. Reed grabbed Jack's gun from the counsel table, the .32 Colt automatic with a steel barrel, and held it in his right hand. The sight of the pistol had the intended effect: the eyes of jurors widened. Standing before the jury box, the two defense attorneys acted out a struggle for the weapon, Reed as Myrtle and O'Sullivan as Jack. They had rehearsed this many times. O'Sullivan (Jack) twisted the wrist of Reed (Myrtle) until the pistol passed under O'Sullivan's armpit. Reed told jurors, "He twisted her arm so the gun was in this position and then it accidentally discharged. Now gentlemen, you have been told that he was shot in the back but the physical facts of this case, and the answer to that charge, is that he was shot in the armpit, accidentally." Page stood next to the two defense attorneys to watch more closely their pantomime of the killing.

Reed said that evidence would also show powder burns on Jack's white polo shirt, burns that could not have been made if this particular weapon had been fired at Jack from a distance greater than twelve inches.

Alone now before the jury, Reed fingered the killing weapon, the pistol's black rubber grip comfortable in his hand. He pressed the pistol under his arm, wheeled before jurors and showed where the bullet exited. "That shot would have been impossible if Mr. Bennett had been trying to run away from the house," he said.

From his chair, Page spoke: "That's a question of argument."

And Reed roared back, "We'll show that!" Then Reed twisted his arm and the gun at a slightly different angle, to demonstrate how the other bullet must have struck Jack.

He described the final scene: Myrtle on the living room floor cradling her dying husband, inconsolable, calling for a doctor. Reed's voice soared, and then broke and trembled, reduced at the end to a whisper. He said, "Then Bennett, still conscious—he only lived a few minutes—tried to speak to Mrs. Adkins—he called her 'Mother'—and reached out and, and [Reed's eyes were moist again, his voice barely audible] . . . took his wife's hand.

"That, gentlemen, is the murder case here.

"Alas, Mrs. Bennett is charged with willfully, deliberately, in cold blood and with malice aforethought murdering the man she loved."

Charles Hofman, the state's first witness, testified, "Bennett dealt and bid one spade. I bid two diamonds. Mrs. Bennett raised to four spades—it was contract bridge. Mrs. Hofman passed, and I, realizing I had a good hand, doubled. Bennett played the hand and naturally I won. He went set two tricks." As that Sunday evening bridge game developed, Hofman testified, "there was quite a lot of criticism as to the card playing between Mr. and Mrs. Bennett—this is a common thing during a bridge game." Hearing this, women spectators tittered. Hofman's testimony about the game and how Jack struck Myrtle and then moved between rooms "like a crazy man," offered no surprises. In his fine dark suit, Hofman stood before the jury box explaining the movements of the players that night, pointing at a diagram of the apartment, even helping the prosecutor hold it. But then, in a critical turn, Page asked, "Is it or is it not a fact that when you went into the bathroom, that Mr. Bennett was rummaging through his dresser drawers and picking up his clothes in his bedroom?"

"The last I saw of Mr. Bennett," Hofman replied, "he was standing right alongside the bed."

Page froze. He was incredulous, furious. Hofman had just changed Jack's position, moving him diagonally across the bedroom, and therefore out of Myrtle's view as she approached from the den, pistol in hand. In the preliminary hearing two weeks after the killing, Hofman had testified that Jack stood by a chest of drawers near the bathroom door. Page's theory of a chase through the apartment that night—his entire case, really—rested on Jack's position. He had to be right there, by the chest of drawers in the bedroom where Myrtle could see him through two open bathroom doors.

Page: "You didn't answer the question and I am asking it again. Answer it yes or no."

Hofman: "I don't know what he was doing."

Reed: "Wait a minute. I object to that. It is an attempt to impeach his own witness."

Page handed Hofman a copy of his testimony at the preliminary hearing, "for the purpose of refreshing your memory." Reed objected again, and Latshaw sent the jury from the room. There followed an hour of spirited arguments between attorneys and the judge. Reed insisted the law did not allow Page to impeach his own witnesses, and Latshaw agreed. But Page said he must be permitted to show jurors how Hofman—Myrtle's good friend—had changed his testimony. Reed accused the prosecutor of "bulldozing and intimidating" the witness, while an exasperated Hofman said from the stand, "Mr. Page, I am a salesman and not a lawyer." Now Page told the judge, "I had a right to believe that the sworn testimony of this witness at the preliminary hearing would be his testimony now . . . It never occurred to me at any time that this witness would testify to anything to the contrary until I heard Senator Reed's opening statement this morning. I made my opening statement as to what the evidence would show based absolutely upon the sworn testimony of this man." Page read from Hofman's earlier testimony about Jack's position: "He was rummaging through his dresser drawers and picking up his clothes." Then, seeing Myrtle approaching, Hofman had testified, "I said, 'My God, Myrtle, what are you going to do?' and she brushed me aside and opened fire . . . I stood right there, glued to the floor in the den . . . She went through the bathroom into the bedroom, no doubt."

"Now, Brother Page," Latshaw said, his tone condescending, "show me wherein he contradicts himself." Page contended that Hofman had moved Jack out of Myrtle's view and so shattered the prosecutor's contention that Myrtle had twice fired at her husband through the bathroom. Page said one bullet had lodged in the bathroom doorjamb and another splintered a hole through the far door that the fleeing Jack had slammed shut to use as a shield.

Myrtle bit her fingernails. The argument shifted. Now prosecutor and judge went at it. Page sought to reword his questions to Hofman in order to bypass Reed's objections, but Latshaw sustained the senator's objection each time. In a huff, Page threw down papers on the counsel table. Latshaw, flushed, rose from his seat and angrily pointed at Page. The prosecutor, enraged, said, "The jury is entitled to know the whole circumstances. I think it would be an absolute injustice for me to have to take the testimony of this man today wherein it is changed as to the material things. I might just as well dismiss this case and walk out of court . . . and I don't think it is the intention of the courts of this country to permit a thing of this kind to happen without the jury knowing all the facts."

With the jury still out of earshot, Reed joined the fray: "The prosecutor would have you understand, I suppose, that she fired shots through this door—blindly through a door—at a man that she didn't know was there at all. Now it is ridiculous, any such argument as that . . . [Hofman] is intelligent, he has told the story in a straightforward manner and he didn't get started to telling it until this proceeding began of attempting to coerce and to prejudice and to mislead this witness in order to get something that it is claimed this witness said at another time, before this jury . . . This man is not testifying to anything today that he has not testified to at this preliminary hearing. Mr. Page is trying to put a construction on some language to suit himself."

Page held his ground, barking and jabbing his arm into the air.

Latshaw, flashing his own anger, said, "Suppose, Brother Page, you do succeed in proving to the jury that this man is a perjurer; that is as far as you can go. Where is your case then? You can't substitute the statement made there for his statement made here. The law says you can't."

Page fought for his case: "You ask me where I would be. I would have to step into another court and prosecute this man for perjury."

Reed objected. Latshaw said, "That sort of idle threat passes as idle wind."

The judge made his decision: "Sometimes the only way a person can see the light is by falling in the darkness . . . I am going to allow you to impeach the witness, against my judgment, and with a firm conviction that you are putting in this record, in case of a conviction of this woman, an absolutely fatal error."

The next morning, the jury back in the courtroom, Hofman returned to the stand. Page handed him a transcript of his earlier testimony. Hofman read it, and then Page led him carefully to this question: "Then as you came through the bedroom and went into the bathroom where was Mr. Bennett?" Charles Hofman answered, "I recollect that he was prancing back and forth between the chest of drawers and the bed." Page took a deep breath, his case once again on more solid ground.

On cross-examination, Reed sought to undo that gain. "You state that Mr. Bennett was moving back and forth from one room to another, you were trying to comfort Mrs. Bennett, and trying to quiet Mr. Bennett down, and he was moving about constantly—it is impossible for you, is it not, at this time, to say where Mr. Bennett was at any particular moment, except when you came back into the room and found him [slumping] on that chair?"

Page shouted his objection, which Latshaw overruled.

Said Hofman, "Yes."

Through other witnesses, Page constructed his portrait of a chase. A maid, Willetta Henry, testified that she and her husband, a Park Manor janitor, lived in the basement beneath the Bennett apartment. At about fifteen minutes past midnight, Henry said, she entered her bathroom, directly beneath the Bennett den and bathroom, and heard two gunshots. Frightened, she ran into her bedroom and awakened her husband. Then she heard two more gunshots upstairs, farther away than the others. Her story supported Page's notion of a chase. The third-floor neighbor Bill Reid took the stand and testified that he heard three shots. He feared a holdup was under way and asked his departing guests not to leave, afraid for their safety. Moments later, he said, he heard a knock at his door, and a woman's voice calling to his wife, "Mrs. Reid, let me in. It's Mrs. Hofman." Mayme Hofman entered and told them what had just happened. Bill Reid and a friend accompanied Mayme to the Bennett apartment, where they saw Jack on the floor, dying, cradled in Myrtle's arms. Reid said he found Jack's pistol on the floor near the front door, and gave it to a patrolman.

That patrolman, G. R. Woodman, testified to seeing blood smeared on the Bennetts' front door, four feet up from the floor. Woodman said he examined the apartment and discovered two bullet holes in the bathroom. On cross-examination, the patrolman said he saw Myrtle holding her dead husband and saying to him, "Jack, why did you do it? Jack, why did you do it?"

Policewoman Frances Trowbridge testified that she spoke with Myrtle at police headquarters, hours after the killing. She said Myrtle admitted to shooting Jack, telling Trowbridge, "I went into the den and he was packing his grip. He said he was going to leave me. I shot him." Jim Reed approached the witness stand and, on cross-examination, asked Trowbridge about Myrtle's condition at the time of that admission. "Wasn't she hysterical?" Reed inquired.

"She was crying," Trowbridge answered.

Reed: "Wasn't she distracted?"

Trowbridge: "She was very nervous."

Reed: "Did the doctor give her a hypodermic?"

Trowbridge: "I don't know."

A deputy coroner, Stanley Hall, testified about Jack's bullet wounds. Page introduced Jack's bloodied polo shirt and handed it to his witness. (Seeing the shirt, Myrtle broke into sobs that shook her body.) Hall identified the bullet holes for jurors. He said either wound alone would have killed Jack. The one in his upper back, he explained, came from a bullet entering beside the second dorsal vertebra, passing so close it nearly struck that vertebra, and exited two or three inches higher through the center of his throat. The second wound, in the left armpit, came from a bullet that ranged downward and lodged in the tenth dorsal vertebra, near Jack's waistline. Each bullet hole in Jack's shirt was at the center of a large brown bloodstain, which jurors examined.

In his cross-examination of Hall, Reed called for O'Sullivan. Once again, the two defense attorneys playacted the killing as they insisted it happened, with O'Sullivan (Jack) seizing the right wrist of the senator (Myrtle), the pistol under O'Sullivan's arm. "Dr. Hall," Reed asked, "with the pistol in this position would it have been possible for the wound under the left arm to have been inflicted?"

Hall thought for a moment. "I suppose so," he said. Just then, a newspaper photographer's flashbulb exploded. With the muzzle of Jack's pistol still held against O'Sullivan's ribs, the explosion startled Reed and O'Sullivan. The two men reacted with a jolt. Spectators laughed, and the bailiff rapped for order. The defense attorneys changed position again, and Hall said he couldn't be certain if the second wound had been inflicted at that range, too.

Jim Page next called a surprise witness, Annie Jane Rice, Jack Bennett's half-sister. Reed objected to her introduction. She had not been mentioned on the prosecutor's witness list, and he had not been permitted to question her before the trial. Out of earshot of the jury, Page argued that he had learned of Rice's connection to the case only two days before. Latshaw, reserving judgment, allowed her to testify.

Under questioning from Page, Rice said she had visited Myrtle at her apartment on November 10, 1929, six weeks after the killing. So close was their friendship in earlier years that Myrtle called Annie Jane "Sis Jane." Now Annie Jane Rice testified, "I said to her, 'Myrtle, you told Brother Tom [Bennett, Jack's brother] when he went to see you that you didn't know why you did it. But you do know why.' "

Page: "What did Mrs. Bennett say?"

Rice: "She said, 'Nobody but me and my God know why I did it.

But I'll tell you, Annie, when this is all over. Then you won't feel so bitter about it.'"

Here was the most damaging testimony yet introduced by the state. Reed sought to undo it, at once. On cross-examination, he stood ten feet from Sis Jane.

"How close was she to you when she said that?" Reed asked, nearly shouting, the volume of his voice exaggerated for effect. Rice didn't understand the question and did not reply. "Did you hear my question?" Reed bellowed.

Rice looked at him. "I beg your pardon," she said.

Reed repeated, louder still, "Did you hear my question?"

She said she did not. Rice asked him to repeat it. He did, and Rice replied, "She was as close to me as this gentleman," and nodded to the stenographer at her left elbow.

With apologies, Rice told Reed, "I am a little more deaf than normally. I have a cold."

Jim Reed smiled. He said he had no further questions.

TEN

Ely in the Crucible

Hard Times and Bridge: When money is scarce for the theaters or talkies, then the joys of Bridge—even though at times tinged with bitterness—are fully realized.
—ADVERTISEMENT
in *The Bridge World,* January 1931

Ely slept late and rose to his first cigarette at midday. He took long hot baths until his alabaster skin turned steamy pink. As governesses and tutors tended to the children, he walked about the apartment suite in pajamas and slippers, or in a thin silk robe, wearing nothing underneath. The tutors, he decreed, would emphasize character, intelligence, physique. They would teach Joyce and Bruce to speak German, French, and English, and to write weekly letters to their parents. Jo wanted no such educational experiments, only happy children. But Ely wanted leaders, perfectionists. He decided his son would become a scientist, his daughter an actress. Jo pleaded against such heavy-handed parenting. But Ely only shook his head and waved her off. He hired a manicurist to buff his fingernails. His clothes hung neatly in a closet, his suits in a row, each garment (socks, handkerchiefs) expensive and European made. He told newspapermen he was a linguist, a scientist, a chemist, a mathematician. He shared autobiographical stories with reporters about defying death, including once after being struck by a Cossack's saber. He liked his coffee ink black, and he carried a special percolator for it on trips. He preferred frozen meats, four or five days old, rare and oozing blood.

As the Depression deepened, Americans had more worries. Contract bridge, a palliative, trickled down from the elites to become a social fad played in homes, hotels, and private clubs, and on ships. Contract bridge columns appeared regularly in hundreds of newspapers and magazines. It arrived on the big screen in the Marx Brothers' 1930 comedy *Animal Crackers*, with Harpo and Chico as cheaters in a game against two women. When Harpo impishly sits in one woman's lap, Chico explains, "He thought it was *contact* bridge!" On radio, the United States Playing Card Company sponsored weekly instruction by the old guard authorities, Work and Whitehead. Visiting America, Britain's Winston Churchill played a few rubbers in a New York home. First Lady Lou Hoover played socially in the nation's capital. In Independence, Missouri, the future First Lady, Bess Truman, played every other Thursday, alternating homes with friends. In Hollywood, movie moguls Samuel Goldwyn, Irving Thalberg, and Louis B. Mayer played for big money. At the Algonquin Hotel in Manhattan, Round Table writers Alexander Woollcott and playwright George S. Kaufman were inveterate players. (Kaufman's bridge partner once excused himself to go to the men's room, and Kaufman famously deadpanned, "That's the only time this afternoon I've known what he's got in his hand.") Syndicated columnists Grantland Rice and Ring Lardner and their wives played contract bridge in their side-by-side homes in the Hamptons. New York Yankees first baseman Lou Gehrig regularly partnered with sports columnist Rice. Babe Ruth played, too, though not competently, usually in his hotel room with sportswriters. Could there have been a less likely bridge player than the brutish Babe, once described by sportswriter Paul Gallico as "kneaded, rough thumbed out of earth, a golem, a figurine that might have been made by a savage"? Ruth interrupted one bridge game with sportswriters when a woman named Mildred called on him. The Babe excused himself and took Mildred into an adjacent room, where he made like the famous man he was. They reemerged in due course, with the Babe telling Mildred, "So long, kid." She left, the Babe returned to the table, and bidding resumed.

The Saturday Evening Post in 1930 suggested that Americans spent more time on bridge "than on any other activity except working, eating, sleeping, traveling, reading and the different methods of expressing affection."

In Babe Ruth's case, there was overlap.

A bridge evangelist, Ely crossed the country by train and automobile, from the Atlantic to the Pacific, with stops along the Gulf Coast. With his derby, walking cane, and quirky mannerisms, he was a persnickety show unto himself. His *Contract Bridge Blue Book* hit number six on the *Publishers Weekly* national bestseller list. He presented his lectures in crowded hotel ballrooms, fraternal lodges, and furniture store showrooms. Nothing would stop Ely, not even when a car he was driving swerved, flipped, and landed upside-down in a roadside ditch near Columbus, Georgia. Ely, another man, and two women bridge instructors suffered bruises, but escaped serious injury. At the lectern that night, unable to stand, Ely quipped, "Ladies and gentlemen, I am sorry to announce that I am a little vulnerable. That is, I have a leg up." He would deliver sixty lectures in two months, sometimes several in a day, losing weight, battling ulcers, yet pleased by the attention. He mastered the art of self-deprecating humor ("I'm half Russian and entirely American. That makes me a trick and a half."), and praised Jo as his favorite partner.

Women, especially housewives, packed his lecture halls, carrying their copies of the *Contract Bridge Blue Book*. At Boston's Copley Plaza, a crowd of 800 filled the main ballroom for one lecture, and, according to *The Boston Evening Transcript*, 748 were women.

Nearly 3,000 showed up for Ely's lecture in Oakland, California. On the podium, his manner was formal and precise, his purpose always the same: to sell his bidding system, and his book. Speaking without notes, he began lectures typically by explaining the Culbertson System. Other bidding measures used "quick tricks" or "sure tricks," but he used "honor tricks" and though his system did not differ fundamentally from the others, it was, Ely said, more accurate and practical. At the end of lectures, women stampeded to the rostrum to shake his hand and to ask him to autograph their books. They posed questions about bridge strategies. He warmed them with his patience, intellect, and charm.

From New England to Atlanta to Cincinnati to Dallas, and west to San Diego and Los Angeles, and north to San Francisco and Vancouver, Ely, with single-minded focus, spread his name, instilled confidence in Culbertson System teachers, and conducted newspaper interviews to emphasize that twenty million Americans—nearly one in four Americans older than the age of fourteen—now played bridge. He could not prove that number was accurate, but the more he said it, the more accurate it became.

Whenever possible, Ely told the story of Myrtle and Jack. It became the star moment of his interviews, writings, and lectures. He would exploit the Bennetts in every way possible, ratcheting up the drama in his telling of the murder at the bridge table. Never mind that Myrtle, to date, had not been convicted. *Murder* better served Ely's needs. The killing of Jack Bennett was a national news story about contract bridge, and Ely seized it for what it was: a fine marketing tool. He was a master of marketing and so it would have been unbelievable had he not used the story to his own advantage. Myrtle's trial had rekindled conversation among players about the vagaries of husbands and wives at the table. And never mind that neither Myrtle nor the Hofmans remembered their cards from that final hand. During lectures, Ely diagrammed on blackboards the so-called Fatal Hand, pure fabrication though it was, first drawn up in his magazine by Sidney Lenz.

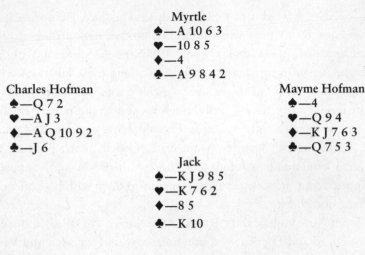

Myrtle
♠—A 10 6 3
♥—10 8 5
♦—4
♣—A 9 8 4 2

Charles Hofman
♠—Q 7 2
♥—A J 3
♦—A Q 10 9 2
♣—J 6

Mayme Hofman
♠—4
♥—Q 9 4
♦—K J 7 6 3
♣—Q 7 5 3

Jack
♠—K J 9 8 5
♥—K 7 6 2
♦—8 5
♣—K 10

In Los Angeles, at a lecture hosted by the Home Economics section of the Los Angeles *Evening Express*, women in the audience listened spellbound as Ely analyzed the Fatal Hand. "His bid was one spade. That was his first mistake," he said of Jack Bennett. About Myrtle, he said, "She raised the bid to four, which was quite proper." He pointed to the blackboard with one hand, his other hand in the pocket of his double-breasted suit. "In playing the hand he [Jack] failed to finesse for the queen of spades. That was his second mistake." Jack failed by one trick, Ely reminded his listeners—"and it caused his death." In truth, Jack failed by *two* tricks, but the idea of one trick increased the drama and made for a better story. It heightened the importance of a bidding system: one misplay at bridge was the difference between life and death. In each new city, on radio and in lectures, Ely cited the story of Jack's demise because it was simply too good not to use. He wrote an article in his magazine, "The Lessons from the Bennett Murder Trial," and surmised, "We have heard of lives depending on the play of a card. It is not often that we find that figure of speech literally true. Here is a case in point. Mr. Bennett had overbid his hand. Of that there can be no doubt, but even with this, so kind were the gods of distribution that he might have saved his life had he played his cards a little better." Analyzing the fictitious Fatal Hand, Ely wrote that when Charles Hofman led the jack of clubs, Jack took the trick with the king, "and started in to pull the adverse trumps. Here again," Ely wrote of Jack Bennett, "he flirted with death as people so frequently do when they fail to have a plan either in the game of Bridge or the game of life."

At nearly every stop along his lecture tour, Ely spoke with reporters, always with a quip at the ready. He told them about his childhood in Russia, and said he could not speak English until he was sixteen. He boasted that he remembered the distribution of cards in bridge hands he had played eight years before. Slyly, he said he refused to be photographed with a pretty woman because it might be "dangerous." Being a bridge expert, he said with a playful sigh, was a *dog's life*. At the stately Mark Hopkins Hotel in San Francisco, he told a local newspaperman, immodestly, that if bridge players alone voted in America, "I'd be president by an electoral grand slam." He emphasized the battle of the sexes at the bridge table. At bridge, he said, "Women trust less to intuition and place their reliance upon concentration and thought. Men fancy themselves to be possessed of an inner capacity for playing and will not study." Wiping shaving lather from his face, and then slipping out of his bathrobe and into a blue suit and derby at the Sutter Club in Sacramento, Ely told a reporter, "I'm all for bridge fights between married couples. It's a fine way to blow off steam and get rid of the millions of little differences and big differences which dam up in both parties and are the real reason for bridge fights." He milked Myrtle and Jack's story for all it was worth. On the day he would deliver two lectures at the Scottish Rite Auditorium in San Francisco, the front-page headline in the *San Francisco Call-Bulletin* blared, "BRIDGE EXPERT EXPLAINS CARD PLAY KILLING: Had Husband Been Good Player He Would Be Alive Today, Says Culbertson."

While Ely was on lecture tour, Dorothy Dix, syndicated women's columnist, pondered the stress points of marriage: "All married people, whether they realize it or not, keep a running account with each other in which they charge up against each other the hurts to their hearts, the wounds to their pride, all the hateful little things that each has done to the other that has taken the joy out of life for them . . . The moral of all of which is that in matrimony as in finance, if we look after the pennies, the dollars will look after themselves. If we avoid the little quarrels there will never be any big ones."

American bridge had never known such a personality. In an earlier age, and on a smaller scale, there was Joseph Elwell. A star of the early auction years, Elwell authored handsome bridge books, with gold leaf and illustrative hands printed in red and black. He insinuated himself into the elite circles of Newport, New York City, Palm Beach, and Lexington, Kentucky, gaining celebrity as an instructor of the stars. Women found him smart, wry, and playful. He taught bridge to the young Harold Vanderbilt, and they played often as partners. He also taught the game to many young, beautiful, married women. Some waited for their husbands to leave for work before rushing to Elwell's New York brownstone for private sessions at his breakfast table and in his bed. A few kept nighttime garments (a pink silk night robe, a boudoir cap, slippers) in his bedroom closet. Then, one morning in 1920, about a year before Ely arrived in America, while Joe Elwell sat alone at a desk in his study, reading mail, someone put a bullet through his head. His maid found him there, slumped in his chair. Without his toupee or dentures, she did not recognize him at first. Elwell made an odd gurgling sound, and the maid ran into the street screaming for help. He died the next day. The tabloids had a big time with the story, trumpeting Elwell as a gambler and rampant womanizer and possibly a bootlegger, and his wife, from whom he was estranged, confirmed that he was all of that and worse. Police never apprehended the killer.

After Elwell, Milton Work, Wilbur Whitehead, Sidney Lenz, and other bridge authorities gained notice through writings and lectures. But times were changing. Now personalities could be shaped three-dimensionally, and packaged to a mass audience. By 1930, more than 40 percent of American households had a radio, and the writer E. B. White commented, "I live in a strictly rural community and people here speak of 'The Radio' in the large sense, with an over-meaning. When they say 'The Radio' they don't mean a cabinet, an electrical phenomenon, or a man in a studio, they refer to a pervading and somewhat godlike presence which has come into their lives and homes." Talkies had arrived in Hollywood, and newsreels, too.

Ely's bridge rivals did not understand him or his publicity methods. They were self-satisfied nineteenth-century men, trapped in the sepia-tone past. They wrote bridge books for posterity and their egos and one another. But Ely was fast becoming a star of the modern multimedia age. He appeared regularly on radio, and had his eye on Hollywood, too. He amazed newspaper feature writers with stories about his life. He said he had been a radical, arrested in Russia, and jailed in Canada. He said that during the war German air raids on Paris were so amateurish that even as Big Bertha bombs exploded in the streets every twenty minutes, he continued playing auction bridge in clubs as if the Germans didn't exist. Down to his last one hundred francs in wartime Paris, he said he put twenty francs on a baccarat table, whereupon a bystander stepped on his toe. They argued, went outside and brawled. When Ely returned to the baccarat table with a swollen eye, the croupier announced that his twenty francs had grown to more than twenty thousand. Ely's mythology grew. He had a compelling if high-pitched voice, an Eastern European sound, plus charm and mystery—and even more than that, he had the elegant Jo. The writer Edwin C. Hill of *The New York Sun* wrote of Ely: "He had the gray matter. He had the personality. And he had his red-haired lady. And the greatest of these was his red-haired lady." Ely's phrase "my favorite partner" amounted to an advertising campaign that sold not only bridge but prestige, and sex appeal. Housewives adored him.

The lecture tour gave Ely firsthand insight into American bridge: who played, and which bidding system they used. Now Ely could play contract at the Knickerbocker and look past his cards, past New York, and see bridge as it existed in the heartland, the South, and the Far West. His teachers carried his system from the metropolises to the hinterlands. Ely would lecture to as many as 225 bridge teachers at his 1931 convention, with each teacher spending sixty dollars for three days, which meant Ely earned $13,500 for less than a week's work. These teachers were paying for the privilege of being associated with the Culbertson name.

Ely used *The Bridge World* to galvanize his teachers' network and to agitate his rivals. His boastfulness could be breathtaking. His magazine described his lecture tour as "a sensational and universal success." It reported that the *Contract Bridge Blue Book* was selling "at the unheard of rate" of four thousand copies daily, "an extraordinary and still mounting tidal wave [and] news of first magnitude not only to Bridge players but to publishers and students of sociology." *The Bridge World* trumpeted that eight hundred teachers taught the Culbertson System now and another four hundred had applied for their Culbertson teaching certificates, abandoning other experts. Per his plan, Ely published his second book: a pocket-size *Culbertson's Own Summary: Contract Bridge at a Glance,* a concise overview of the *Blue Book*. That sold briskly, too.

In his magazine, Ely grew more excessive, more self-absorbed, and more egregious in the sexual suggestiveness of his writings: "This new [Culbertson] Contract system has splashes of romance in it. It is thrilling. Take Forcing bids for instance. Partner is held by the throat and willy-nilly must obey your sovereign commands. At last you can satisfy your inferiority complex through the thrill of an absolute, inexorable command over another being, thus reviving the feeling of godly omnipotence lost in the dim childhood."

Secretly his rivals plotted. They would take back their industry—their books and lectures and syndicated columns. To do that, they joined forces and created a new blended bidding system and gave it a convincing name. They sought to destroy Culbertson—the system, and its irritating creator.

Their announcement came on June 23, 1931, in a news release prepared by Shepard Barclay, bridge writer for the *New York Herald Tribune* and *The Saturday Evening Post.* Twelve authorities, including Barclay, had united to form "Bridge Headquarters," and were in the process of creating the "Official System" of contract bridge. According to Barclay, the avowed purpose of Bridge Headquarters was "to preserve the game of contract bridge, protect it from the advance of unsound ideas, to end the confusion of countless bidding systems and enable anyone to obtain pleasure from playing it." Ely read the names on the Bridge Headquarters list and, except for Harold Vanderbilt,

R. F. Foster, and Hal Sims, who were above such treachery, nearly all of the stars of contract bridge were there including Whitehead, Work, Lenz, Liggett, Barclay, George Reith, E. V. Shepard, and Charles True Adams. "This constitutes the first time in the history of bridge," Barclay's news release read, "that such an aggregation of recognized experts has ever agreed so completely on any matter of a technical nature and marks a new epoch in the history of the game."

The Official System, while acknowledging the Culbertson Approach-Forcing System, simply added the pet devices of Lenz, Milton Work, and others to set up a "new" system to challenge Ely's juggernaut.

Ely released his own statement, calling the new group "Elder Statesmen and Minor Luminaries." Their new venture amounted to "a merger of ex-authorities." He charged that Bridge Headquarters was thinly disguised altruism. It was a commercial enterprise, he announced, owned by the Embosograph Corporation, which manufactured bridge supplies. Each of the experts of Bridge Headquarters would receive Embosograph corporation stock and would participate in the profits created by "junior lecturers" trained by them. The Bridge Headquarters also intended to publish a magazine, and sell bridge supplies and accessories (lamps, tables, scorecards, pencils, duplicate boards). Ely choked out the words, "This will be Mr. Lenz's system No. 5. In the course of the last two years he has published books on four different systems. This will also be Mr. Work's system No. 4."

In the days that followed, New York's newspapers burned with bridge controversy.

Ely took the offensive. He returned to a tactic that feuding Americans and Europeans had used for centuries: a duel. It had worked for him against Buller, and he would do it again, this time on American soil. Using New York's newspapers, he challenged any two members of Bridge Headquarters to a match. He said he would wager $5,000 against $1,000 that he and a teammate, preferably Jo, playing the Culbertson System, would win, thereby proving the superiority of their system. Ely proposed that proceeds from the match go to charity.

Even as Jo privately urged caution, Ely vowed to bring his rivals to their knees. He would challenge them all by challenging one, but which one? Milton Work would not play in a challenge match. Whitey was in declining health. What about Sidney Lenz? Jo's bridge teacher from a dozen years earlier was now fifty-eight. Lenz had won fourteen national titles, though that was many years before, and in whist and auction bridge, none in contract. "If we can pull down Lenz," Ely told Jo, "we'll pull down the whole bazaar." Ely revisited Lenz's books and bridge columns, and studied the hands bid and played by Lenz. He believed Lenz won through his card play, not his bidding system. Ely's eyes brightened. Sid Lenz would be their target.

Privately Ely admitted to fears that he and Jo might be nothing more than "ephemeral little bridge gods." But he concealed these fears behind bravado in announcing to the New York newspapers his challenge of Lenz to a bridge contest of two hundred rubbers. Ely or Jo, or both, would play Lenz and a partner of his choosing in a battle of bidding systems: the Culbertson System versus the Official System. Ely said he would wait patiently for Lenz to respond, and emphasized that his challenge was "good until the cows come home. The place? Bridge Headquarters, Inc., if they want it," he said. But F. D. Courtenay, president of Bridge Headquarters, declined Ely's offer, saying he preferred a nationwide match that pitted twenty couples playing the Culbertson System against twenty couples playing the Official System. Ely laughed. "Very silly," he said.

He appeared on radio station WJZ and the NBC Blue Network and again challenged Lenz. "My lady listeners will not be displeased to hear that this is the first time in the history of whist and bridge that a woman is challenging an international expert and even, in addition, offers extraordinary odds," he said. "Now this challenge is not made out of the spirit of braggadocio, but because I am sincerely convinced that to advise hundreds of thousands how they should bid or play, is a serious responsibility and any well-known authority must be sure of his technical grounds, and be prepared to defend his methods by playing himself rather than having others play for him."

For Ely, the stakes against Lenz would be huge. To lose would be catastrophic. The Culbertson empire was growing at an astonishing rate. Ely's daily and Sunday column (ghostwritten by magazine staffers) was syndicated now in sixty American news-papers, including *The Washington Post, The Atlanta Constitution, The New York Sun, The Boston Globe, The Seattle Times,* and *The Chicago Daily News.* He was about to begin a weekly column in *Life* magazine. Two books bearing his name were selling in huge numbers. And no more dilapidated offices for *The Bridge World*: his eighteen-member magazine staff moved into the swanky new fifty-story General Electric Building on Lexington Avenue and Fifty-first Street.

Ely and Jo, meanwhile, rented an enormous apartment suite at the Hotel Chatham, where their servants sometimes served lunch or dinner to fifteen guests and more. (Like Jack Bennett, Ely was every bit the flamboyant host.) The Culbertsons' few friends also lived in privilege, on Park Avenue and in the Hamptons. At a time when the nation's unemployment rate had reached 16 percent, Ely reportedly was earning $200,000 a year. He and Jo became conspicuous consumers. They dined, dressed, and entertained as if the Depression wasn't happening. It was part of their celebrity image: cool, elegant, happily married. They played only tournament bridge now, except for an occasional social game at Harold Vanderbilt's home.

Though no reply had come from Lenz, Ely was not worried on June 30 when he and Jo, with Joyce and Bruce in tow, boarded the SS *Bremen*. They would spend the next seven weeks in Europe, making a lengthy tour of Russia.

On the high seas, as smoke from his Melachrinos blew in the stiff ocean breezes, Ely could only imagine what Lenz would say when he laid his eyes on the next issue of *The Bridge World*.

The tectonic shifts in bridge stirred even the deep waters of the Atlantic. On the very week of the Bridge Headquarters' announcement, Wilbur Whitehead, aboard the SS *Île de France* with his granddaughter, collapsed and died at sixty-five. He was en route to Paris, where his wife and daughter lived. That Whitey had signed on as a member of Bridge Headquarters did not keep Ely from showing proper respect. *The Bridge World* office closed in honor of Whitey's memorial service at a New York City chapel. Though Ely and Jo were in Europe, the rest of the magazine staff attended. "An irreparable loss to bridge," Ely wrote in his appreciation of Whitey. He cited Whitehead as the first to develop simple yardsticks for auction bidding, a system of valuation, and a quick-tricks table. "Bridge players owe to him countless hours of enjoyment," Ely wrote. "Writers and teachers owe to him ideas and much of their success.

"I, more than anyone else."

As he looked at the cover of *The Bridge World*, Sidney Lenz understood, more clearly than before, the magnitude of Ely Culbertson's ambition. There, two words exploded in boldface capital letters: **A CHALLENGE.**

Beneath, Editor Culbertson cited his conditions:

> Mr. or Mrs. Ely Culbertson challenge Mr. Sidney Lenz to a refereed match of two hundred rubbers at Contract Bridge. Mr. Lenz may select his own partner and play any published system. He may change partners at will but he must play throughout. He may choose a partner for Mr. or Mrs. Culbertson from a list of six players to be named by Mr. Culbertson.

According to Ely, the match would be played at the Hotel Chatham, where Ely and Jo lived and lectured. Ely would put up $5,000 to Lenz's $1,000 and the winnings would be donated to the New York Infirmary for Women and Children. Ely allowed that if Lenz preferred a team-of-four duplicate match, both men would choose their own three teammates (Ely would take Jo, Lightner, and von Zedtwitz), with the stakes rising to $10,000 for Ely and $1,000 for Lenz.

> This Challenge by Ely Culbertson offers to Sidney Lenz a golden opportunity for a show down. Doubtless, Bridge players throughout the world will greatly benefit from the elimination of theories and methods which fail to stand up under the acid test of competitive play.

Ely filled the issue with mud-slinging, name-calling, and petty derision. "Our reaction to the combination of gentlemen formerly regarded as authorities is a mixture of sorrow, tinged with a little shame," he wrote. "We respect honest views, however mistaken they may be." He called his rivals a "paradoxical attraction of opposites." He wrote, "The whole thing can be fixed, for those who are interested in definite historical data, as beginning about the day when sales of the *Blue Book* began to take on best-seller proportions. . . . Authors are sensitive souls. Their nervous systems are curiously polarized in royalty checks . . . Players of 'chaotic' systems have found that there is no 'Royal road to Learning' Bridge. They seem to be at the point of discovering, however, that there is a 'Royalty' path to Stupidity.

"Personally," Ely added, "I am sorry that my colleagues, instead of getting together on a system which is already 'official' are trying to stir up even more confusion and uncertainty, and all to annoy that fellow Culbertson. Really, he is not worth it."

Finally Lenz agreed to Ely's challenge. He posted a certified check for $1,000 with his publisher, Simon & Schuster. "And if Mr. Culbertson means business and this challenge is not just another bluff, let him also post a certified check," Lenz told *The New York Sun*. "Now he has got to put up or shut up." Lenz said he would choose "any of several hundred bridge players who already have expressed a willingness to play." He said, "I would select Mrs. Culbertson as one opponent. Her husband calls her the greatest woman bridge player in the world; certainly she is a much better player than he and . . . much more pleasant to play with."

Ely's reaction to Lenz's acceptance was a vintage piece of showmanship—no reaction at all. He acted as if Lenz still had not answered him. The challenge was generating so much publicity Ely would keep it going for as long as possible.

How startled Sidney Lenz must have been four weeks later when he saw on the cover of the next issue of *The Bridge World* the same two-word challenge as before. To Lenz, it was a rogue's act, ungentlemanly. Just plain rude.

ELEVEN

Myrtle's Murder Trial, Part 2

Snow came to Kansas City, and so did Albert Einstein. He stepped from a train at smoky Union Station wearing a black slouch hat, overcoat, and trousers several inches too short. As Einstein strolled with his wife, Elsa, through the station plaza, awed newspapermen, tipped off to his intermediate stop in Kansas City, took down his every word. "What is this you say, that only twelve men in the world understand my theories? Dummheit! Idiocy. It is not so. Everybody who understands mathematics understands my theories," Einstein said. En route from Pasadena, California, to New York, Einstein would arrive in Chicago the next day and read a speech, from the back of the train, advocating resistance to military service. Then, in New York, he would examine a test tube containing what was said to be the first example of artificially created life (calves' brains, dried and separated chemically, the cells broken down into proteins, fats, and ash; these substances, when placed in ether, re-formed and showed characteristics of living cells). But now, bundled up against the Missouri cold, Einstein strolled past the newsstands where the headlines called out: "A Bennett Climax" and "Tragedy by Steps" and "The Bridge Quarrel Again." The physicist had spent his third visit to America conducting research at the California Institute of Technology in Pasadena—a wonderful city, he said, with lovely Spanish moss. In Hollywood he had met Chaplin, a charming man. Now the winner of the Nobel Prize in Physics shivered in the chill. "What time does the train go?" he said. "These trains: I never remember the time." Einstein considered Kansas City, if only for an instant. "What a sober town," he said, looking off into the distance. "How very sober." Had he stopped at the Criminal Courts Building, he would have had a different view.

As the trial moved into its third day, the crowd grew in size and impatience, once surging against the padlocked front gate until it buckled inward. Some spectators sneaked through a side door. One tried to climb through a window. Another hid beneath the overcoat of a reporter. Denied admittance, one man demanded to know "who Mrs. Myrtle Bennett was" for the court to transform her trial into a society event. The man said he had attended the 1910 Hyde murder trial. "And," he insisted, "surely the principals in that were as important socially as Mr. Bennett." Women came to the musty old courtroom to hear about bridge, to experience a real murder trial, to watch the famous Senator Reed in his final courtroom drama, and especially to hear Mrs. Bennett tell her story. Women seemed more interested than men in the testimony of a maid, one reporter wrote: "For what woman has not at some time cross-examined her own maid if it were over no greater matter than how much butter she put in the cake? . . . 'What testimony would my maid give?' every woman asked herself and wondered." One woman explained why she was attending: "I suppose I might have a tiny interest in finding out how far one might go in punishing one's husband for failing to make a bridge bid."

Harry S. Truman, Jackson County's administrative judge, a courthouse post in Independence, had little time for the travails of Myrtle and Jack. With Myrtle's trial under way, Truman held a press conference to show local newspapermen a sketch of the proposed new county courthouse. His report went mostly unnoticed during the Bennett circus.

Jim Page's wife attended the trial every day. She dreamed one night she was delivering the closing argument, telling jurors she was neither a judge nor a distinguished senator, only a prosecutor armed with the truth. It was, she said, a nightmare.

Each day, it happened the same way: at the morning opening and the late-afternoon adjournment, Myrtle walked down the courtroom aisle past Jack's brothers and sisters. For a decade and more, they had shared visits, stories, laughs. Now Myrtle caught the eye of Jack's brother Tom Bennett and nodded slightly. He returned the nod, but his expression was stern.

On Saturday morning, the prosecution rested, sooner than expected. Jim Page chose not to call either Alice Adkins or Mayme Hofman. Charles Hofman had been troublesome enough, answering many of Page's questions with "I don't remember" and "I can't say exactly." If Page could not cross-examine his own witnesses, he would let Jim Reed call Adkins and Mayme Hofman, as surely he would, and then Page would go to work on cross. Page's case thus far was built on compelling circumstantial evidence: a wife slapped by her husband at a bridge table, a pistol in the wife's hand, and her expression and movement sinister enough to prompt a friend to ask, "My, God, Myrtle, what are you going to do?"; her admission in jail that she had shot her husband; evidence supporting a chase, namely two bullets fired into the bathroom door and doorjamb, and two others striking the victim's back and armpit.

Now it was Jim Reed's turn. His courtroom style was different from that of his friend Clarence Darrow, the famed defense attorney. Big, broad-shouldered, and slightly stooped, Darrow often spoke with his thumbs tucked beneath his suspenders. And he often took cases for posterity. He had kept Leopold and Loeb from hanging in Chicago in 1924, and a year later, in the Scopes trial in Dayton, Tennessee, he placed on the witness stand William Jennings Bryan—and the believability of the stories in the Bible—to dramatic effect. In his courtroom orations, Darrow spoke to the press every bit as much as to the jury. His arguments were meant to be read, not heard. (They were often edited *after* he'd delivered them.) Reed did not need Darrow's homey suspenders, or the morning coat and striped trousers favored by some attorneys. He dressed in a black or blue serge suit. He spoke directly to jurors, up close, playing on their emotions. As a cross-examiner, he was intrepid, hostile, meanspirited. In defending Henry Ford against charges of libel and anti-Semitism, Reed, assisted by a team of seven attorneys, kept plaintiff Aaron Sapiro on the witness stand in cross-examination for thirteen days. He probed, badgered, and denigrated Sapiro, and consistently mispronounced his name. Mencken's description of Reed as a maverick senator—"The forensic talents of the man are really almost unparalleled. He is, for our time, the supreme artist in assault"—applied to Reed in the courtroom as well.

Reed spent most of the first day of his defense introducing character witnesses who were, for the most part, well-heeled and who moved in impressive social circles. Reed announced that some "came all the way from Memphis," or Little Rock, as if those cities were at the distant ends of the earth. Friends, old and new, and former bosses, from Texas, Illinois, New York, and South Dakota—places where Jack and Myrtle had lived or traveled—testified to Myrtle's admirable qualities as a devoted wife, hard worker, and woman of high character and integrity. They testified to having played bridge or golf with Myrtle and Jack. For several hours, the lines of worry disappeared from Myrtle's expression. Her face softened. In his slow, easy drawl, Judge Abner McGehee of Little Rock testified that he had known Myrtle for twenty-eight years. He evoked the life story of the rural Arkansas girl in pigtails. Mrs. Elmena Ebert of San Antonio described Myrtle as "a peaceful, quiet and ladylike woman," and said Myrtle and Jack always appeared very much in love. From New York City came C. A. Pennock, Jack's boss, general sales manager for the Richard Hudnut Company. Pennock said he had known Myrtle and Jack since 1919 and, with his wife, had socialized with the Bennetts in Kansas City and New York, and once on a fishing vacation in Wisconsin. He testified that Jack habitually carried a gun in his car, and once had shown a pistol to him. Pennock could not identify the murder weapon, though, since he said he knew little about guns. He said Myrtle seemed amiable, gentle. Reed asked if Jack had made a lot of money at Hudnut. "That depends what you term a lot," Pennock replied. He said Jack, during the last four years of his life, had earned between $15,000 and $18,000 a year.

Reed attempted to show Jack's high-tempered nature, with Page

objecting at every turn. The prosecutor knew Reed was trying to put
Jack Bennett on trial. Myrtle's longtime friend Mrs. E. M. Houston of
Memphis testified, "They always seemed greatly in love with each
other and got along fine, except when he got ugly." Reed asked for
details about Jack's ugliness, but Page cut him off. The prosecutor
argued before the bench that since the defense was attempting to
prove the shooting accidental, Jack's character had nothing to do
with this case. Latshaw ruled that defense witnesses could tell of
Jack's disposition but could not relate specific manifestations of his
temper.

Reed had other ideas. His defense was elaborately constructed.
Guy Baker, a wallpaper hanger, took the stand. He testified that,
while hanging wallpaper in the Bennett apartment at Ward Parkway,
he witnessed a quarrel between husband and wife. He saw Jack slap
Myrtle in the face, and "slap her hard." Page erupted with an objection, the attorneys bickered, and Latshaw again sent the jury from the
room. In an impassioned plea, Reed said he intended to show that
Myrtle had suffered violence from Jack before the night in question
and that in a state of fear she retrieved his .32 Colt automatic to protect herself. "Because of the peculiar circumstances in this case it is
necessary for the defense to show the relations of Mr. and Mrs. Bennett," the senator said. He insisted the wallpaper hanger's testimony
was necessary and proper. It would show Jack's temper, his violence,
and that Myrtle had not fought back in the past. That was not her
way. Reed was preparing four separate defenses for the shooting of
Jack Bennett: accidental, emotional insanity, self-defense, and quali-
fied self-defense, the latter generally meaning too much force was
used by the defendant to repel an assault. He would demonstrate that
Jack had struck Myrtle before the night of the bridge game and that
Myrtle had not retaliated. He would demonstrate that these previous
attacks amounted to communicative threats and caused Myrtle to
fear for her life, so that either she wrestled with Jack for the gun to
keep him from taking it, or shot him deliberately in an understand-
able act of self-defense. (O'Sullivan joined this argument, and
explained to Latshaw, "She had a right to shoot under the theory of

self-defense . . . She had the right to apprehend danger when he seized the gun.") These theories connected neatly with the emotional insanity defense for, depending on the turns of the trial, Reed might also portray Myrtle as temporarily deranged from the humiliation of being struck in front of guests.

Page questioned Reed's right to inject an irrelevant new motive into the trial. Latshaw told Page he was inclined to admit the testimony, which he viewed as relevant to the case. He gave Page until Monday to look up the law on the case. He also gave jurors a much-needed break. For a few hours Sunday afternoon, Latshaw announced, a bus would show them the newest paved roads in Jackson County, a respite from the interminable hours of sequestration at the Gladstone Hotel. There, fighting late-night boredom, one juror had been teaching two others how to play contract bridge.

A letter arrived at the law offices of James A. Reed, in it a mocking poem:

> *One Spade he bid,*
> *Poor dud, he is dead.*
> *She sits in widow's weeds.*
> *He went down one,*
> *She got her gun.*
> *One Spade is all he needs.*

This is what we are up against, Reed said as he spat out his cigar tip. That kind of rot!

On Monday, O'Sullivan told reporters the defense was seeking the right moment to put Myrtle on the stand. As anticipation built, bailiffs crammed extra chairs into the courtroom. Members of Boss Pendergast's family, hoping to hear Myrtle's testimony, got front-row seats. Tension was building within Jim Reed. News photographers bothered him until Reed obtained a ruling from Latshaw that forbade photographs during testimony. The spectators bothered Reed, too.

"If this sightseeing crowd shows up tomorrow, I'll have a brain-storm," Reed told Page. "I'll have it and give them a good cussing out when I do."

Page had done his reading, and said, without explanation, he would withdraw his objections to allowing defense witnesses to discuss the manifestations of Jack's temper. (Page might have concluded that the evidence was admissible and decided that to improperly exclude it would entitle Myrtle, upon conviction, to a new trial; or he might have determined that jurors would know that Jack's prior mis-conduct had nothing whatsoever to do with Reed's *accident* defense.)

Reed smashed ahead with his defense. Witnesses told stories about Jack's temper and how, on two previous occasions, he had slapped Myrtle. Ernest Olrich of the National Bella-Hess Company in Kansas City testified how Jack had cursed and slammed his briefcase shut in anger in Olrich's office after he refused to sell Hudnut per-fumes at the prices Jack sought. Olrich also testified how Jack, in a huff about his poor shot-making on the golf course, had once heaved his golf bag over a fence. Mrs. E. M. Houston testified that in Mem-phis, while Myrtle was "in a delicate condition" (Reed clarified, "You mean in a family way?" and Houston said, "Yes"), they posed in her backyard for Kodak pictures. A small boy put a puppy in Jack's lap. "Hold him, Jack," Myrtle said, smiling for the camera. Jack became enraged over the dog, cursed, and stalked into the house where he remained, away from guests, all day. Guy Baker returned to the stand. Baker, the wallpaper hanger, testified that as he worked in the Bennett kitchen in September 1928, he saw Jack emerge from the master bedroom and ask Myrtle where to find a certain dress shirt. Check the closet, Myrtle replied. Jack said he "couldn't find the damned thing." Then wear another shirt, Myrtle told him, where-upon Jack scoffed, "Oh, to hell with it," and slapped her in the face. Baker testified that he watched Jack grab his hat and coat and leave the apartment while Myrtle dashed into their bedroom and wept for thirty minutes. In the summer of 1929, a repairman named Nelson Duss had witnessed a similar scene: Jack strode into the Bennett kitchen holding a necktie. "Look," he demanded, pointing at the tie.

"What is it, Jack?" Myrtle said, with indifference. At that moment, Duss testified, Jack slapped his wife so hard she nearly fell over. "Damn you, I'll knock some sense into your head," Jack said, and strode off. Page did not cross-examine Baker or Duss.

Now Reed called Mayme Hofman to the stand to discuss the most relevant slapping of all. Dressed in a striking sport suit of burnt orange, with matching hat, sheer hose, and low-heeled pumps, Mayme testified in a voice small and timid. Reed brought her along gently: "Mrs. Hofman, describe the game. I do not mean how all of it was played, but how the game went and bring us up to the time of the last hand. Tell it in your own way."

Mayme: "Well, we played Mr. and Mrs. Bennett partners and Mr. Hofman and I partners. During the course of the game, the last hand, the bid went around. Mr. Bennett opened the bid, a spade, I believe. Mr. Hofman bid two diamonds."

Reed interjected: "Was that higher than a spade?"

Mayme: "Yes, and Mrs. Bennett raised him to four spades because in contract you have to have four spades to make game. Mrs. Bennett, of course, laid down her hand and was dummy and Mr. Bennett played the hand. He went set on the hand and Mrs. Bennett said that he should have made it. Mr. Bennett said she had no business raising it to four spades. She said that she laid down a beautiful hand, which she really did, and before we realized what was happening, Mr. Bennett reached across the table and grabbed her by the arm and slapped her hard and almost upset the card table. We were astounded and—"

Reed: "How many times did he slap her?"

Mayme: "I cannot say exactly, four or five times." She said they rose from the card table as Myrtle sobbed uncontrollably. "She seemed stunned and hardly knew what to do. She was embarrassed, naturally, at being slapped in front of guests and we were embarrassed, too. . . . [Jack] began running here and there about the apartment. I don't know what he was doing."

Reed introduced Myrtle's two-piece sport suit with vest and skirt, and when Mayme identified it her voice choked with emotion.

(From her defendant's chair, Myrtle, seeing her outfit, wept loud enough to be heard across the courtroom.) Reed showed Mayme a long rip near the arm hole and another in the sleeve. Mayme said she had noticed these rents when she and her husband accompanied Myrtle to the Country Club police station the night of the killing; Latshaw admitted the outfit as evidence. (Reed intended to tell jurors it was torn in the struggle for the gun with Jack.) Reed asked Mayme to recall the last moment she saw Jack alive. Again, Mayme fought tears, and across the room so did Myrtle. Mayme needed several moments to compose herself. Then she told of seeing Myrtle bent over her dying husband and hearing her plead, "Jack, talk to me."

On cross-examination, Page peppered her with questions, with Mayme often answering that she didn't remember. Page asked, "You said, didn't you, that you heard Mrs. Bennett say she would not have any man hitting her?"

Mayme: "I can't say."

Page: "You didn't answer the question." Page repeated his question.

Mayme: "I don't remember the exact words. I may have."

Page: "Answer the question."

Mayme: "I don't remember."

Page asked about the statement she had signed at the Country Club police station on September 30, 1929, only hours after the killing. "Did you read the statement before you signed it?"

Mayme: "I glanced through it. I was too frightened to read much of it."

Page asked if she had made any written corrections to that statement.

Mayme: "I don't remember any that I made."

Page: "Did you make that correction in it?" He pointed to a correction made in pen and ink on the copy of her statement.

Mayme: "No, I didn't."

Page smiled. "Will you take a pen and print the words 'rear bedroom'?"

Reed objected, and was overruled.

Mayme Hofman sensed a trap. "Let me see the statement a moment, just to refresh my memory," she said.

Page: "No, just print the words 'rear bedroom' on this sheet of paper. I want to see if you did or did not make this correction."

Reed protested and Latshaw told Page to let Mayme Hofman see the statement. "I don't remember," she said after a quick review, "whether I made this correction or not."

As Page began to read from a transcript of Mayme's statement to police, Reed objected and Latshaw warned the prosecutor, "You can't impeach a witness's memory. You can impeach if they answer 'Yes' or 'No' and the answer is false. But when she says she doesn't remember, you can't impeach."

Page roared back, "I object to your honor's telling the witness how she can avoid impeachment."

Latshaw rolled his eyes. "Proceed. You can't impeach memory."

With the witness Mayme Hofman, the prosecutor had hit a wall.

Edward Hickman, pistol expert for the defense, testified he had performed tests, firing Jack's pistol into a cloth similar to that in Jack's shirt from a distance of one foot, two feet, and three feet. Only the bullet fired from one foot left powder marks around the hole similar to those left in Jack's shirt, Hickman said. To Reed, this expert testimony confirmed that the shots had been fired during a physical struggle between husband and wife. On cross-examination, Page asked Hickman if he would participate in more tests with the state's own pistol expert, firing the .32 Colt automatic into Jack's shirt from a distance of three inches, six inches, nine inches, fifteen inches, eighteen inches, and twenty-five feet. Hickman said he would happily participate in such tests, and Page told the judge and jury he would abide by the results.

Then, with Hickman still in the witness chair, Page suddenly turned on his heels and said: "Now I want you to come down here in front of the jury and show me how you could shoot me in the back if I had hold of your wrist."

Reed leaped from his chair to object.

Page, ready for battle, said, "Here, then, senator, you take the gun and show me. You said it could be done. You tried to show the jury last week, but the jury didn't see it because your back was turned. Take the gun and show me. I'll stand with my back to the jury."

Caught off-guard, Reed replied, "That's all nonsense."

From the bench, Latshaw said, "Proceed, gentlemen."

Reed fired back, "I'm willing to proceed if Mr. Page will sit down and act like a lawyer."

Page, glowering at Reed and O'Sullivan, said, "I'm acting like a lawyer. *I'm trying to act like two lawyers.*"

Now Page's voice exploded with a challenge: "I'm willing to make the test with the senator, with the judge, with the witness, any member of the jury"—Page looked around the room—"or anyone in the courtroom." The judge told him that only a witness could make a demonstration, no one else. "All right then," Page said. "Mr. Hickman, come down here and take this gun and try to shoot me in the back while I have hold of your wrist."

Hickman stood to comply, but Reed waved his hand and objected. He said, "I'll show Mr. Page how it can be done if he'll sit down." His objection was sustained.

Page jabbed an index finger at the senator and said, "Fine. I'm going to hold you to that promise."

"The defense calls Mrs. Alice Adkins." Whether it was the sound of those six words or the appearance of the old Mississippian walking in small steps toward the witness chair, or the very idea of her mother coming to her rescue, Myrtle went to pieces. Tears stormed down her cheeks and fell to the table. Her anguished sobs filled the courtroom. Quietly, Page asked Latshaw to send the jury from the room "until the defendant can calm herself." "I'll be all right," Myrtle protested as jurors walked out, but her sobs grew deeper. Jim Reed's eyes filled with tears. O'Sullivan threw his arm about Myrtle's shoulder as she slumped over the table. O'Sullivan waved for Myrtle's bridge friend Mrs. Benjamin Shires. In her wide-brimmed hat, Shires sat beside Myrtle until finally she quieted.

On the witness stand defending her only child, wearing a dark overcoat with fur collar, and a bulky wool hat that perched curiously atop her head like a thick biscuit, Alice Adkins seemed a tower of strength. Each day, she came to court prepared to testify, mounting two flights of stairs, jostled by curiosity seekers in the hallways. Her craggy face suggested the rocky soil of Arkansas, her voice the rural rhythms of her native Coahoma County, Mississippi. The sympathies of spectators were with her.

"They were a loving couple; never had any serious trouble of any kind," Adkins testified about Myrtle and Jack. Reed asked if once, when Myrtle had returned from a business trip with Jack, one of her eyes was discolored. "Yes," Adkins replied, "and he apologized to her about it after they got home and said he was sorry he had struck her in the eye."

Reed: "Then how were they after that?"

Adkins: "Fine and loving toward each other."

Once, Adkins said, Jack turned his temper on her after she had tailored his lounging pajamas. "He wanted them taken up a little in the waist—Mr. Bennett was small in the waist—and when I had them done they weren't small enough, and they didn't please him. I said to him, 'Jack, I fixed them the best I could,' and he said to me, 'Well, I guess I'm a liar then,' and he got mad."

Reed asked, "He swore at you?"

Yes, Adkins said.

Reed: "What about after that?"

Adkins answered, "Oh, he was just quick-tempered. He soon got over it and was very nice to me."

Reed turned to the night of Jack's death. Adkins testified to watching the bridge game before turning in. Much later, awakened by a bright light in her bedroom, she testified she heard Myrtle rummaging through her chest of drawers. She asked Myrtle what she was after. "Jack wants his gun. He is going to St. Joe," Myrtle replied. Her daughter, Adkins testified, was sobbing when she took the pistol. Moments later Adkins heard two gunshots. She rose from her bed and, in her confusion, ran through the wrong door—into her bathroom—

before turning and running down the hallway toward the bright light of the living room. Reed pulled out the diagram of the apartment and Adkins put on her tortoiseshell glasses. She traced her movements for the jurors. Once she reached the living room, she said she saw Jack step toward the open front door, put his hand against the doorjamb, then step back into the living room and sit in a chair.

Reed: "Where was Mrs. Bennett when you saw her?"

Adkins: "Standing right there"—she pointed to the diagram indicating near the master bedroom door—"just like she was frightened almost to death, paranoid." Later, when the doctor arrived and pronounced Jack dead, Adkins recalled, Myrtle said, "Jack's gone and I want to go, too." Adkins told the others not to let Myrtle get hold of the pistol.

Page cross-examined Adkins, his tone gentle even as she fell back on the reliable standby answer—"I don't remember." He asked about Jack as a son-in-law: "Mrs. Adkins, how did Mr. Bennett treat you?"

She replied: "He was very kind to me."

Page: "He took good care of you in your old age, didn't he?"

Adkins: "Yes. He was always good."

Assistant prosecutor John V. Hill, working with Page, interrupted: "I want to object to Mr. O'Sullivan standing there shaking and nodding his head at the witness. Let the witness answer."

O'Sullivan boomed: "I resent that! I was doing nothing of the sort."

Latshaw waved his hand and said, "The jury will disregard it. Mr. Hill, suppose you tell me when you think you see anything like that."

Page asked Adkins if she told Myrtle, as she rummaged through the chest of drawers for the pistol, "Jack won't need his gun tonight."

Adkins said she didn't remember.

When she saw Myrtle in the living room with the gun in her hand, Page asked, did Adkins say to her daughter, "Myrtle, what on earth are you doing?"

Adkins said she didn't remember.

At one point, Page said, "Now, Mrs. Adkins, I'm going to ask you if it isn't a fact that—" Adkins didn't let him finish. "I don't remember," she said. The courtroom broke up in laughter. The frowning deputy sheriff waved his arms in a call to order.

It was a stalemate.

Finally, Latshaw said, "You can't impeach this old woman by what she doesn't remember."

As Page battled to introduce discrepancies from Adkins's earlier sworn testimony, Reed insisted there were none. Though eager to get Myrtle on the stand as soon as possible, he suggested adjournment to give Page time to identify discrepancies to show to the court. "It's a good suggestion," Page said, adding defiantly, "and I'll find the discrepancies."

Reed sneered and told the prosecutor, "You ought to wear petticoats. You always get the last word."

The next morning, Jim Page arrived laden with law books. He read aloud Missouri Supreme Court rulings that showed he had legal precedent to impeach the memory of the witnesses Mayme Hofman and Alice Adkins. With the jury out of the courtroom, Page and Reed sparred on this issue for two hours. "Judge, you know more criminal law than Page ever thought of," Reed said, nearly fawning. The judge replied, "The fact is, Senator, I'm such a good friend of yours that I can hardly give you a fair trial." Latshaw had long admired Reed, and was among the few Missouri Democrats to stand by him in 1919 during the League of Nations fight for "his courageous, forceful and honest stand." Now Latshaw said he was inclined to rule for the state for fear of being partial to his old friend. This time, he ruled in favor of Page. Latshaw would admit witnesses' earlier testimony, but only for the purpose of impeaching the witnesses. Their previous testimony could not be used against the defendant. (Page could only hope jurors would not compartmentalize this earlier testimony, per the judge's ruling. At the very least his case demanded that they hear it, and decide for themselves its relevance to Myrtle Bennett.) Latshaw smiled at Page. "I'm glad to see you read a little law last night," the judge said.

Good news came to Page from the new pistol tests. Jack's bloody shirt had been laid against cakes of soap in the gallows room of the county jail, and his .32 Colt fired at it from the newly prescribed distances. Back on the witness stand now, Hickman admitted to Page during cross-examination that the holes in Jack's shirt were surrounded by not powder burns but bullet burns. By examining the bullet holes in Jack's shirts, therefore, Hickman said he could not tell the distance from which the shots had been fired. Here was a victory for Page.

Reed got some satisfaction, though, when Hickman admitted from the witness stand that, yes, the killing shots could have been fired from close range, as if during a struggle.

Myrtle suffered in silence. Her private life observed and exposed, each day she gnawed at her fingernails and failed to get enough food or sleep. Her pallor grew sickly, the circles under her eyes darkened, and her outfit, which she had worn all eight days of trial, began to look as wrinkled and exhausted as she did. On Tuesday, two of Reed's associates burst into the courtroom. They interrupted the senator, whispering into his ear. Reed sidled over to the bench and quietly spoke to Latshaw, who dismissed the jury. Reed and O'Sullivan approached Myrtle, delicately, knowing her emotional imbalance. Only a few moments ago, they told her, Alice Adkins, while waiting in a room upstairs to be recalled as a witness, had collapsed. Myrtle panicked and rushed from the courtroom, her attorneys in tow. A murmur passed through the courtroom, spectators uncertain of what was happening. Myrtle ran up the courthouse stairs calling, "Mother! Mother!" Overwhelmed by the trial's pressures, Adkins had suffered a nervous breakdown. Myrtle found her prostrate, mumbling. Adkins was carried to a waiting ambulance and taken to the home of Mr. and Mrs. H. E. Woods.

A train through the heartland arrived in Kansas City earlier that morning carrying a young man with a story. He proceeded directly from Union Station to the courtroom. The prosecution had telephoned him only a few days before. He told them his tale straight, as if it had happened only yesterday. The assistant prosecutor pleaded with him to come to the trial to testify, promising to pay for his train fare and lodging. The young man obliged. His story was a bombshell, the last and most important trick in Jim Page's bag, and would be delivered from the witness stand during rebuttal. The young man, still in his twenties, small and angular, with dark veiled eyes, was Byrd Rice. He was Jack Bennett's nephew and had lived for a time with Myrtle and Jack. The family knew him as a good-time Charlie, young and carefree, and devoted to his uncle Jack, whom he admired. In the courtroom he exchanged handshakes and hugs with Bennett family members, including his mother, Annie Jane Rice. The family told him every detail about the trial, including how his mother had already testified that Myrtle had told her: "Nobody but me and my God know why I did it."

All of Kansas City awaited Myrtle Bennett's testimony, and when she finally gave it, Byrd Rice would understand instantly that it was at odds with the story he knew.

He also knew her story was at odds with the truth.

At last Myrtle Bennett came to the witness stand in an attempt to save herself from prison. The senator wasted no time, taking no chances, diving into questions about the Fatal Hand within two minutes of her swearing in.

Myrtle, in nearly a whisper: "He slapped me several times. I don't recall how many."

Reed: "Where did he slap you?"

Myrtle: "In the face."

Reed: "Were they hard or easy blows?"

Myrtle: "Hard."

Clutching a large white handkerchief, she spoke softly, her eyes focused on her attorney. She trusted Jim Reed completely. She testified that she had packed Jack's grip during that night, and said it was resting in the den on a large English lounging chair. Fighting her emotions, she told how she approached her husband after he had slapped her and after he had announced he was leaving at once for St. Joseph. She asked him to apologize to the Hofmans. "I felt that they had been embarrassed and . . . I thought it would be better if we would try in some way to make them feel better and I walked over and asked him not to go [to St. Joseph] and to apologize to them, too, for his conduct," Myrtle testified. "And he told me that he was going, to go and get the gun back from my mother's room; that he was going to go that evening."

With the gun in hand, Myrtle testified, she walked into the den and saw Charles Hofman. "He said something to me, as he says, 'My God, Myrtle, what are you going to do?' and reached for me or in some way, I don't know just how it happened, I couldn't tell you—but there was a chair—a large chair, one of the dining room chairs sitting there." Her lips trembled, and the pace of her words quickened as if she were in a race to reach the finish. "It hit my arm in some way or I stumbled over it, or in some way." Her breaths deepened. "I don't know how it happened, and the gun discharged." She buried her head in her white handkerchief and wept.

Several women friends in the courtroom wept with her. Jim Reed stood beside the witness chair and waited, allowing the widow's emotions to pour over the jurors. Then, softly, Reed asked, "Did that frighten you?"

Myrtle answered, "Why, it nearly frightened me to death."

Reed: "Where did you go from there?"

Myrtle: "I went on through the bathroom and through my bedroom—or *our* bedroom, rather—and when I got in there Mr. Bennett was running towards me or coming—"

Reed: "Into where?"

Myrtle: "Into the bedroom. Mr. Bennett was coming towards me and when he got right to me, right near the door leading from the living room into the bedroom, he caught hold of me and grabbed hold of me, and then he caught hold of my arms and twisted them and in some way in the scuffle, I don't know how, the gun discharged, I don't know how it happened. I don't know in what position, or just how it happened, but that is how it happened." She told Reed, "When he grabbed hold of me I said, 'Oh, Jack, be careful, be careful of the gun'—because it had just discharged and I was frightened to death when he came toward me. I didn't know what he was going to do. I was just frightened when he took hold of me and that's all I know. I was simply frightened to death."

She said she saw Jack recoil from the gunshots, stagger backward, away from her, sit on a chair, and then slump to the floor. She remembered asking her mother, the Hofmans, anyone, to call a doctor, to call Jack's aunt Nellie. She remembered putting a pillow beneath Jack's head.

Reed asked if she had ever handled the .32 Colt. "No," she said.

The senator angled toward the finish: "Now, Mrs. Bennett, did you intentionally or consciously fire that gun at your husband that night?"

"No, indeed, I did not. I'd rather have been dead myself."

"You may examine," Reed told the prosecutor.

Reed had intentionally covered little ground, leaving few openings for Page.

The prosecutor barreled forward. "Did you say you were so excited that you didn't know how it occurred?"

"I did," Myrtle replied. "I don't know what position we were in exactly when it happened. It was in a scuffle. It would be impossible to say."

"If you don't know how it occurred," Page said, "how do you remember that he grabbed you *hard*?"

Reed objected, and Latshaw sustained.

Page pressed on. "The only thing you know about it, is that he grabbed you hard, is that right?"

Myrtle: "No, that isn't all I know about it."

Page asked if Jack was facing her when she fired the last two bullets, or if his back was turned. "It would be impossible for me to say. I don't know," Myrtle said.

Page asked about the dining room chair that struck her arm. Where was it positioned in the den? How tall was it?

"One of those large, heavy upholstered chairs," Myrtle said.

Page: "Did you fall down before you fired the first two shots?"

Myrtle: "I don't know what you mean 'fall down.' I had

stumbled over this chair. I was not down on the floor, no." She said the first two shots discharged from the den, before she reached the bathroom.

Page asked if the bathroom door was closed.

Reed objected, saying, "I didn't ask any questions about that."

Latshaw: "Objection sustained."

The legal wrangling intensified, prompting Latshaw to send the jury from the room.

Page's eyes grew tight at the corners. "You said in your answers to Senator Reed that you did not intend to fire the shots."

Yes, Myrtle said, that is true.

Page asked if she had had a talk with Jack's brother Tom Bennett soon after the shooting.

"Yes," Myrtle replied, "at the county jail."

Page said, "Did you mention to him how you happened to shoot your husband?"

Reed's protest prevented her answer.

Then Page asked if she knew Byrd Rice, and despite Reed's loud objection, Myrtle was permitted to answer.

Yes, she said, Byrd Rice is Jack's nephew.

"Did you have a conversation with Mr. Rice after the shooting?"

But Reed intervened, with another objection that Latshaw sustained.

Page erupted. "If Mrs. Bennett told other persons that she did shoot him and that she intended to shoot him, the state has a right to show that."

But Reed countered: "If the state had any such evidence it should have been shown in its case."

Latshaw ruled without delay: "The defendant can be cross-examined only on those points brought out in the interrogation in chief. The law throws special protection around defendants in criminal cases and there is a specific way in which they must be examined. We recognize that intent is a necessary ingredient of a crime. Yet it must be proven by the state in its case in chief. The defense objection is sustained. Bring in the jury."

Even before jurors returned, Page cited case law supporting his position.

"I'm not going to be subjected to argument every time I rule on a matter, Mr. Page," Latshaw thundered. The jurors reappeared and took their seats. "Proceed, Mr. Page," the judge said.

"Under the ruling of the court," Page said, "I can't ask any more questions of this witness."

Reed bounded to the witness stand. "That is all, Mrs. Bennett," the senator said to his client, solicitously. He extended his hand to her and escorted her to the defendant's chair. Myrtle sipped from a glass of water, her hands trembling. Her testimony, including cross-examination, had lasted only forty minutes.

An agitated Page announced that he would bring courtroom observers to the witness stand to testify how Latshaw had thwarted the prosecutor's pursuit of justice: "I'll call bystanders to show that I tried to read the law into the record."

"Bystanders, bah!" Latshaw said. "I'll rule it out!"

On opening night of the ballyhooed Bridge Battle of the Century in December 1931 in the Culbertson suite at The Hotel Chatham in New York, the press gathers around Ely and Jo as they challenge Sidney Lenz *(seated right)* and Oswald Jacoby *(left)*.
The Bridge World

TWELVE

Bridge Battle of the Century

*The practical attitude toward all partners should
be that of a philosophical sincere and sympa-
thetic friend. Partner must never be allowed to
feel that his loss is taken too hard by you. During
bidding and play, partner, however weak, must
feel that you sincerely respect his intelligence and
efforts.*

—ELY CULBERTSON,
in *Contract Bridge Blue Book*

The Culbertsons returned home on September 18, 1931, on the RMS
Mauretania. A newspaperman asked Ely his view of the new Official
System. "Their so-called system," Ely replied, "is eighty percent Cul-
bertson, twelve percent Work and Lenz, and eight percent rubbish."

Not coincidentally, upon his return, Ely taught a weekly bridge
class with key members of the New York media: the president of
NBC Radio, the president of the Bell Newspaper Syndicate, the gen-
eral manager of the Associated Press, the syndicated sports columnist
Grantland Rice, the editor of *Vanity Fair* magazine, the editor of *The
American Magazine*, and Bruce Barton, the celebrated adman from
Batten, Barton, Durstine, and Osborn. Ely nurtured these relation-
ships, and they would serve him well.

The Bell Syndicate soon placed Ely's bridge column in 120 American newspapers with a combined circulation exceeding six million. While other magazines likened Ely to Napoleon, the Prince of Wales, Einstein, and golfer Bobby Jones, *The American Magazine* suggested him as "a youngish David, [who] has risen up to defy the Goliaths of hearts and spades." In this article, writer Jerome Beatty asked members of his wife's bridge club about Ely. "He's grand! I heard him speak in Miami last winter. You can have Rudy Vallée. Give me Culbertson," one woman replied. They told Beatty they played the Culbertson System because Ely described a complex game with humor and philosophy and warmth without getting bogged down in technicalities. Beatty's wife estimated that Ely was responsible for more than a half million bridge quarrels across America. Beatty wrote, "He—virtually alone—has stirred up a nation-wide bridge war; a war so intensely exciting that normal citizens who debate calmly on politics or prohibition have been known to go berserk in discussions of Culbertson and his veteran rivals in the art of bidding."

By October's end, Ely's *Summary* appeared at number two on the national bestseller list, and his *Contract Bridge Blue Book* at number eight.

Despite Sidney Lenz's reputation as a gentleman and bridge maven, Ely badgered and belittled him. A graying, bespectacled bachelor, tall and wiry, with a prominent nose, Lenz possessed a droll sense of humor and raging competitiveness. He had been a tremendous athlete, excelling in tennis, swimming, golf, and bowling. His apartment at 240 West End Avenue held so many trophies it resembled a whist and auction bridge museum. He once was offered $1,000 for a lesson from a woman who simply wanted to be able to say that Sidney Lenz was her bridge teacher. (He declined the request.)

Lenz had learned bridge in 1911 when he traveled to India to study magic and Hindu culture. There, British army officers taught him the game, and its complexities absorbed him. He would play auction bridge in nearly every nation of the world, including once in Holland with three diplomats, each speaking a different language. He loved magic, especially sleight-of-hand tricks, some learned from his friend Harry Houdini. A master of card tricks, he could pull honors from a deck or deal himself a suit's thirteen cards.

On October 14, Lenz told *The New York Times* that Ely had ignored his earlier acceptance of his challenge. Lenz bemoaned that Culbertson "lays down all the conditions, even unto the eighth dimension, going so far as to make disposition of my winnings, if any, and claiming the right of selecting his team and also mine." The Lenz wit leavened any bitterness. "It is a bit analogous," Lenz said, "to challenging your adversary to a duel and insisting upon giving odds of ten-to-one—the challenger taking the first ten shots, after which he graciously permits his late opponent a hundred."

Each day, Ely and Jo spent hours at the Hotel Chatham in their silk pajamas, taking breakfast in bed; this was lounging time for Jo, maybe, but not for Ely, who jotted notes, conducted business by telephone, and kept his secretaries busy. He typically arrived at his magazine office in midafternoon and stayed late. Thanks in part to the Lenz controversy, Ely had sold several hundred thousand copies of his books with translations in German, French, and Scandinavian.

The New York Sun's Edwin C. Hill wrote, "Would it be extravagant to assert that if these giants do face each other over the bridge table—each with a partner of his own school of thought—that at least 20,000,000 American citizens will burn with the fever of the fray?" By comparison, Hill wrote, the recent seven-game World Series between the Philadelphia Athletics and St. Louis Cardinals would have been a mild affair. He reminded readers of Italian heavyweight Primo Carnera's recent loss in the ring to Jack Sharkey at Ebbets Field, adding, "The shock of great Carnera's fall over in Brooklyn, a fall which gyrated the earth upon a mighty axis, was a dull and colorless incident compared to the ferocious onslaught of Culbertson upon Lenz."

At a press conference in mid-November, Ely and Lenz agreed to a contract bridge pairs match of 150 rubbers, beginning on December 7 in the Culbertsons' apartment suite at the Chatham, and moving to the Waldorf-Astoria. Lenz chose as his partner one of the celebrated Four Horsemen, Oswald Jacoby, a twenty-eight-year-old actuary. Rules required Jacoby to play with Lenz for at least half the match.

"Whom will I choose as my partner?" Ely asked. "Whom does a dutiful husband choose in moments of stress? My wife, Josephine, of course." He said Jo would play at least half of the rubbers, and Lightner and von Zedtwitz each would substitute in one fourth. Ely added, "My wife is the only person, woman or man, whom I have never seen crack under the strain of the most grueling competition."

NBC delivered in an important way. Each night the network would air a fifteen-minute national radio broadcast about the match. Meanwhile, as new ads in *Publishers Weekly* called for booksellers to enjoy "A Culbertson Christmas," Ely pondered how best to promote the match. He remembered the 1921 Dempsey-Carpentier heavyweight title fight when ninety thousand fans jammed a wooden arena in Jersey City and a radio audience of several hundred thousand heard the world champion Dempsey win by knockout. The fight promoter Tex Rickard called it the "Battle of the Century."

Even before the ink had dried on the agreement with Lenz, Ely spoke of the "Bridge Battle of the Century." The newspapers ran with it.

II

On December 7, 1931, Ely walked into his drawing room and into an explosion of light. Newspaper photographers and Hollywood film cameramen rushed down the corridor of the Culbertsons' ten-room suite, past silver cups and tournament trophies and beneath signs asking ABSOLUTE SILENCE because there are CHILDREN ASLEEP AND DREAMING. At the center of the carbon arc lamps of motion picture newsreels and the smoking bulbs of flash cameras, the incandescent Ely Culbertson, a colossus of cards, in dinner jacket, a gardenia pinned to his lapel, moved continentally. He greeted tuxedoed admirers and enemies alike. Bridge rivals smiled and wished him luck, even as they despised him. The stakes were never higher: the winners would enjoy the financial spoils of contract bridge, on which, in 1931 alone, Americans would spend an estimated $100 million on lessons, books, and supplies.

The Culbertson drawing room was brightly lit with a fireplace, mulberry velvet curtains, plush carpeting, and a wooden table covered by green felt, and with four ashtrays inlaid for the occasion. Dark leather screens were carefully positioned with slight cracks between them to allow kibitzers—card-table onlookers notorious for giving players unwarranted advice—to peek, three at a time, for up to five minutes. "The Greatest Peep Show in History," Ely called it. (The United Press correspondent Henry McLemore deadpanned that the screens permitted him to achieve an ambition to become a "crack reporter.") Now Ely stepped past the table to stand beside Josephine, in taffeta gown with a corsage of orchids.

In the lobby of the Chatham, a skyscraper on Vanderbilt Avenue and Forty-eighth Street, bridge fans and inebriates tried to sneak past security to see the famous foursome. Already squeezing into the drawing room were reporters, kibitzers, Western Union telegraphers, army officials, security guards, maîtres d'hôtel, radio men, famed sports columnists Ring Lardner and Grantland Rice, referees, bridge elites, social and executive secretaries, editors, book publishers, plus thirty stenographers and clerks. Telegraph would flash results across the country and to Europe. In the press room, newspapermen were well satisfied with sandwiches, chicken à la king, and alcohol, a feast that astounded the syndicated columnist Westbrook Pegler, who walked the halls asking the same question: "Who's pickin' up the tab?" The members of the press would receive match updates on a bulletin board, and while away time playing cards themselves. Down the hall, in *The Bridge World* room, clerks would record and make copies of each hand as that information arrived from the playing room by courier. Joyce and Bruce Culbertson, in their pajamas, rushed in for one last good-night embrace from Jo before a nanny took them to bed.

This was Ely's defining hour, a moment of high-art ballyhoo he

had imagined. The light of the modern technological age appealed to
his sense of self and theater. The four players had signed with newspaper syndicates to do nightly columns (ghostwritten, naturally). Ely and
Jo shaped their story as the near-impossible struggle of a young married couple fighting a historic empire. Jo knew that housewives rooted
for her while their husbands waited for the inevitable marital spats.

On this glittering night in the gathering darkness of the Depression, the Bridge Battle of the Century, with its high style and carnival
excess, was a final roar of the 1920s. More than the Myrtle Bennett
murder trial, a local sensation in Missouri spurring ripples of gossip
and headlines across the nation, this drama was played out over five
weeks in the media hub of New York, where the radio networks, wire
services, a dozen and more local dailies, and many of America's leading syndicated columnists were based. More than two million words
(by Ely's count) would be published in American newspapers on his
battle against Sidney Lenz, more than had been published on Lindbergh's historic flight across the Atlantic.

The *New York World-Telegram* called it "the most amazing card
battle in history," and *The Sun* trumped that with "the contract
championship of the world, the planetary system, the milky way and
the fourth dimension, according to Einstein." Grantland Rice, in the
financial doldrums as he watched his Goldman Sachs stock plummeting from $121 to $3 a share, showed up in evening attire and suggested to his readers that beyond 20 million bridge players, another
40 million kibitzers would want to watch—this, in a country with a
total population of 120 million. "So, if there were room enough we
might have had an attendance approaching 60,000,000," he wrote.

Festivities started downstairs at the Chatham with an eight-
course meal for fifty guests and a national radio hookup on NBC.
Sidney Lenz humbly predicted over the airwaves that the match
would prove that experts could drop tricks as easily as any beginner.
Jo's voice trembled as she said she aimed to prove that a woman
could play as well as any man. Ely praised Lenz and Jacoby, saying
they could win the match "in spite of the handicap of the so-called
'Official Bidding System.'" He also told listeners he would spend

more time with his family in the future and that "win, lose or draw this is my last big match."

One discordant voice was heard. In his syndicated column, Milton Work reminded readers that the British writer Cavendish once had asserted that luck would not equalize itself in cards in less than ten years of play, and that Ely and Lenz would be playing *less than one hundred hours*. Of course, Cavendish was writing about whist, which, with no bidding or dummy, had a greater element of luck than bridge. Ely estimated the luck factor in the match at 8 percent, but Work suggested it was more like 80 percent. "The chances are that the respective bidding systems will have little to do with the victory or the size of it," Work wrote. But this view, at least for the moment, was lost in the melody of bubbling champagne.

Photographs and more photographs were taken of the four players. "Ay," a drawing room cynic said, "now I know why it's called the Battle of the Century." At long last, the head referee, army lieutenant Alfred M. Gruenther, in his formal West Point dress with gold epaulets, cleared the card area. In the mid-1950s Gruenther would serve as Supreme Commander of NATO forces in Europe and sometimes play as President Dwight Eisenhower's partner in the regular Saturday afternoon bridge game at the White House. Now just thirty-two years old, Gruenther had as his primary responsibilities overseeing the record-keeping of this bridge battle and adjudicating any written protests filed by the players.

At 10:07 P.M., the match began. Its 150 rubbers, spanning 20 sessions, would be front-page news in the morning and would remain so for nearly five weeks.

The first news announcement of the Bridge Battle of the Century came before the first hand was played, with an official emissary rushing into the press room and calling the gathering of reporters to rapt attention. "Gentlemen of the press!" he reported. "The contest has started. I have the first words spoken in this historic match." With all pens and notebooks at the ready, the royal courier added, "The first words were spoken by Jo—I mean Mrs. Culbertson. She said, 'Where do you wish to sit, Ely?' "

Initially nerves trembled. During the first rubber, Lenz made a beginner's blunder by forgetting the contract. He contracted for game at no trump (and could even have made a slam, though not having been bid, no slam bonus was available), but played the cards thinking that diamonds were trump. As a result he was set two tricks, an embarrassment he later blamed on the distraction of Ely taking six minutes and twenty-six seconds to make a bid. "I'm sorry, Jo," Lenz said, so flustered after the hand that he apologized to an opponent. Three times on this night Lenz and Jacoby lost large bonuses by making slams they failed to bid. (In auction bridge, Lenz's true game, players need not have worried about bidding and would have scored these slams, anyway.) The results spread quickly. After each deal, Capt. Ernest Brown, head of the hotel service, whispered to a waiter, who reported to the nearest bellhop, who told the elevator boy, and within minutes word had reached the Chatham's lobby. Even with the miscues, Lenz-Jacoby led by 1,715 points at the end of a session in which, experts agreed, Jo, with a jeweled cigarette holder in hand, had been the calmest and most competent player.

Ring Lardner, a master humorist, had reported too many sporting events to be fooled by hyperbole. "According to the diffident Mr. Culbertson, this event is more important to the world at large," Lardner wrote in his syndicated column, "than the signing of the Armistice on Nov. 11, 1918." He evoked Jack "Legs" Diamond, the gangster and former lieutenant to gambler Arnold Rothstein. "As I left the gay party," Lardner wrote after the first session at the Chatham, "I heard a rumor that some of those secretaries were really Capone gunmen brought on from Chicago to keep the peace. They certainly flopped if that be true. It was said that Mr. Culbertson wanted Jack Diamond as a bodyguard, but Mrs. Culbertson doesn't like minor suits."

Damon Runyon did not appear at the Chatham, but from Broadway his presence was felt between deals. Writing for *The New York American*, Runyon issued a challenge to Ely and Lenz. Runyon said his team of four of Broadwayfarers—players named "Reno," Mike

Cohen, Artie Adelman, and Louis Mart—would play any team of four offered by Ely or Lenz, and for big stakes, five dollars per point. "You can see my proposition runs into money," Runyon wrote. Runyon said his team played "practical bridge," and didn't know "book bridge," and that his men played in a room on West Forty-fifth Street, "where Gilda Gray had her night club years ago and used to shake a mean shimmy." No lady, including Josephine Culbertson, could play in this proposed challenge match, Runyon wrote, since one of his players, when exasperated, often said, "Oh, pshaw!" Runyon feared that, in the presence of a lady, "my man might be sorely exasperated." Runyon's colorful challenge brought smiles, but only one reply from the Chatham. Jacoby said the Four Horsemen would play anyone, anytime.

Ely kept the newspapers busy. He said he might play a session with Harold Vanderbilt as his partner, or perhaps Mrs. Emily Smith Warner, daughter of former New York governor Al Smith. At another moment, Ely proposed a session be held in an auditorium with an electronic scoreboard and broadcasters, the four players inside a soundproof glass case, with all revenues to benefit the unemployed. His idea gained the support of Mrs. David Sarnoff, wife of the president of Radio Corporation of America (RCA), but Lenz said the scenario was beneath the dignity of bridge. In the press room, Ely offered quotes pithy, ironic, conceited, and cutting. He reveled in the noise he generated.

Now more than ever Ely *needed* the press and, therefore, he needed the press to be happy. McLemore of the United Press surely was that, writing of opening night:

> I wish you'd have been there. I like to died. This mighty duel between Messrs. Sidney Lenz and Ely Culbertson opened amidst more hoopla, hullabaloo and fol-de-rol than you'll find at an ice cream sociable, a gangster's funeral, or the Broadway premiere of a Chaplin picture. . . . I never enjoyed an assignment so much as I enjoyed this Culbertson-Lenz thing. All you need to do is slap your feet upon a desk, aim

your eye at the big bulletin board and wait. And the nice part of it is, nothing ever shows up on that bulletin board . . . All you got to do is sit down and wonder, "When is that guy going to bring around some more cocktails?" The press boys have a huge room and before the battle started the pressers had a stud poker party, a crap game, two games of checkers . . . going full blast.

Even the Culbertsons' butler, Charles (William) Natcet, "with special permission from his employers," wrote a story for the newspaper syndicate. "Mr. Culbertson is by far and away the best card player. I'd say that even if I wasn't the Culbertson butler," Natcet wrote, "and I'd only say it a little more discreetly if I was the Lenz butler."

Ely knew how to get into Sidney Lenz's head, irritating and disrupting, his manner distinctly anti-Hoyle. During the second session, he ordered a rare broiled porterhouse steak and ate it at the table. "Ely, we're playing cards, you know," Jo said. Ely's knife and fork squealed against the plate. He smacked his lips. Lenz howled, "My God, Ely, you're getting grease all over the cards. Why don't you eat at the proper time like the rest of us?" Ely dabbed a napkin at the corners of his mouth, and said, "My vast public won't let me, Sidney." Each night, before the first hand was dealt, Ely asked his opponents, "Have you changed your system yet?" Finally, Jo scolded him: "Ely, that's getting awfully monotonous." He showed up late for nearly every session. He hung a large wishbone for good luck near the card table. He brought a toy Scottish terrier and posed it atop a bridge lamp. Each time he laid down his hand as dummy, he left the table to visit the press room. "Doggone, Ely," Lenz would say, waiting to deal the next hand. Or, to referee Gruenther, biting off each syllable, Lenz would howl, "Page E-lee!" Lenz charged Ely was deviating from his bidding system. (He was.) Ely counter-charged that Lenz and Jacoby were deviating from the rules of Lenz's 1-2-3 system, the cornerstone of the "Official System." (They were.) Once, Jacoby alleged Ely and Jo had both broken the rules of their system, at which point Ely pulled from his jacket a copy of his *Summary*, showed Jacoby the relevant paragraphs, and gave him the book. He also offered to autograph it. Again and again, Ely delayed his play—five minutes, six, seven— prompting Lenz once to plead to Gruenther, "He's been sitting there for 10 minutes without moving—acting like he was studying when it's plain there's only one play he can make." Ely snarled that Lenz ought not be allowed to protest during play. "It's just like letting out a yell at a golfer just as he starts to swing," Ely said. Lenz could not bear the tedium of such delays, and once stormed from the room. Small wonder that, after the third session, one writer thought Lenz had aged ten years. Heywood Broun, the *World-Telegram*'s crusading columnist, admitted that studying a hand for five minutes was excessive: "Hamlet required a shorter interval to argue the problem of 'to be or not to be.' "

Broun played contract bridge at the Algonquin with writers George S. Kaufman, Alexander Woollcott, and Franklin P. Adams. He believed that experts such as Ely and Lenz were making contract bridge too confusing for the masses. Even among the legions playing the Culbertson System, Broun wrote, "we have the reformed Culbertsonians, the fundamental and the neo." Broun sought a simpler time. "Give me then, no experts, I beg of you," he wrote, "but people who play with celerity and who can smile when everything goes wrong." Broun stopped by the Chatham during the match, accepting an invitation to serve as Lenz's honorary referee. "The match, beyond argument, constitutes the overemphasis of a pastime, but from my point of view contract of this sort is more thrilling for the spectator than either college football or professional hockey," he wrote. He had assumed that the Ely-Lenz spats as reported in the newspapers "constituted nothing more than a flair for showmanship and publicity on the part of the performers," but now he changed his mind. "Now I am prepared to acquit all members of the troupe from that accusation. Even in the role of a deaf and dumb kibitzer I could feel the blood congeal along my arteries at all the tight points in the match," he wrote.

The run of cards stayed with Lenz and Jacoby, with their lead building to 7,030 points in the fourth session, though Walter Malowan of *The New York Times* insisted "neither side has yet demonstrated anything like conclusive superiority either in bidding or in play." Once, Ely flipped a card, saying, "I always lead this way for no trump." Sidney Lenz's expression brightened. He reminded Ely that this was a suit contract, and added gleefully, "That's the second time you have done that." Lenz smiled and said grandly, "Send it to the press." Ely tried to explain, but Lenz wagged his finger and said, "It was a boner." At another moment, Jo felt the eyes of kibitzers peeking between the screens. "I can't stand them any longer," she snapped, and the room was cleared.

From the outset, Ely believed that Jacoby and Lenz were an ill fit, like merging "an express-train and a hansom cab." At the table, Lenz never varied: always the lean-faced brooder as he examined his cards, with nary a twitch or tremor, always sober and pragmatic. Jacoby preferred aggressive, imaginative bidding. He sometimes used "psychic bids," bluffs that were, by definition, anti-system and designed to mislead opponents about the strength and distribution of his hand. However, such psychic bids could also mislead a partner, and undermine partnership confidence. Jacoby had entered Columbia University at fifteen, aspiring to become a mathematics professor. Instead, he became at twenty-one the youngest ever to pass the Society of Actuaries examination, and went to work for Metropolitan Life. He accepted Lenz's invitation even though they had played as partners only once. Studying Lenz's game, Ely noted his preoccupation with achieving perfection and a refusal to take risks. Though a highly skilled auction player, Ely believed that Lenz was a weak bidder in contract. Lenz would make his brilliant technical plays, but he would make few, if any, penalty doubles. And Lenz would underbid—that would be his undoing.

As his early deficit mounted, Ely told reporters the Culbertson luck would turn—and it did. In the sixth session, he and Jo won 6 of 8 rubbers, wiped out a 4,840-point lead, and moved into the lead by 745 points. Before the next deal, Ely scribbled a note and passed it to his favorite partner. Jo read it in silence: "Darling, you are wonderful, but *à la guerre, comme à la guerre*—do not be demoralized by success."

♣ ♣ ♣

As Jo's fatigue deepened (one writer thought she looked on the brink of illness), Ted Lightner, Ely's appointed first substitute, bit his fingernails in the press room, impatiently waiting for his call. By the match's stipulated rules, Jo had to play at least 75 rubbers, half the match. At 2:00 A.M. on December 16, having finished the forty-eighth rubber, the Culbertsons stood 410 points ahead. C. C. Nicolet, the *World-Telegram*'s bridge writer, assessed: "At the conventional suburban tenth-of-a-cent this margin of superiority amounts to just forty-one pennies."

The Sun's Edwin C. Hill, like so many other reporters, admired Jo. "She seems detached, immeasurably removed from bickering and backbiting—gentle, tolerant, forbearing, slightly superior," he wrote. "No visitor to Ely Culbertson's Greatest Show on Earth and Educational Exhibition can fail of that impression." On the afternoon of December 16, with no session scheduled for the evening, Hill spoke with Jo. He noted her sallow complexion, but also her resolute spirit. She said, "Did you know, by the way, that Mr. Lenz was my teacher at bridge? It almost looks as if I were biting the hand that fed me, doesn't it? But I'm very fond of Sidney. He's a delightful man and has been very sweet all through this match." Then, Jo rose and said, "Well, good afternoon. My maid is making faces at me. There's no braving her out. The woman means business." Hill, smitten, wrote, "Her calm composure under the strain that has cracked masculine restraint must be pleasant in the sight of the gods."

But Jo needed time off from the match. She was exhausted. Ely announced that she was "homesick," ironic given that the match was being held in her home. She said she wished to be free until after Christmas to spend time with the children and finish her holiday shopping. On came the bespectacled Lightner, the Yale and Harvard Law graduate, a stockbroker by profession, pessimistic by nature, though brilliant as a bridge theoretician and player. Lightner played, Ely explained, "with an air of studied boredom." Playfully, Jacoby asked, "If Lightner smiles, is it a signal?" No, Ely replied. "Well,

Mr. Lightner never smiles," Jacoby said, "and I just wanted to know whether a smile tonight would be a signal."

In the second rubber, sixth deal, of Lightner's first session on December 17, Lenz-Jacoby suffered a catastrophic failure. In what referee Gruenther later would call "one of the most grotesque hands of the entire match," Jacoby, as dealer, opened at one heart with a weaker hand than Lenz might have expected. Holding all four aces, Lenz could think only of no trump, and bid three no trump. Lenz's bid sent his partnership on a race, with the two players running on opposing tracks, betraying a lack of trust. When Lenz raised to six no trump, Ely, sensing an opportunity to nail him with penalty points, doubled. In a bind, Jacoby bid seven hearts, and Ely doubled again. Jacoby failed to make his contract by one trick. After the hand, Lenz called for a recess, and held a ten-minute private conversation with Jacoby. Another psychic bid by Jacoby later on this night played at one spade, doubled, cost him 1,000 points. Ely and Lightner moved out to a lead of 4,965 points, and Lenz muttered to a reporter, "Ozzie promised me faithfully that he wouldn't bid a vulnerable psychic tonight. And look at him."

Ely had seen Lenz shooting looks at Jacoby, and was gleeful. "Another session like tonight's will show Lenz and Jacoby as the world's worst losers. I have never seen so much petty squabbling, unknowing gestures and petty despairs as in tonight's game," he said.

A day later, in the ninth session, Ely and Lightner gained nearly 3,000 points more, and their lead ballooned to 7,915 points. In one week's time, covering 244 hands, Ely's team had gained 14,945 points. Now Ely was calling Lightner "my other favorite partner."

His rivals saw the match—and their place in the bridge industry— slipping away. F. D. Courtenay, president of Bridge Headquarters, decried, "The whole thing is a publicity stunt organized by the successor of Barnum." Courtenay said the only fair test of the bidding systems would be to deal hands face up and to permit a committee of experts to bid them, first by one system and then by the other, determining which system was better.

Meanwhile, Lenz brushed off Ely's criticism, saying, "I believe I may safely allow the American people to judge what constitute the tactics and actions of a gentleman, especially when he is winning at cards."

Waldemar von Zedtwitz, about to depart for a three-week South American tour with Hal and Dorothy Sims, played the tenth session as Ely's partner. He held remarkable cards all night, and the Culbertson lead grew by 3,205 points, to 11,120. Jacoby deadpanned, "Baron, you played a perfect game. I hope your boat doesn't sink until you are at least three days out."

Lenz once questioned whether Ely's jump raise from one to three hearts was according to his system, and Ely snapped, "Why don't you read my *Blue Book*? Every sucker in the country has read it except you."

From behind a kibitzer screen came a quick retort: "I haven't!" It was one of the Marx Brothers, Chico. He got the desired laugh.

For nearly five weeks they played in a brilliantly lit cocoon, every move critiqued, as if the world were paying attention only to them. But during these thirty-three days, newsreels captured hardship, gunfire, deprivation, and strife. In West Virginia, sixty white men lynched two black men and riddled their bodies with bullets. In India, Mahatma Gandhi was arrested at his home on the eve of a new civil disobedience campaign that he predicted would plunge his nation once again into "the fires of suffering." In New York, Governor Franklin Roosevelt criticized the Hoover administration for failing to aid business and called for new leadership that would recognize "the right of the individual to make a living out of life." The Chicago Crime Commission declared that city's notorious gangsters beaten, with all but five of the twenty-eight "public enemies" under wraps, including Al Capone. In Germany, Adolf Hitler promised a day of reckoning with the authors of the Treaty of Versailles and proclaimed himself the spokesman of the German people in defiance of the Bruening government. In New York, Babe Ruth insisted he would not accept a pay cut from his $80,000 annual salary, and New York Yankees owner Jacob Ruppert, reminding the press about the Depression, answered, "Who does he think he is?" The bootlegger and racketeer John "Legs" Diamond was shot to death as he slept in a lodging house in Albany, New York. Winston Churchill, in New York on a book tour, suffered head injuries and two broken ribs when struck by an automobile on Fifth Avenue.

Consigned to bed rest, his head bandaged, the recuperating Churchill moved to the Waldorf-Astoria two days before the Bridge Battle of the Century arrived there. But for doctor's orders, Churchill, who adored bridge, might have become a kibitzer himself. (He had been playing auction bridge at the Admiralty House in London on August 1, 1914, when a messenger arrived with a large red dispatch box. Churchill unlocked it and read its one-page message: "Germany has declared war against Russia." He rang a servant to bring him a lounge coat and departed at once for 10 Downing Street.) As a kibitzer at the Waldorf, Churchill would have rubbed shoulders with steel magnate Charles Schwab, cartoonist Rube Goldberg, columnist Franklin P. Adams, the British golfer Cyril Tolley, the Grand Duchess Marie of Russia, Mrs. Marshall Field III, Mrs. Vincent Astor, and lawyer Henry W. Taft, brother of the former American president.

As host for the second half of the match, Lenz had arranged for a dozen rooms on the fifth floor of the Waldorf's east wing, with luxurious accommodations for the press and telegraphs. Lenz might have hoped that the new location, one of New York's gilded, ornate landmarks, would change his luck. But his partnership with Ozzie Jacoby was in freefall. As the Culbertson lead built after the thirteenth session to more than seventeen thousand points, Ely chirped to Lenz, "You're going down with flying colors, Sidney, but you're going down."

On December 28, Jo returned to the table just in time to witness the disintegration of the express train and hansom cab. The hand that broke the Lenz-Jacoby partnership occurred in the 102nd rubber. As the midnight hour passed, and with the Culbertsons vulnerable, Jacoby made a psychic bid to confuse the Culberstons. But his bid confused Lenz. The Culbertsons made their five no trump contract easily, and Lenz, boiling over, said to his partner, "Why do you make these rotten bids?" The kibitzers, in white shirts and ermine coats, instantly perked up. Lenz said to Jacoby, "You're having a lot of fun.

Give me a chance. I can't tell whether you have anything or not when you bid." It was 12:28 A.M. Under assault, Jacoby was livid, but remained silent. Match rules stipulated that no new rubber could start after 12:30 A.M. Gruenther asked the foursome about playing one more rubber. "Not with me in it," Jacoby snapped. He agreed to remain for a final rubber, but he could not contain his anger. With the first hand in play, he glared at Lenz and said, "Sidney, in a hand in the second rubber tonight you made an absolutely stupid defensive play, and then you criticized me. I am resigning right now as your partner."

Lenz's face sagged. He said, "Well—well, sir, well, sir, all right, sir!" Jacoby continued, "The play you made was absolutely stupid and there was no excuse for it." Lenz waved his cards and shut down his young partner. "Why talk about it?" the old master said.

Minutes later, at session's end, Jacoby rushed out of the drawing room. He told reporters he was finished with Lenz. "I was criticized merely to cover up his own bad plays," Jacoby said. He would go on to a brilliant bridge career lasting more than fifty years, by which point the disintegration of his partnership with Lenz no longer obscured the fact that Jacoby had been the best and most adaptable contract player among the luminous four at the table. That night, pale and visibly affected by the breakup, Lenz walked through the corridors, hounded by reporters, telling them, "I have nothing to say."

Commander Winfield Liggett, Jr., veteran of the bridge table and the high seas, replaced Jacoby for the final forty-seven rubbers. Playing with old friend "Lig," Lenz seemed calmer, happier. Liggett was a steady player from the old school—also a member of Bridge Headquarters—and had ghostwritten Wilbur Whitehead books. Inseparable as partners for years in whist and auction tournaments, Lenz and Liggett might have played as partners from the start but for a misunderstanding. Lenz had believed, incorrectly, that Liggett preferred a new partnership. Liggett waited for Lenz to ask him to play against the Culbertsons. Their pride came between them. Neither made an overture to the other, and Lenz chose Jacoby. Now partners again, they whittled away at the Culbertsons' lead. Still, to Liggett, convoying soldiers to Europe on the USS *Montana* during the war must have seemed an easier task than eradicating a seventeen-thousand-point deficit in only six bridge sessions. Ely played with two new partners, Michael Gottlieb and Howard Schenken, rising bridge stars. Then Jo came back for the Culbertson coronation.

The newsreel and newspaper cameras returned en masse on January 8 for the final session at the Waldorf. The photographers asked Ely and Sid to shake hands before the twentieth session. Posing, Ely asked Lenz why he wouldn't smile. "Looking at you, how can I?" Lenz replied. Then he grinned and offered a firm handshake.

Jo won the final hand of the 150th rubber, making her five-diamond contract. Gruenther leaned forward, checked the scoring, announced the completion of the match, and said the Culbertsons had won by 8,980 points. Lenz thrust his hand across the table. "Congratulations, Ely. Congratulations, Jo," he said. Liggett extended his hand as well. Well-wishers rushed in, including Oswald Jacoby, who congratulated Ely and then approached Lenz. They shook hands, but said nothing. Jacoby checked the score sheet: Liggett had advanced the Lenz cause by 7,860 points during the final six sessions. "Looks like I'm the goat of the match," Jacoby said. Jo hurried through the crowd as gentlemen kissed her cheek. It was nearly one o'clock in the morning. Jo wanted to go to the children, but Ely said, "We have newsreels and radio and supper and all kinds of things yet." Jo sighed, and ducked into a private room to freshen up.

Bridge analysts made much of the match statistics: during the 879 hands in the match, Ely's side held 1,745 aces and 1,775 kings, and Lenz's held 1,771 aces and 1,741 kings. But Lenz said, "Aces and kings don't mean a thing. It's distribution that counts . . . The cards speak for themselves. When the players are about equal, system means little."

The *Chicago Tribune* highlighted the fallibility of both bidding systems, and believed that the only point proven was "that Lenz is just as apt to bid two tricks too few as Culbertson is apt to bid two tricks too many." *The Virginian-Pilot* in Norfolk, meanwhile, clucked that Ely "is to contract what John D. Rockefeller was to oil . . . Culbertson is the greatest exploiter of contract that the world has ever seen, and Lenz in his own way is not far behind." The *Brooklyn Daily Eagle* believed the match proved nothing about the superiority of one system or the other, but saw a dramatic watershed in the bridge movement: "More citizens than ever are now talking bridge and playing bridge and buying bridge cards and taking bridge lessons and reading books on bridge." And *Collier's* magazine playfully chimed in, "No such excitement had been felt in the United States since the experiment with yeast an' raisins. . . . It stands proved that a husband an' wife can play together without the development of those homicidal tendencies that have done so much to make Contract a Dark an' Bloody Ground."

On NBC Radio at 1:30 A.M., Ely Culbertson stood with his favorite partner and announced his genius confirmed.

He said the Bridge Battle of the Century had proved nothing he did not anticipate or predict, including the superiority of the Culbertson System. Exultant, he said his system was about two hundred points per rubber better than any other system.

He praised Sidney Lenz and his partners for their sportsmanship and "their almost angelic patience with me."

He said he was convinced that, Depression or not, people naturally will work harder for their pleasures than for their necessities.

"It has been stated several times that I am one of the greatest showmen living today and even the elder statesmen of the 'Official System' announced that I appeared to be an illegitimate child of Barnum, who, incidentally, I greatly admire for his unquestioned genius.

"People who talk a great deal about publicity and ballyhoo, as some do, seem to miss the most important point in the art of mass psychology," Ely said. "Nothing can be ballyhooed which is not worthwhile. Bridge, an intellectual game, has become a powerful social factor for good, mainly because there is a great need and a great desire on the part of millions to forget, to relax, to quiet down the emotional waves aroused by everyday fears and worries."

Returning to a central theme, Ely told listeners, "To women the most satisfying feature of this match is, and should be, to see a member of their sex exchange the most subtle inferences and out-maneuver, in the strategy of an intellectual struggle, the greatest of men experts." Ely and Jo had played as partners for 85 rubbers and in aggregate won by a razor's edge, 365 points, only 4 points per rubber.

But the ballyhoo artist understood his craft. Ely knew the margin of victory didn't matter. Americans would remember only this: that Ely Culbertson had played with his wife, his favorite partner, they had used the Culbertson system, and they had won.

"What's that, Sweetka?" Ely said on air. "Excuse me, please, my wife, who is standing by my side, is whispering something to me." Five seconds of dead airtime passed. "No, darling, please don't worry, I won't say anything dreadful? What?" More silence.

"She says I am overbidding. I sign off."

Hidden, even from Ely, was the truth that Jo could no longer tolerate her husband's insensitivities and self-delusions. The Bridge Battle of the Century was over. Ely's unraveling was about to begin.

The First Couple of Bridge: Josephine and Ely Culbertson. Ely called Jo "my favorite partner," and together they galvanized the bridge movement in America. *AP IMAGES*

A Memphis belle, striking, statuesque, and headstrong, Myrtle Bennett, circa 1918, the year of her marriage.
Personal files of Carolyn Scruggs

Myrtle approached him on a train and the smitten soldier, Jack Bennett (photo, circa 1918), proposed after only three dates. A hard-charging perfume salesman, he was, in the business term of the day, *a producer*.
Missouri Valley Special Collections, Kansas City Public Library, Kansas City, MO

Below: Upstairs neighbors Mayme and Charles Hofman played against Myrtle and Jack Bennett on September 29, 1929, in the most infamous contract bridge game in history. The Hofmans witnessed what writer Alexander Woollcott would call "the Four Shots Heard 'Round the World."
Missouri Valley Special Collections, Kansas City Public Library, Kansas City, MO

Ely Culbertson decreed that his daughter Joyce Nadya would become an actress, his son Bruce a scientist. As part of that design, he filled their home with governesses and tutors. Josephine pleaded that she wanted their children to be not perfect, but happy. *Personal files of Steve Culbertson*

Below: On opening night of the ballyhooed Bridge Battle of the Century in December 1931 in the Culbertson suite at the Hotel Chatham in New York, the press gathers around Ely and Jo as they challenge Sidney Lenz *(seated right)* and Oswald Jacoby *(left). The Bridge World*

In this 1937 cartoon and in many others, H. T. Webster features the tensions between husbands and wives playing as bridge partners.
Wisconsin Historical Society, Image No. WHi-61552

H. T. Webster bridge cartoon from the *New York Herald-Tribune*, 1945.
Wisconsin Historical Society, Image No. WHi-61551

Waldemar von Zedtwitz *(left)* and Ely Culbertson study their cards. A member of the Culbertson team, von Zedtwitz was an inscrutable nobleman with a pedigreed bloodline. His father was a German baron (a title his son inherited) and his mother a Kentuckian descended from John Breckinridge, vice president under James Buchanan, and candidate for the presidency in 1860 against Abraham Lincoln. *Personal files of Steve Culbertson*

Below: In September 1930, at New Almack's in London, Ely and Josephine took on the British team-of-four captained by the blustery Lt. Col. Walter Buller *(standing, third from left)*. The victory started the Culbertsons on their meteoric rise. *Also pictured:* American Ted Lightner *(far left)* and British players Mrs. Gordon Evers *(seated, right)*, Dr. Nelson Wood-Hill *(standing, second from left)*, and Lt. Cedric Kehoe *(standing, second from right)*. *The Bridge World*

A scene in the Jackson County criminal courtroom during the Bennett trial. Myrtle (in black) sits at lower right, in foreground.
Missouri Valley Special Collections, Kansas City Public Library, Kansas City, MO

Jurors in the 1931 Myrtle Bennett murder trial included a night watchman, railroad conductor, storekeeper, and telegraph operator. Eleven years after women won the right to vote, twenty-six states, including Missouri, still categorically excluded women from juries.
Missouri Valley Special Collections, Kansas City Public Library, Kansas City, MO

Byrd Rice admired his uncle, Jack Bennett. He visited his aunt Myrtle six weeks after Jack was killed, and she escorted him through the apartment, telling and showing him what happened. *Missouri Valley Special Collections, Kansas City Public Library, Kansas City, MO*

Former U.S. Senator James A. Reed addresses jurors in the Myrtle Bennett murder trial in Kansas City, 1931. Reed's emotional plea infuriated the prosecutor, who asked for a pause to give "counsel for the defense and his client a chance to finish their cry." *Missouri Valley Special Collections, Kansas City Public Library, Kansas City, MO*

Jim Page (papers in hand), the pugnacious prosecutor in the Bennett murder trial, was a Pendergast machine Democrat, same as Judge Ralph Latshaw *(seated behind Page)* and lead defense attorney, James A. Reed *(at right).*
Missouri Valley Special Collections, Kansas City Public Library, Kansas City, MO

Hollywood paged Ely and Jo after their victory in the Bridge Battle of the Century. Ely wrote and starred in six film shorts released in 1933 by RKO Radio Pictures. *Personal files of Tim Bourke*

When syndicated gossip columnist Walter Winchell wondered aloud in November 1932 if Nell Donnelly and Jim Reed might "merge," Reed, whose wife had died just six weeks earlier, fired off a letter to Winchell, calling him "about the lowest order of animal life." A year later, all calm, Jim and Nell married. *Personal files of Terence O'Malley*

THIRTEEN

Myrtle's Murder Trial, Part 3

They were liars, Mayme Hofman and Alice Adkins. That's what Jim Page wanted to tell the jury. He wanted to scream it not only to jurors and Latshaw, but also to the holy heavens: "THEY LIE!" Loyalty to a friend or daughter was one thing, but these lies were protecting a murderer.

When Latshaw, at long last, ruled that he would permit the prosecutor to impeach his own witnesses, Page stood before jurors on rebuttal and said, "I want to read to the jury a part of the statement made by Mrs. Hofman early in the morning following the tragedy. *'The next thing I saw was Mrs. Bennett rushing into the front room. Before I knew what happened the shots were fired. I jumped out of the door and ran upstairs.'* "

Standing before the jury box now, Page said, "Mrs. Hofman testified at this trial that she saw no shots fired and that she did not see Mrs. Bennett rush across the room with the pistol in her hand. She testified that she left the apartment before the shooting began."

Then Page said, "I want to read from the statement signed by Mrs. Adkins on the morning after the tragedy: *'. . . and I said to her, "There's no need of your getting it [Jack's pistol] tonight. He is not going away tonight"'* . . . Now I want to read from Mrs. Adkins's testimony given at the preliminary trial. This question was asked by Mr. O'Sullivan. *'Question: And you ran into the living room and Mrs. Bennett still had the gun in her hand? Answer: "Yes."'* " Page said, "And in another place is this answer: *'And [Myrtle] said, "He hit me, he was fighting me and twisting my arm."'* " However, in this murder trial, Page reminded jurors, Alice Adkins had testified differently. Adkins said she did not remember whether her daughter had the pistol in her hand when she first saw her in the living room, nor did she remember what Myrtle said to her at that moment.

There, Page thought. Even though Latshaw had ruled earlier that testimony could be used only to impeach witnesses, and not to prove the guilt or innocence of Myrtle Bennett, Page felt better. At least jurors knew the truth.

His rebuttal had only begun. Page introduced seven character witnesses so that jurors would not believe, as Reed hoped, that Jack Bennett came home every night and struck his wife. Jack's aunt Nellie Scyster, his brother Tom, a colleague at Hudnut, and several friends in Kansas City testified to his work ethic, civility, and honorable nature.

At last came the moment, according to Jim Page's script, to drop the bombshell.

There was a sparkle in Byrd Rice's eyes as he took the witness stand. Reed and O'Sullivan, sensing high drama, pulled their chairs closer to the counsel table. Assistant prosecutor Hill questioned Rice, though he did not get far, only a couple minutes, when he asked this question: "Mr. Rice, did you ever have occasion to talk to Myrtle Bennett since the homicide?"

Reed, rising to his feet: "Wait a minute."

Latshaw: "Gentlemen of the jury, step to your room a moment."

The purpose of Rice's testimony, Hill explained to Latshaw, was to rebut what Myrtle had said on the stand. She had testified that she did not intentionally shoot her husband. Now, Hill told the judge, "I want to show through this witness, through conversation had with the defendant—"

"Ask the question," Latshaw said, interrupting.

He did and, with jurors out of the room, Rice answered directly. He said on November 10, 1929, six weeks after the killing, he visited his aunt Myrtle at her apartment and they discussed the shooting.

From the counsel table, Page added, "[Myrtle] testified on the witness stand that she didn't know what happened. We want to show by this witness that she told him exactly how it happened."

"Then it was a part of your case in chief," Reed argued.

"It could not be," Page replied, "until she had testified."

Reed demanded to know if Byrd Rice had told his story to the prosecutor's office long ago.

Rice said he had.

He said the day after he spoke with Myrtle, he shared her story with George Charno, then an assistant prosecutor investigating the case. (Charno resigned from the prosecutor's office seven weeks before the trial started.) "You told him all you know now, didn't you?" Reed asked.

"I think so," Rice said.

Latshaw had heard enough. Once more he excoriated Jim Page, this time for failing to place Byrd Rice on his list of witnesses before the trial. "It is one of the safeguards the law has seen fit to throw around a defendant to protect him. This is a part of the case in chief. You put the sister of the deceased [Annie Rice, Byrd's mother] on the stand to show these same matters, knowing that they were in chief. At that time the question came up as to whether or not the sister had talked to the prosecuting attorney and she had not, and the court very properly permitted you to use her . . . [But] to allow the state sixteen months after it had knowledge of the witness and had not indorsed the witness's name on the information, to use that witness, is to use the court as a trap, to take away from the defendant the constitutional right which [she] has."

The prosecutors insisted they were unaware of Byrd Rice's conversation with Myrtle until only a few days before, during the trial's first days. His mother, Annie Rice, told them about it. The prosecutors said George Charno had never mentioned his conversation with Jack's nephew. Hill phoned Byrd Rice immediately and heard his story. He wired money to Rice and told him to come to Kansas City at once.

That Charno had left the prosecutor's office before the trial mattered not at all, Latshaw said. "The knowledge of one prosecuting attorney is the knowledge of all," he said.

Pointing at Myrtle, Page countered, "I am not bound by this woman's testimony. If I have a witness who says—"

"I will not argue with you now, Brother Page," Latshaw fumed.

He ruled Byrd Rice could not testify and said, "You knew it sixteen months ago. Objection sustained. I am trying this case according to the law. Bring in the jury."

Strategically, Page had hidden his most important witness and waited for the optimal moment to call him. This proved to be a grave miscalculation.

Jim Reed could barely contain his glee.

Rice stepped from the witness chair and walked past Myrtle Bennett, who diverted her eyes. As he left the courtroom, spectators buzzed, wondering foremost, "What did Myrtle say to him?"

The prosecution's bombshell remained in the hands of Jack's young nephew, unexploded.

That night, away from the courtroom, Byrd Rice told his story to a reporter from the *Kansas City Times*. Six weeks after the killing of his uncle Jack, Rice said he visited his aunt Myrtle. She told him essentially what she had told his mother, Annie Rice: "After the trial I will tell you why I shot Jack and then you won't feel so prejudiced against me. Nobody but my God and I know why I killed him." But then Myrtle went a step further. She walked Byrd Rice through the apartment and narrated the chase as she remembered it. In the den, she pointed to the spot where Charles Hofman had stood, near the bathroom, when she appeared with the pistol. Of Hofman, Myrtle told her nephew, "He could have stopped me." She demonstrated how she had chased Jack with a pistol in her hand. She told Rice she fired four times, the first two from the den, just as Jack closed the bathroom door as a shield. She said she chased him through their bedroom and into the living room, where she fired twice more, the last bullet striking him in the back as he reached for the front door.

The next morning all of Kansas City knew Byrd Rice's devastating story—except the jurors.

The suffragists notwithstanding, women always turned out for James A. Reed. His oratorical eloquence and rough-hewn Andrew Jackson–like handsomeness commanded their attention. Now would come

Reed's closing argument in the Bennett case—the senator's last criminal trial, according to the newspapers. So day nine of the trial became a society event, attracting women from the Junior League and Kansas City's arts and theater circles. Some of the city's old legal lions, lawyers and judges who had watched Reed as prosecutor twenty years earlier, wangled choice seats. During a recess, Latshaw waxed on to a newspaperman, comparing the Reed from the 1910 Hyde trial to the Reed defending Myrtle Bennett. "Just a trifle slower than in former years," the judge said of Reed, though "still a fighter and still a flashing star in a firmament of stars." His closing argument would be yet one more quintessential Kansas City moment for James A. Reed, reminiscent (on a smaller scale) of the Century Ball, December 31, 1900, when more than ten thousand Kansas Citians, in ball gowns and tuxedos, gathered at Convention Hall and bid adieu to the nineteenth century, while their energetic young reformer mayor wrote a letter (placed in a time capsule) to Kansas City's first mayor of the twenty-first century. Reed was the thirty-nine-year-old mayor then, and with typical flourish that night, he called his Kansas City "Queen of the West and Southwest . . . wielding a scepter of supremacy over a territory vaster than the empire of Germany, richer than the valley of the Nile in the days of the Pharoahs." In his letter to the future, Reed bowed solicitously to the ladies of his day, and wrote, "In 2001 you may have greater concourse of people at your ball, but the flower of your womanhood will not exceed the congregated loveliness here tonight." Now, in the cold of winter, at the padlocked front gate outside the Criminal Courts Building, a few such Kansas City flowers, 1931 vintage, vied to get inside, some even offering guards five-dollar bribes. Radio station KMBC announced that as soon as the Bennett verdict was known, it would cut in on programming.

That morning, attorneys met with Latshaw to discuss jury instructions. Despite Page's arguments, a first-degree murder charge was eliminated. Latshaw ruled that the evidence did not support it. The most severe charge the jury could assess was second-degree murder, which carried a sentence of ten years to life imprisonment. The jury's other options were manslaughter or not guilty. According to

Latshaw's instructions, jurors could find Myrtle not guilty only if they believed the homicide had resulted from an accident or a mistake committed in the heat of passion and without unlawful intent.

From the four lawyers, the jury would hear four hours of closing arguments. The two assistant counselors outlined the case for their sides. Hill went first and, standing before jurors, lit into Charles Hofman's credibility. "And this man, Hofman," the assistant prosecutor said, "Hofman said he was paralyzed, 'glued to the spot' . . . [He] stood 'glued to that spot,' while the life of one of [his] friends was destroyed." O'Sullivan's turn came next. He said the Bennett case had drawn wide attention because it involved a young, wealthy couple playing the popular game of bridge. Then he said, "You've heard it said that I was a friend of the dead man. That is true. I played golf with him on that Sunday of the tragedy. I had visited at his home and at the home of this good woman [Myrtle]. My wife and I associated with them and had them visit us in our home. You've heard that I represent this woman because of that friendship, and that is true. I'm here because I know that if John Bennett were alive he would order me to protect this wife."

Then it was Reed's turn, the main event. Before Reed began, though, the judge called for a five-minute break to allow spectators to stretch, and smoke. A rocking chair was brought in and set behind Latshaw, and in that chair now sat R. R. Brewster, the Republican lawyer who had lost to Reed in the 1922 Missouri senate race, for decades Reed's ardent admirer and implacable foe. Alone now, Reed stood in a small room behind the jury box. Gathering his thoughts, he smoked a cigar and stared out a window. More chairs were added in the courtroom, filling the center aisle. The break grew to fifteen minutes, with Reed standing, smoking, thinking. At last he returned to his seat, Latshaw nodded to him, and the senator approached the jury box.

Newspaper photographers stood poised, ready to take his picture. "Get it over," Reed told them, gritting his teeth. All at once, the flashbulbs exploded, loud and brilliant, as if a meteor had struck the courtroom.

And then: "If your honor, please, and you, gentlemen of the jury . . ." Reed began his argument by reading from notes, and then removed his glasses. The rest he would do strictly from memory. There was fire yet in Reed, and now he unleashed it. He sneered and threw acid on the prosecution's case. His chest puffed out, his right arm shot skyward, and twice he clapped his hands together with a bang to emphasize a point. He took Jack's .32 Colt automatic in his hand, twirled it before jurors, walking in front of the jury box, this way and then that way. He pulled the trigger, and his body recoiled in horror, just as Myrtle's must have. He was part scold, part friend, a thespian performing his high art. Reed called for O'Sullivan and for the third time in this trial they pantomimed the physical struggle for the weapon between Myrtle and Jack, Reed's face—or, rather *Myrtle's face*—writhing for effect. "Could you say if you were struggling," the senator said softly to jurors, "that you could *not* get a bullet here?" He pointed to his upper back. "Nonsense."

"The state started out to hang this woman," Reed said. "And then they said they guessed they wouldn't hang her, they would just send her to the penitentiary for life. That was all they wanted. The court tells you there isn't a scrap of evidence of murder in the first degree. . . . There has been something said here about your duty to enforce the law. There are people who think that the law is a sword to be held in the hand of some cruel monster to chop down through bone and sinew and muscle, that that is the business of the law. The law is more shield than sword. And you twelve men are in this box today as much to shield as you are to punish. And you have no right to punish, no right to penalize, no right to create human suffering in the future, no right to destroy this woman's life, unless under the evidence she is a guilty woman."

He turned to portraiture, painting Myrtle with splashes of color and insight, up from poverty, both tragic and heroic: "The story of her school-day life, of the hard toil and labor of this pathetic figure [Alice Adkins], working to take care of her baby girl, brought moisture to the eyes of more than one of you," Reed told jurors. He had been watching, and hoping, for their tears all along, of course, and he neglected to mention that Alice Adkins—"this pathetic figure" on this reference, "that old woman" on earlier references—was four years *younger* than he. That was not part of his script. Reed reminded jurors of Myrtle's marriage to Jack, how she had worked in those early years, "and this old mother moves down her furniture—I expect it was pretty shackling stuff" to live with them. Of Jack, Reed said, "Years run on and he begins to have these fits of anger. Trifles light as air throw him off his balance. Where he got it, I don't know. Inherited it, perhaps. Then we run along. Men of that kind and of that disposition are liable to tie themselves with hoops of steel to the affection of a woman." Jack Bennett had slapped Myrtle twice previously, Reed said, "under the evidence. How much oftener I don't know. But the point of the matter is she showed no hatred or resentment. She showed no disposition to kill or strike back. A crushed woman—the humiliated woman, sobs, 'I cried.' 'I cried.'

"Did he handle her roughly that night?" Reed pulled out Myrtle's sport suit and handed it to a juror, who studied it, and passed it to the next juror. "Here are the clothes she had on," Reed said. "They speak to you with voiceless lips with a strength that nothing I can say will supplement." Those rips in the outfit, Reed said, resulted from a man trying to physically overpower his wife.

Reed veered toward the peroration's emotional center:

Impose any penalty whatever upon her, place the brand of the unlawful killing of her husband upon her and you destroy her. She is not the type of woman that is graduated from penitentiaries. If you are going to give her one ounce of penalty, give her the limit.

She will be sent into the world, after a sentence of any kind, with bowed head and crushed heart, to her old mother, and do the best she can in the few days left her in this world, and then she will go to her grave, rest and be destroyed.

You can do that. Or you can say to this woman: "You are simply the victim of misfortune that took your husband

and your support, and left you a widow to take care of yourself in this world. That is misfortune enough." And send her back to her sad tired mother, who cared for her from babyhood and who she in turn has cared for.

As a cold winter rain fell on Kansas City, and pelted noisily against the courtroom windows, the senator was nearly sobbing, his voice breaking, as he said, "All I can say, gentlemen, is read the instructions and find, if you can, where there was intent to kill in this case. Find the evidence to sustain it. You will not find it. It isn't there. And, now, gentlemen of the jury, I thank you."

In the hushed silence of an old courtroom, with all eyes upon him, Reed walked to the counsel table. He reclaimed his unlit cigar, bit off the tip. He strode off into an anteroom, head high.

In his closing argument, his last chance, Jim Page's emotions ran hot. Emotion pent up over nine days erupted from within, like lava from a volcano. "If this had been an accident," Page said, "why didn't she explain it immediately after *the accident*?"

Reed objected.

"But isn't it the most natural thing on the face of the earth if you had killed somebody by accident to say so immediately after it happened?" Page asked, rhetorically.

Latshaw waved off Reed's objection, saying, "The jury heard the evidence."

"Did she say it was an accident?" Page continued. "No, this is what she said to Mrs. Trowbridge. [Reading] 'I shot him. He slapped me. I went into my mother's bedroom and got the gun. I went out of the bedroom and into the den. He was packing his grip. And he said he was going to leave me. I shot him. I followed him into the bathroom and out into the living room.'" Page then cited Myrtle's conversation with Jack's sister, Annie Jane Rice. "Does she say it is an accident? And this is undisputed even though it was given by a good old deaf lady who sat up on that stand—and the senator stood back there and bellowed at that old woman like you wouldn't holler at a common dog." Page looked at Reed with accusing eyes, and said, "Why were you so disrespectful to [her] . . . just because she was telling the truth and it showed that this wasn't an accident?"

He read Annie Rice's testimony, and recalled Myrtle's reply: "Only me and my God know why I killed him."

Page asked jurors, "Is there an accident in that woman's testimony? Nobody knew it but her and her God, but after she had talks with her mother and these two distinguished members of the bar, she concluded it was an accident."

Page scolded and mocked Mayme Hofman. "She ought to be called 'Mayme I Don't Remember,' " Page said, his brows arched.

"Now, men, those are the facts of the case. There aren't any of the senator's tears in those facts. But they are the facts without his tears just the same. And he is seeking, in my judgment, to cry in the presence of you men and overcome the facts by tears."

Page pointed across the table at O'Sullivan. "He said he knew what the man she shot in the back would want him to do if he was here. Now, Great God! I wonder how long he has been receiving messages from the dead and using them as testimony to keep this woman from being punished. He said that this case has news value. Why? He says because these people were rich and were *somebody*.

"It has news value because this man was making $18,000 a year and was a bum bridge player."

The prosecutor defended Jack's bridge game: "He was a bum bridge player because he had to work and couldn't learn to play bridge!"

Now it was Page's turn to finger the killing weapon. He play-acted the motion of firing four shots, pulling the trigger each time and using his free hand each time to illustrate how the .32 Colt automatic ejected cartridges. In his pantomime, Page falsely made it seem as if two hands were required to shoot the automatic pistol. "She went through the bathroom, just as she told Mrs. Trowbridge she did. This man was fleeing from her, fleeing for his life. Then she fired two more shots. Her finger was on the trigger. The pistol had to be pointed at this man. She pulled the trigger and the shot struck him either under his arm or in the back."

There was blood on the outside of the front door, Page said. Then Jack Bennett came back inside his home to die. His wife stood six or eight feet from him. With mock incredulity, Page asked, "Where is the *intent to kill*?"

Uneasy with the prosecutor's theatrics, Reed interrupted. He asked Page why the state had opted not to place Mayme Hofman on the witness stand.

"I'll tell you why," Page said, spitting out each word. "You gentlemen heard her sit there and to everything I could ask her, her only answer was—she would look up at the judge and smile, and say, 'I don't remember.' That is the reason why I didn't put 'Mayme I Don't Remember' on the stand."

"The court didn't see those smiles, Mr. Page," Latshaw said.

"Well, the jury saw them," Page replied.

"I didn't see them," Latshaw reasserted.

"Well, you were not fortunate," the prosecutor answered. "They were pleasant smiles."

Page was on the prowl now.

Decide the case on the evidence as it came from the lips of witnesses and the judge's instructions, Page told jurors, and not from O'Sullivan's fictions or the senator's crocodile tears.

At long last, with the dinner hour past, Page was done. The jury left to begin its deliberations. Newspapermen raced to their typewriters to tap out a beatification of Reed, the old master of the legal drama. "He came to sing his swan song in the old courtroom where the triumphs of his young manhood sent him hurdling to fame," wrote the *Kansas City Times*. *The Kansas City Star* recalled the young Reed from the Hyde trial: "He found pathways in the clouds never before trodden by orators in criminal cases . . . That golden voice could be as plaintive as a lute or as bold as thunders, ringing from mountain peaks." All around Kansas City, small wagers were made that Myrtle would be freed. According to one columnist,

"Much more censure was heard about town for Mrs. Bennett's counsel and for the court than for Mrs. Bennett herself."

The jury deliberated for more than three hours that night without reaching a verdict. Jurors reentered the courtroom and lined up in a single row behind Myrtle's chair at the counsel table. Uniformly, and one by one, they answered Latshaw's question about the possibility of reaching a verdict: Not tonight, they said. Latshaw sent them back to the Gladstone Hotel, and to bed.

For Reed, the jury's failure to reach a quick acquittal was a personal affront. The senator and his client had walked to his law office for a quick dinner. Myrtle was tense and picked at her food. Then they returned to their favored spot in the back of the now-vacant courtroom.

By 11:20 P.M., only newspapermen and a few stragglers remained. Reed put on his overcoat and talked in hushed tones with Myrtle and O'Sullivan. Just then, Reed heard a shutter click and saw a quick flash of light. He turned, thrust out his finger, and demanded, "I want to see you." George Cauthen, photographer for *The Kansas City Journal-Post*, folded up his tripod, snapped shut his camera case. Reed hastened across the hallway and gave Cauthen a verbal whipping. He used brawny language, the *Journal-Post* later reported, "liberally sprinkled with hells, damns and stronger terms." Cauthen explained to the senator he was only doing his job. "I want you to understand that if this picture is published I'll knock your _____ head off!" Reed said.

As Cauthen turned away, Reed suddenly reached back and slapped him in the face. Cauthen did not retaliate. O'Sullivan stepped forward and pulled Reed from the photographer. As he did, Reed's voice reverberated in the courtroom hallway: "Now, listen, if you don't like that, by God, I'll hit you with my knuckles and knock you out."

Fightin' Jim was still Fightin' Jim. He was sixty-nine, Cauthen only thirty. An irony was not lost on observers of the Bennett trial: Reed had struck Cauthen in the face with a hard slap, Jack Bennett–

like. The next day, Cauthen playfully claimed to be the most distinguished newspaper photographer in the nation, reasoning, "I'm the only one who has ever been attacked by a one-time candidate for president of the United States." In a front-page editorial, the *Journal-Post* was less playful, saying that if the senator were a younger man, it would have upbraided Cauthen "for not breaking his camera over his assailant's head.

"Irascibility, which not infrequently comes with age, may be indicative of many things—inflated ego, waning powers, a sense of frustration, loss of a sense of proportion or whatnot," the newspaper editorialized. "We do not know what it is symptomatic of in James A. Reed, former United States senator. But whatever the trouble in his case, it is deep-seated."

The *Journal-Post* published Cauthen's photo the next day, Jim Reed be damned.

The verdict came the following afternoon, a Friday. After more than eight hours of deliberations, the jurors formed in a semicircle in front of Latshaw's bench. Standing beside the defendant's chair, wearing the same black wool outfit for the tenth day, Myrtle held a handkerchief in one hand and J. Francis O'Sullivan's hand in the other. O'Sullivan placed an arm about her shoulders. She leaned into him as the clerk read aloud from a yellow sheet of paper: "We, the jury, find the defendant not guilty." Myrtle fell into O'Sullivan, trembling, and through the handkerchief said to jurors, "I thank you, gentlemen." Those in the crowded courtroom received the verdict, per Latshaw's orders, in silence.

Jim Reed beamed. The verdict was no surprise to him, except this, *Why had it taken so long?* News of the acquittal hit the radio airwaves within minutes: "Mrs. Bennett freed!" In an anteroom moments later, Myrtle's friends embraced her and sobbed with her. "I want to tell mother," Myrtle said repeatedly. O'Sullivan dialed the Woods residence where Alice Adkins was confined to bed. "Please tell Mrs. Adkins, it's not guilty," O'Sullivan said. Jim Page, not in the courtroom for the verdict, told reporters later that it had not been a fair trial. His assistant, John Hill, said, "It looks like an open season on husbands."

Jurors explained their decision. "It was not that the defense proved her innocent of murder," the jury foreman, Leslie Choate, explained. "It was that the state did not prove her guilty beyond a reasonable doubt." Jurors took eight ballots, the first seven with the same result: three for conviction, nine for acquittal. The three hold-outs for conviction found especially persuasive the testimony of policewoman Frances Trowbridge, who said Myrtle had told her on the night of the killing that Jack slapped her and she had gotten his gun and followed him through the bathroom, and then shot him. But the other nine jurors, with Jim Reed's story still in their ears, countered that Myrtle had been given a hypodermic injection and ought not be responsible for what she said that evening. As pressure came to bear on the three holdouts, they conferred in a corner of the jury room. Later they conferred in a washroom. Finally, after lunch on Friday, the three announced they were convinced: the eighth ballot brought unanimity.

According to Choate, the nine jurors who were for acquittal believed that the first two shots had been fired accidentally. They remained uncertain whether the next two shots were fired accidentally or by a hysterical woman struggling with her husband for the pistol. Either way, those nine said, the state had failed to show premeditation.

In short, the jury believed Jim Reed.

"We agreed early that the lawyers' speeches should be thrown aside," Choate said. "What they said was not considered."

But their speeches were considered. Jurors accepted Reed's version of events that night: that the pistol discharged twice only because Myrtle stumbled in the den, and that Myrtle could not have seen Jack through the offset bathroom doors. In fact, from studying the locations of the bullet marks in the bathroom door and molding, jurors believed that the far door had been closed, disregarding completely

Page's contention that Jack had slammed the door shut as he fled. They believed Jack was shot to death during a scuffle for possession of the gun.

From the courthouse, O'Sullivan rushed Myrtle out a side door and into a waiting car. A small crowd saw her and fell back. Reed emerged through the front door moments later, the crowd slapping him on the back, shouting huzzahs. The once and still legal champion climbed into the backseat of his car, his trusted chauffeur, George Dugan, as happy as he. At a brief press conference in Reed's office at the Telephone Building, Myrtle pulled off her wool beret, loosing chestnut curls upon her neck. She opened her black coat, which had been tightly fastened throughout the trial, threw it back to reveal a frock of black crêpe. "Plans? Well, I—I haven't any," she said. Reed said, "I'll tell you what she's going to do. She's going to take care of that old mother of hers, that's what."

Hearing the verdict, Tom Bennett remained stoic. "I think the prosecutor did all he could," Jack Bennett's brother said. "If I had not been here to see and hear the trial I expect I would have blamed him, but he isn't to blame. It was a case in which he had fourteen men to fight: the judge, the jury and Senator Reed." He headed for the train station. "There's nothing for us to do now, but take the medicine they gave us."

Jim Reed's wife missed the dramatic moment. Lura was in Washington, staying at the home of former congressman William Rodenberg of Illinois and his wife. Reed dashed off a Western Union telegram to her: VERDICT IN BENNETT CASE, NOT GUILTY (STOP) LOVE. JAMES A. REED. How the buoyant senator shared the great good news with Nell was not recorded in writing.

Snow blanketed Kansas City on verdict day, a happy development for the unemployed that would bring hundreds of jobs to men who needed them. On that day, the Kansas City Country Club announced that at its upcoming mixed contract bridge tournament husbands and wives would not be permitted to play as partners. No explanation was needed.

A car dropped Myrtle at the Woods residence and she dashed upstairs to her mother's bedside. They shared tears and a long embrace. Then Myrtle slept fifteen hours. The next afternoon a reporter inquired about her future. Myrtle told him she wanted people to forget her. But she had made herself unforgettable. She would not be forgotten.

PART 2

♠

The Search

FOURTEEN

Miami

Here the author enters the story. Myrtle wanted to disappear. I wanted to find her, or at least find her well-covered tracks, to see what she had made of her freedom. I wondered if she had ever found redemption, and so in searching for her footprints seventy-five years after her acquittal, I would search also for how she tried to make peace with herself and get right with Jack's memory.

A woman of Myrtle's resolute nature would find a way to live. Of that I was certain. But how? Where? Anita Loos's fictional Lorelei Lee, after shooting her man, created a rich new life of adventuring. I imagined Myrtle had used her second chance to do much the same.

And if driven by endless curiosity about Myrtle, I had to know about the others, too. The braided stories of Myrtle, the Culbertsons, and Jim Reed ended with Myrtle's trial and again became three streams, this time diverging. When I left them in 1932, Ely and Jo—and contract bridge—were national sensations. Senator Reed had one more presidential run in him. Myrtle was a young woman, only thirty-six. But now in the early years of the twenty-first century, they were long gone from center stage, enveloped by the shadows of time.

Myrtle's fame endures in the dim light of the microfilm readers at the Kansas City Public Library's central branch. Her acquittal prompted an avalanche of cynical, even caustic, letters to the editors of Kansas City's newspapers. "Why go to Arkansas and stay ninety days to get a divorce when you can stay in Missouri and get one overnight by getting your husband into a bridge game?" one said. Another took a swipe at Jim Reed and Judge Latshaw: "The senator should have snapped his finger at the judge when the trial was over and brought him out from under the spell. The way it was, the judge congratulated the senator over his victory—adding more disgrace and shame to the occasion. Well balanced judges don't do those things." From the pulpit in Jefferson City, Missouri, a Presbyterian minister castigated Latshaw, contending that his court "has deliberately obstructed the introduction of evidence, has belittled itself by arguments with the prosecutor and has generally conducted itself in a manner ill befitting any court of justice." Latshaw reacted harshly. "Some people are preordained and predestined to be fools," he said. "This reverend gentleman seems to be one of them." Later, for the only time in his judicial career, Latshaw dictated a public statement. In it, he cited several critical instances during the trial in which he had sided with the prosecution.

The *Kansas City Times* would have none of it. Nearly aghast over the handling of the Bennett trial, the newspaper editorialized, "It was representative of a good many American trials, in which essential facts are kept from the jury through the technicalities of law and procedure, the resourcefulness of counsel for the defense or the blundering of the state's attorneys. In such cases there are often two verdicts, that of the jury and that of the public. As to the merits of such cases, the public is likely to be much better informed. . . . If the jury had been permitted, or could in law have been permitted, to have all the essential facts in the case, the verdict might have been different."

Deaths at the card table are few and famous. Wild Bill Hickok was shot dead playing poker in a saloon in Deadwood, South Dakota, in 1876. Legend says Hickok held two pair, aces and eights, the "dead man's hand," when a bullet from a Colt .45 crashed through the back of his head. In November 1928, only ten months before the Hofmans sat at the Bennetts' bridge table, the gambler Arnold Rothstein, a much-feared man, was shot through the stomach with a Colt .38 while playing poker at New York's Park Central Hotel. A shadowy figure believed by some to have fixed the 1919 World Series, Rothstein stumbled from the hotel room and lived long enough to be able to tell authorities who had shot him. He chose not to, though. He took the name of his killer to his grave. To this short list was added an obscure name from the bridge table: the Kansas City perfume salesman Jack Bennett.

Myrtle's unwanted celebrity as a femme fatale kept her name in the news for about a year after her acquittal. Alexander Woollcott, a devoted bridge player who spent some of his boyhood in Kansas City, rose from the Algonquin Round Table in November 1931 to write in *The New Yorker* about Myrtle and what he called the "four shots heard round the world." At the time of the 1929 shooting, Woollcott wrote, "There was probably not a literate household in Europe or the three Americas [in] which the emotional seismograph had not recorded its tremors." He noted the theatrics of Senator Reed in his "more than adequate performance" in trial, and poked fun at Mayme Hofman on the witness stand as a dainty and pitiable emblem of the "now devitalized society of a once rugged community." (In his 1934 book, *While Rome Burns,* Woollcott republished his Bennett column and, as an addendum, suggested that Myrtle later played with a bridge partner who, unfamiliar with her history, put down his hand as dummy and told her, "I'm afraid you'll want to shoot me for this," at which point Myrtle fainted. This story, repeated so often as to become part of the Myrtle Bennett legend, carries the certain aroma of apocrypha.)

Months after the criminal trial, Myrtle settled out of court with Jack's family to avoid a civil trial. She had received about $30,000 from Jack's life insurance policies, plus about $15,000 more from his estate. The attorney for Jack's dozen heirs said Myrtle paid his clients $10,000, a sizable amount in 1931.

The trial participants soon faded. Latshaw became ill several months after the trial. When he died in May 1932, Jim Reed was among his eulogists. Jim Page would achieve his goal in becoming judge of the circuit court in Jackson County early in 1933; he died late the following year. Though his failure to convict Myrtle Bennett was a stain upon his record, during his five years as county prosecutor, 7 men were hanged and 3,088 were sentenced to the penitentiary, largely as a result of Page's efforts.

Stories, such as Woollcott's, took root in the years after the trial. One had the defense attorney O'Sullivan reporting that Jack "ran around on his wife for years." Jim Reed was said to have told Myrtle that he regarded Jack's death as an alcohol-driven accident. "There can be no more terrible accidents in your life," the senator warned Myrtle, "because the second time something like this happens no one will be able to defend you." In Carmi, Illinois, Jack Bennett's sister, Annie Rice, refused till her dying day to believe that her brother ever slapped Myrtle. "He was such a gentleman," Rice insisted. She despised Myrtle, and told her granddaughter, "Can you imagine someone who would commit murder because of bridge?" In her home, Rice kept a cartoon showing a wife leaning over a bridge table, a smoking gun in hand, and her husband across the table, slumped over, dead in his chair. Rice told everyone she thought Myrtle should have been imprisoned forever.

Then, undoubtedly by her own design, Myrtle Bennett vanished, with not a word about her in Kansas City's newspapers. She lived on, though, in myth and legend. Down through the decades her name has cropped up at bridge games, even today, usually as a laugh line or as a wife's stern warning to her husband/partner to straighten up, or else "I'll pull a Myrtle Bennett on you!" On the Internet, I found several dozen references to Myrtle, most filled with embellishments and inaccuracies, and some depicting the fictitious Fatal Hand.

I told myself that somewhere, beyond the myths, embellishments, and inaccuracies, the real Myrtle Bennett was there to found.

I searched online for "Myrtle A. Bennett" in the Social Security Death Index (SSDI), and found three women by that name: one born in 1918, the others in 1895, the year of my Myrtle's birth. I located Myrtle in the 1930 Census, still living with Alice Adkins in Kansas City, and followed her back to the 1920 (South Dakota), 1910 (Tennessee), and 1900 (Arkansas) censuses. Each census provided different personal information—some facts (age, birthplace, parents' names) were strengthened by repetition, others were called into question by contradictions. The Myrtle A. Bennett born in March 1895 had obtained her Social Security card in Missouri and died in 1992. I could not find a published obituary for her in microfilm or electronic databases.

A search for her death certificate, though, brought a remarkable finding: a will for "Myrtle A. Bennett" in a Miami-Dade County,

Florida, clerk's office database. A stroke of researcher's luck, here was the first gold nugget in my sifting pan. Though wills typically are public records, it is unusual for the complete text of a will to be scanned, page by page, in a database free to the public. When the death certificate from Florida showed up in the mail weeks later, it confirmed that I had found my Myrtle. More gold came in the date of her death.

Born in Tillar, Arkansas, to Alice B. (McReynolds) and Henry F. Adkins, she had died on January 21, 1992, in North Miami Beach. Myrtle had walked from the Jackson County courtroom and lived another sixty-one years. At age ninety-six, she had lived from the nineteenth century to the cusp of the twenty-first.

How had she come to live and die in Florida? What was her life like after Jack? Did she ever play bridge again? Her will listed beneficiaries, and I hoped to find them—if they were still alive—and fill in the blanks of her life.

I followed the public-record trail to Miami.

Myrtle's death certificate from 1992 carried the embossed gold seal of the state of Florida. It showed she had died at her apartment at 5:27 A.M., no cause listed. It offered a few clues to her life: name ("Myrtle A. Bennett"), marital status ("Widowed"), and occupation ("Administrator—Hotels"). Apparently, never marrying again, she had been resourceful enough to build a managerial career.

Her will offered more details. Filed in the Probate Division of Dade County Circuit Court in Florida, it reported that Myrtle's estate would distribute an estimated $850,000, mostly in bonds and securities. According to my cross-checking in the SSDI, all beneficiaries had died except for three people with the last name of Armshaw, and a cousin named Carolyn Scruggs, living in Little Rock. The estate was administrated by a William Armshaw, a name listed in a South Florida phone book.

I contacted Bill Armshaw. He told me he was Myrtle's stockbroker. The mere mention of Myrtle's name made him laugh. He said she insisted on thanking him for his friendship by leaving money to his three children, though she'd never met them. Armshaw first saw Myrtle in the middle 1970s, when she came to his office in Surfside,

Florida. "She was a fascinating woman, very bright," Armshaw told me. About her personality: "Myrtle was a bit acerbic. Basically she was very suspicious, but she was also capable of real warmth."

Only near the end of her life did Armshaw learn (from Myrtle's extended family in Oklahoma) about the killing of Jack. But that Myrtle had it in her to shoot a gun did not surprise Armshaw. He called her tough, fiercely independent, and quick to anger. He said she bickered with maids, firing them for petty infractions, cashiering one for dusting incorrectly. That was Myrtle Bennett, Armshaw said with a laugh. Well dressed, he said, carrying her personal dignity impressively—but always domineering, "one of the most domineering women I ever met."

On the off chance Armshaw might have known the Hofmans— the Bennetts' bridge companions from the Roaring Twenties—I mentioned that Charles and Mayme Hofman had left their country club life in Chicago in 1960 for Fort Lauderdale. Both Hofmans died in 1970, but Armshaw said Myrtle had never mentioned them. In fact, she told him little about herself other than that she had worked in New York hotels, for years at The Carlyle.

She invested her money conservatively, Armshaw said, mostly in public utilities. Jack had always handled their money in marriage, but during her decades alone, Myrtle proved her own good business sense. Her investment portfolio grew handsomely. In the early 1980s, she handed Armshaw a check for $72,000. "Did someone die?" he asked. No, Myrtle said, but with gold and silver prices skyrocketing, she had sold her jewelry. "I'm too old to be wearing these, anyway," said Myrtle, then in her late eighties. She added, "They're pretty and nice, but they don't pay a monthly check."

I contacted Miami-area bridge clubs to ask about Myrtle, dead fifteen years by this time. No one remembered meeting her, though one woman asked me, "Myrtle Bennett? Isn't that the woman who shot her husband in Kansas City?"

For a journalist, nothing can replace putting boots on the ground of his subject, to walk in his subject's footsteps, and to imagine breathing his subject's air. This, I would do.

I would begin with Myrtle's gun.

FIFTEEN

Kansas City

I

It took me months to locate a Colt .32 automatic pistol. Gun dealers and gun shop owners told me that Colt had stopped production of this gun more than a half century ago. But now, finally, I held one in my hand. Small and lightweight, it fit snugly in my palm, as it must have in Myrtle's. With a gun shop owner, I had come to an indoor shooting range in San Rafael, California. I needed to know the sensations that Myrtle must have felt on that long-ago night. We put on hearing protection—the reports from a .32 were loud, he warned me—and then he fired at a target twenty paces away. These were smokeless bullets, but there was a discernible smell, the chemicals superheated by the gun's firing. Now it was my turn. I explained that Myrtle fired at Jack while on the move, from about six or eight paces. The paper target, showing a man's torso and head, was mechanically moved closer, to about ten paces. Just then, I took a deep breath, bolted two steps forward, raising the gun to chest level, and fired. I was a novice—I had never fired a handgun before—but my first shot hit the X on the target, beneath the paper man's solar plexus, a bull's-eye. This was pure luck, but it proved how easy it was for Myrtle, a first-time shooter, to hit the mark from close range, twice. Now, I pulled off my hearing protection. "Don't do that," the gun shop owner warned. But I needed to hear the gun blast, no matter how loud, to know what it must have sounded like inside the Bennett apartment. I fired twice more in rapid succession, and in an enclosed area the reports sounded like cannons. For several minutes, I could not hear anything but the cannons.

No wonder Charles Hofman said he never heard the third and fourth shots.

During my research I consulted with Bill Worley, a Kansas City historian. A delightful conversationalist in love with local history and lore, Worley has portrayed Boss Pendergast and Harry Truman in local one-man stage performances. He informed me that the Park Manor cooperative apartment building where the Bennetts lived still stands at the intersection of Ward and Roanoke Parkways.

Thrilled at the prospects of visiting the most infamous living room in the history of contract bridge, I flew to Kansas City.

With the current owner's permission, a Park Manor neighbor escorted me, Worley, and a local historic preservationist, Susan Jezak Ford, inside Myrtle and Jack's apartment. I brought a photocopy of the diagram used as a trial exhibit. Jim Reed was correct: the Bennett apartment was not big and sprawling. In fact, the current owner was merging it with the adjacent apartment. A few wall beams were exposed as a carpenter explained to us the structural changes already made. The long hallway Myrtle traversed, past the dining room, to her mother's bedroom, was no more. But the high style of the cooperative building, and of the Bennett's first-floor apartment, remained, including the decorative molding and the wrought-iron railing in the front foyer. I had stared at the diagram of the apartment so intently and for so long—a copy of it was taped to my office desk— that being in Myrtle and Jack's place riveted and haunted me. It brought chills.

Now, walking through the apartment, I see and feel and know that Byrd Rice's story about the explosive moment is the way it must have happened:

Go get my gun, Jack ordered. He stood by the living room closet, inflamed, his words and emotions fired by alcohol and contempt for his wife. Myrtle had embarrassed him in front of the Hofmans. No woman would excoriate him like that.

Myrtle did not think to defy him, not yet. She sobbed as she walked the forty-five feet down the hallway toward her mother's bedroom. In her wifely obedience, she grew smaller with each step. That Jack had asked for his gun was one more slap of humiliation. With robberies in the neighborhood recently, it was as if he were saying, *You and your mother can fend for yourselves.* Myrtle turned on the light in Alice Adkins's bedroom, rummaged through the chest of drawers, and reached beneath the linens until she felt the four-inch gun barrel, smooth against her fingertips. She took the weapon in her hand. Her mother, groggy from sleep, heard Myrtle sobbing, and asked, "What are you after?" Myrtle replied, "Jack wants his gun. He's going to St. Joe."

It was well past midnight, and Adkins said, half-statement and half-question, "He's not going away tonight."

In response Adkins heard nothing, only her daughter sobbing and slamming the bedroom door.

The .32 Colt Automatic Model 1903 Pocket Hammerless, designed by John Browning, weighed just twenty-three ounces. It held eight bullets in a magazine inserted in the handle, a ninth bullet in the chamber. On its hard rubber handle was the company insignia, a rampant colt kicking up its forelegs. "Equipped with safety features that absolutely prevent accidental discharge," the Colt advertisement boasted of the .32. "It is always reliable . . . It is accurate. For target practice, small game shooting or personal protection and in the defense of Law and Order, Colt accuracy will serve you best."

Holding the weapon gave Myrtle a sense of shifting dynamics, a new power. "Abe Lincoln may have freed all men," the old saying about the gun maker went, "but Sam Colt made them equal." Now his pistol made a woman equal. Myrtle felt more than equal.

She turned into the den.

Charles Hofman stepped from the small master bathroom, a door on each side, and saw Myrtle, sobbing still, moving toward him, and toward Jack, her right elbow slightly bent, and in her hand, held slightly below waist level, a gun, Jack's pistol, pointed obliquely at the floor. "My God, Myrtle, what are you going to do?" Hofman said.

He reached out to her, but Myrtle sidestepped him. She saw Jack through the two offset bathroom doors. For one instant, their eyes met. Jack pulled the far door shut just as Myrtle fired twice in rapid succession, flames erupting from the gun barrel, the recoils surging into Myrtle's forearm, two cartridges ejecting, one bullet embedding in the bathroom door casing, the other splintering through the door itself. Myrtle pursued Jack through the bathroom, into their bedroom.

From behind, still in the den, Charles Hofman heard those two explosions. In the small room, the sound became a siren deep in his inner ear, a shrill scream. In a few moments, confused, he saw, to his right, Myrtle's mother, in her nightclothes, stumbling down the hallway, the siren still spiraling in his ear, so loud he did not hear the two explosions that came next. Hofman followed Mrs. Adkins down the hallway and through the archway into the living room.

Myrtle chased her husband through their bedroom and into the living room, Jack six or eight paces ahead, sprinting for the front door, reaching for it.

On the run, Myrtle, a few steps from the folded-up bridge table, raised the pistol, fired twice more. One bullet lodged beneath Jack's left arm, the second ripped through his upper back, slicing past the second vertebra, and exiting through his throat. Blood spurted on the door and floor.

Jack stopped. He put his hand to the doorjamb and staggered back into the living room.

Charles Hofman emerged from the hallway, standing beside Myrtle's mother, blinking into the living room light. Alice Adkins asked, "Myrtle, what on earth are you doing?"

"He hit me," Myrtle said. "He was fighting me, and twisting my arm."

Jack leaned against a chair in the middle of the room, reached toward his back, and fell to the floor, blood on the chair, blood on his back.

Myrtle, across the room, her voice a disembodied shriek: "Oh, what will I do?"

She rushed to Jack and dropped Sam Colt's equalizer. She knelt beside her husband, cradled his head, called for a pillow, called for him: "Talk to me, Jack! TALK TO ME! " Her mother joined her, and cradled Myrtle. Jack, on his back, reached for them, one hand to Myrtle, the other to Adkins. He tried to say something, but no words came, only gasps of air through the hole in his bloodied throat. Myrtle screamed, half hysterical, "Call a doctor!"

Charles Hofman reached for the phone, and dialed. The doctor's wife answered and Hofman told her that something terrible had happened, and to have the doctor come quickly.

Mayme Hofman, still in her evening wrap, reappeared at the front door with an upstairs neighbor. In time, the doctor hurried into the room and felt for Jack's pulse. There was none.

Myrtle's wail filled the room.

Passing through the Bennetts' handsomely arched front door splattered with Jack's blood was a policeman from the Country Club station and a reporter from *The Kansas City Star*, notepad in hand. They were responding to reports of gunshots.

From the living room floor, Myrtle called out again, this time not for Jack, but for his gun. Her mother held her tight, keeping Myrtle from the Colt .32.

Alice Adkins demanded, "Somebody get that gun."

I walked from the Bennetts' den through the small bathroom, a door on either side, and into Myrtle and Jack's bedroom. In my mind I saw Jack slamming the bathroom door shut and running past the bed. I imagined his racing heartbeat, and Myrtle's fury. The living room where Jack died was smaller than I had realized. The upstairs neighbor who escorted me here, curious about the long-ago killing, asked,

"Where did the guy die?" I sized up his position, and replied, "You're standing on Jack Bennett right now."

Instinctively, he took a step backward.

II

With local historians Worley and Ford, I walked past the decrepit structure at 1908 Main Street in downtown Kansas City, and looked up at Boss Pendergast's second-story window, listening for the distant echoes of a vanquished political machine. We returned later to the Country Club District, lovely still with its upscale shopping plazas, bubbling fountains, and tree-lined streets. We passed Jim Reed's sprawling house on Cherry Street, owned by his descendants until recently. Behind, I saw Nell and Paul Donnelly's house, transformed into the Toy and Miniature Museum.

Jim Reed's political isolation was intensifying in 1931, his personal life increasingly complicated. Politically he was seen as old and obstreperous, with too many enemies. Though no longer a senator, and a pariah to the national Democratic Party, he determined to make one more run for the White House in 1932, against Franklin Roosevelt. At home, he waited for his elderly wife Lura to die, while Nell and his infant son lived next door in another man's house. Reed immersed himself in a lucrative law practice and in his private trysts with Nell, who was anxious to become his second wife.

During a visit to Kansas City in May 2006, a headline in *The Kansas City Star*'s Sunday magazine caught my eye: "The Secrets of Nelly Don: KC Once Whispered About the Private Life of This Dressmaker." The story told of a new ninety-minute documentary about Nell's life that disclosed publicly for the first time her extramarital romance with Senator James A. Reed and the birth of their son in September 1931—when both were married to others. The documentary filmmaker was Terence O'Malley, Nell's great-grandnephew. Nell's affair with the senator was only a small part of O'Malley's otherwise loving documentary. Even so, not all Reed family members were happy about O'Malley's decision to tell Nell's secret. I saw the documentary and interviewed the affable O'Malley and also two of the senator's grandsons, Peter Reed and James A. Reed II.

They told me about a harrowing family story passed down to them. In December 1931, they said, Nell was kidnapped, and it became a national sensation. Word reached Reed in federal court in Jefferson City, Missouri, where he was prosecuting a million-dollar damage suit. He sped 160 miles to Nell and Paul Donnelly's house. There, he learned that kidnappers had used their car to block the Donnelly driveway. When chauffeur George Blair pulled up in the Donnellys' 1928 Lincoln convertible sedan, his millionaire employer in the backseat, Blair sounded his horn. While one kidnapper rushed to the car, jabbed a gun into Blair's ribs, and took the wheel, others stormed the backseat, where Nell screamed and fought gamely, her lip bloodied as they put a muslin sack over her head. The kidnappers drove Nell and Blair to a remote farmhouse in Kansas where, by candlelight, they dictated a ransom note. Nell wrote to her husband, Paul, telling him to get $75,000 in unmarked bills or her kidnappers would blind her and kill Blair. She wrote a second such note to her company's attorney, James Taylor, Reed's law partner, knowing with certainty that word would reach the senator. Reed paced in the Donnelly living room, gnawing his cigar. He told the gathered newspapermen, "I will say this, if a single hair of her head is harmed, I and Mr. Donnelly will spend the rest of our lives running the culprits to earth and seeing that they are given the full extent of the law, which in this state is hanging."

Paul Donnelly stood by Reed's side, emasculated but putting up a good front. He knew that Nell no longer loved him, fed up with his serial philandering, drinking, and idle threats to commit suicide if she became pregnant. Reed had masterminded a fiction for public consumption that Nell had traveled to Europe to adopt the infant named David Donnelly. That was a ruse. She returned from Europe and gave birth to the senator's son in Chicago. Paul had agreed to keep quiet about the boy's paternity. Their reputations were at stake, along with the well-being of the garment company.

Reed knew the levers of power in Kansas City. He phoned

Johnny Lazia, the genial, cologne-dipped chieftain of gangster corruption in Kansas City. Lazia had served time in a state penitentiary at the age of eighteen for an armed robbery conviction, and later returned to Kansas City, where he ascended to political power at the North Side Democratic Club. Pendergast could not ignore Lazia, so he co-opted him. While Lazia delivered votes on Election Day, the Boss used his police control to help protect Lazia's vice and gambling operations in town. Lazia told Reed he had no idea who had kidnapped Nell, though certainly they were outsiders. He said no locals would dare kidnap a woman as prominent and politically connected as Mrs. Donnelly. Reed presented Lazia an ultimatum: find Mrs. Donnelly within twenty-four hours or Reed would purchase a half hour of time on national radio and expose Lazia's corruption.

An extraordinary hunt for Nell was carried out by Boss Pendergast's underlings, both lawless and lawful. Two dozen carloads of Lazia's men and at least that many police automobiles crisscrossed the city, working both the Misssouri and Kansas sides of town. Lazia's men found Nell and her chauffeur walking near an all-night roadside diner. Feeling pressure, their fearful captors had released them after thirty-four hours, and fled. Lazia allowed Police Chief Lewis Siegfried to get the credit. Siegfried drove Nell and Blair home.

The next summer Reed's dream of the presidency died in the bright lights of Chicago Stadium. A tidal wave of adoration crashed down on Franklin Roosevelt at the 1932 Democratic National Convention. FDR was former assistant secretary of the navy in the Wilson administration, and his camp was populated by more than a few former Wilson men. Nominated as an "Apostle of Americanism," Reed sat in the Missouri section, and Nell was there, too. Days earlier she had engaged in a tense exchange with a St. Louis woman who wanted to put Missouri's standard with Roosevelt. "You go and sit down and think it over," Nell said. The woman replied, "You go and sit down and think it over yourself." Nell stood firm: "Well, this standard is not going to be moved. It would be accepted as a slight to Senator Reed." Shortly thereafter, though, Missouri, and its standard, went to Roosevelt. Amid thunderous cheers, a voice was heard, the voice that would soothe Americans in radio Fireside Chats for the next dozen years. His jaw set, a cigar clenched in his teeth, the defeated Reed perspired and blinked up at the stadium lights. There he might have seen an apparition of Woodrow Wilson smiling.

That October, Lura Reed died at eighty-eight. Her husband of more than four decades was at her bedside, and *The Kansas City Star* reported the senator "crushed by the sudden loss of the wife to whom his devotion had been proverbial." FDR sent a telegram: "Heartfelt sympathy from your old friend and Mrs. Roosevelt goes out to you in your great loss. I wish there was something I could do to be of service."

Thirty-four days later Nell filed for divorce, citing her husband's "acts of cruelty and neglect." She purchased Paul's half interest in the Donnelly Garment Compàny for nearly $1 million. She also took custody of David.

No matter their discretion, rumors about the senator and Nell had spread, even into the most widely read syndicated newspaper column in America, Walter Winchell's. On November 27, 1932, six weeks after Lura Reed's death, and two weeks after Nell filed for divorce, Winchell mused in his column of one-liners, Broadway news, and chatter about otherwise secretive romance: "Wonder if there is anything to the buzz that Mrs. Donnelly of Kansas City, who was kidnapped last year, and Ex-Senator Jim Reed may merge? . . ." At the University of Missouri–Kansas City archives, reading through the James A. Reed Papers, I found a letter Reed fired off to Winchell: "You may think what you said was witty, but I think that a man who will couple another's name with a woman when the ashes of that man's wife are scarcely cold, is about the lowest order of animal life, and I shall be glad to tell this to your face if ever I meet you." A year later, in December 1933, at Nell's fashionable apartment at The Walnuts, she and the senator married in front of twenty guests who had no idea a wedding ceremony was about to occur. By New Year's Day 1934, the senator, Nell and two-year-old David were living together on Cherry Street. Nell, fearful of another kidnapping, placed metal bars on the second-story windows. Their marriage must have haunted

Paul Donnelly, now in Hartford, Connecticut, perhaps as much as his new young wife's pregnancy, because he entered The Hartford Retreat, a hospital for nervous disorders. There, in September 1934, in a manic depressive state, he hanged himself.

Jim Reed legally adopted his own son, and David Q. Donnelly became David Q. Reed. In the process, the boy earned the unusual distinction of having been "adopted" by both of his biological parents. Cocktail-hour whispers passed through the *Kansas City Star* crowd, and the Kansas City Club. On Independence Day 1935, U.S. senator Harry Truman, a risen star in the Pendergast machine, wrote to his wife, Bess, from Washington to say he was preparing speeches on farming, foreign trade, the bank bill, Social Security, and bureaucratic government. Truman must have expected criticism from Reed, always a voluble critic of Roosevelt. "If Mr. Reed gets smart," Truman wrote to Bess, "I'm thinking of telling him what I know about him." The secret Truman knew, one can only guess.

Reed turned from Tom Pendergast even before the Boss was brought down on income tax evasion charges in 1939 by Roosevelt's prosecutors and sentenced to fifteen months at Leavenworth. Reed lived long enough to see what once seemed impossible: Jackson County's Harry S. Truman nominated as vice president. A party loyalist, Truman never forgave Reed for his assault on Wilson and the League of Nations. "I am happy you find my logic infallible," Truman had written Reed in 1937 about the proposed reorganization of the Supreme Court. "Logic which takes into consideration loyalty to party and friends is rather unusual in a United States Senator from Missouri." In 1942, in a crowded elevator at the Kansas City Club, a friend whispered to Truman, "There's Reed. Don't you want to speak to him?" Truman later reported in a letter to Bess that he had answered his friend by saying of Reed that "the old so-and-so didn't mean a thing to me, and unless I had to I didn't care to notice him." Stepping from the elevator, Reed said, "Why, hello, Harry! I didn't see you." Truman replied, "Hello, Senator, it was always hard for you to see me."

The stories about the extramarital romance between the senator and Nell, and the birth of their son, went untold for decades in the Reed family. The silence created problems. In the mid-1970s, a family friend told Peter Reed, grandson of Nell and the senator, that his father David had been adopted by Nell in Europe. Peter Reed had never heard that. He needed to know the truth. He put to good use his education (Andover and Cambridge University, with a master's degree in art history) and his journalistic skills as a critic of art and design. He read old newspapers and magazines, and interviewed members of both sides of his family, the Reeds and the Warricks. He told me he learned about the extramarital affair between the senator and Nell, and much more. When he had gathered his stories, he approached Nell, then in her middle eighties.

Grandmother and grandson shared a close relationship. They talked plainly, honestly, though Peter knew that, in her formidable way, Nell would reveal only as much as she chose. (Peter learned that his father, a Kansas City lawyer for thirty-nine years and a one-term Republican legislator, had promised Nell not to disclose the story of his birth during Nell's lifetime, a promise he kept until his own death in 1999.) Nell had told Peter about the Bennett trial. She said that Jim Reed told her that Myrtle and Jack had had too much to drink on the night of September 29, 1929—a fact that never made it into the trial, or the newspapers. "They were drunk as skunks," Peter Reed told me. A great admirer of his grandfather, Peter said, "He was Sir Galahad coming to rescue Myrtle Bennett, who wasn't going to get a fair trial."

Peter and Nell once shared a pedal boat on a lake at the property the senator purchased during the 1930s, Reed Ranch in northern Michigan, where he and Nell had hunted and sat by a great log fire on cool summer and autumn nights. "Grandmother, I need to talk to you about something that is a bit personal," Peter said that day. "People have been trying to tell me that you and I are not related. People are saying that Dad is adopted." For two hours, they talked about life. Nell confided her story, the way it happened. As Peter slowly pedaled in the fading sun of late summer, he was transported to the early 1930s. He learned about Paul Donnelly and his threats to kill himself if Nell became pregnant. He heard of the senator's first meeting with Nell in his office on the nineteenth floor of the Telephone Building. From Nell herself, the grandson heard how the senator had met Paul Donnelly, man to man, to discuss the pregnancy that sent Nell to Europe.

Peter told Nell he understood why she and the senator had kept the birth quiet. "But I don't understand," he said, "why later in life you didn't just start to whisper into a few ears what the real story was so that the people who really counted in the community understood that he was *really* your son." Peter saw his grandmother look at him "as if I was a great deal more stupid than she had ever imagined." Nell Donnelly Reed would die in 1991 at the age of 102 after 47 years as James A. Reed's widow. On the pedal boat, she only shrugged and answered, "We expected them to figure it out."

The eighty-two-year-old senator died on September 8, 1944, at Reed Ranch, two days before his son's thirteenth birthday. He had fished in a rainstorm at six o'clock in the morning, against Nell's better judgment, and caught pneumonia. Nell later said, "There were some things you could tell him and some things you couldn't."

SIXTEEN

New York

I

"Mrs. Bennett was so good-lookin'." This narration, delivered in a sunny Irish brogue, came from Michael O'Connell, a ruddy-faced native of County Limerick, Ireland, and for fifty-seven years a doorman at The Carlyle. So good-looking was Myrtle Bennett, O'Connell told me, he couldn't resist flirting with her, even though she was thirty-seven years older than he. "I kidded her once and said, 'Mrs. Bennett, how come a beautiful lady like you isn't married? You should be married and have a husband.' She smiled at me and said, 'I'm doing just fine,' and she made a big joke of it."

Following Bill Armshaw's lead, I had phoned The Carlyle to ask about its long-ago employee Myrtle Bennett. A hotel spokeswoman told me she was not permitted to comment on any current or former employee, but amiably suggested I might speak with a soon-to-retire doorman who had served at the elegant hotel for more than a half-century. Perhaps, she said, Michael O'Connell might have known my Myrtle Bennett.

So I took a taxi through New York's Upper East Side to The Carlyle at Seventy-sixth Street and Madison Avenue, a high-rent district. Built in 1930, and named for the Scottish essayist Thomas Carlyle, the storied hotel offers glamorous views of nearby Central Park. Its neighbors include the Whitney and Metropolitan museums. I asked at the front desk for O'Connell, and was told to wait for him in the polished marble lobby. Just then, an older, still spry doorman, in uniform, returned from a walk in the park, holding a schnauzer on a leash. It was O'Connell, who introduced himself, handed off the schnauzer to another doorman, and escorted me to a comfortable couch near the entry to the hotel restaurant.

"Yes, Mrs. Bennett—we all called her that, even Mr. Robert Huyot, who hired her. She was a very elegant person," O'Connell said. He arrived from Ireland in 1949, just seventeen years old, and started work in the hotel's package room. Over time O'Connell became The Carlyle's griot, his memory filled with the history of the hotel, and its people. He was given a PT-109 pin by Senator John Kennedy and White House cufflinks by Ronald and Nancy Reagan. O'Connell reveres The Carlyle, and devoted his working life to it.

Myrtle Bennett worked as executive head of housekeeping at The Carlyle after World War II, and throughout the 1950s. Classified advertisements in *The New York Times* seeking chambermaids and linen room attendants at the hotel appeared during these years, touting "pleasant working conditions," and listing the contact as "Mrs. Bennett."

O'Connell recalled the luminaries during Mrs. Bennett's tenure, some hotel guests, others apartment owners, a Who's Who of American celebrity: David O. Selznick, Myrna Loy, Judy Garland, Mr. and Mrs. Gary Cooper, Tyrone Power, Senator John Kennedy (and later his brother Robert), Henry Ford II, Harry Truman and family. O'Connell remembered the president's daughter, Margaret Truman, later a novelist, and her husband, Clifton Daniel, of *The New York Times*, living in 29A. Former president Truman, during one visit, asked O'Connell about the crowd lurking outside the lobby. "They're photographers, Mr. President," O'Connell replied. Truman smiled and said, "Well, I'll give them a hell of a walk," and, like a Pied Piper, led them down Park Avenue.

O'Connell said Myrtle took care of The Carlyle clientele's needs while living rent-free in 3B, a third-floor apartment. From O'Connell, I learned that Myrtle did play bridge after Kansas City. She liked cards, he remembered, and often played bridge with friends in her apartment. He said she was as classy as The Carlyle's guests, dressed and coiffed immaculately, always patient with the staff. He once saw her leaving for dinner with film stars Mary Pickford and Buddy

Rogers. He also saw her lunch with Broadway star Nanette Fabray. He watched her help interior designer Dorothy Draper put up chandeliers in the lobby and saw her chat with Henry Ford II, whose thanks for her work included a kiss on the cheek. The girl from Tillar, Arkansas, had made it on her own as a hotel administrator in the biggest city of all, awash in elegance and surrounded by politicians, movie stars, and millionaires. She poured her life into her work. And she held her secret, telling no one—a form of denial, but also a show of power. She flourished.

While O'Connell was serving an army stint in Korea in 1952–53, he said he received a box of cookies from The Carlyle's housekeeping department with an attached note from Myrtle Bennett. She wrote about the latest doings at The Carlyle, and added, "We miss you! Hurry back!"

Upon his return, Myrtle asked, "Michael, did you meet any Geisha girls?" He kidded, "No, but I was thinking of you when I was over there." She said, "Boy, you must have kissed the blarney stone!" O'Connell told her, "I wish you were younger," and she laughed and said, "I wish I was younger, too."

There were limits to her conversation, though, as made clear when I asked O'Connell what Myrtle had told him about her background. "Nobody knew anything about her life," O'Connell said.

It made sense that Myrtle would seek a new life far from Kansas City, though it surprised me that, after the trial, she kept the Bennett name. Reverting to her maiden name or even adopting an alias would have freed her from answering to the curious who knew the details of September 29, 1929. But hers was a simple, common name that called no attention to itself. And the media was more fragmented then and did not reach into every corner of America at all hours. So while it remained well known that a housewife had once shot her husband over a bridge game, the woman's name faded until it became almost incidental to the story. Besides, I believe that Myrtle held on to Jack's name as one more act of stubbornness and strength.

As we sat together on the couch, I brought from my briefcase some clippings from Kansas City newspapers in 1929 and 1931. O'Connell read the headlines, and saw the photos of the young Mrs.

Bennett. He gasped: "Oh my God!" His pallor momentarily whitened. "This is amazing." He read in silence about Myrtle Bennett's acquittal, his eyes tight at the corners. He shook his head, and said he never knew about any of this. "There were a lot of old Irish people working here," he said, finally, "and if they had known this they would have told me." I told him about Myrtle's upbringing in Arkansas, and this triggered a memory. O'Connell recalled telling Myrtle that he had trained in the army at Camp Chaffee, Arkansas, and spent time in Little Rock. "Tell me more about Arkansas, Michael," Mrs. Bennett said. "Did you know anyone from there?"

He told her Irving Pratt was his barracks mate, and often took him to his home on weekends. Mrs. Bennett smiled, and said she knew the Pratts. She wanted more details about Arkansas. "Well," O'Connell replied, "it was very clean and wide open. The people in Little Rock were very nice. Were you from there?"

Mrs. Bennett skillfully dodged the incursion into her past. She said, cryptically, "Oh, I've been around there."

Michael O'Connell said, "I'm glad I didn't know about all this when she was here. It's amazing. She was so happy. I would never think—" O'Connell hesitated, and said, "Well, I guess she left it behind."

II

Only fourteen blocks from The Carlyle, the international bridge celebrity Ely Culbertson lived mysteriously in a hideaway he had designed: a soundproof five-room apartment secreted behind a sliding bookcase. When a hidden button was pressed the bookcase swung backward, revealing a dimly lit room with plush rugs, a bar and kitchenette, and, behind glass bricks, a card corner. This hideaway had no telephones and no ringing doorbells, and eliminated the sounds of city life in New York. Secretaries and servants were allowed to enter only when paged by the master.

As he floated above the Great Depression, there were signs that

Ely was, in fact, a man descending into megalomania. His need for self-glorification, always there, became insatiable. He lived increasingly alone with his ideas and ambition. He had become king of a world he had created, a world strange and forbidding. All who entered his world, as Jo had, soon found no air to breathe.

Rather than confront rising rivals at the table in 1938, Ely left contract bridge altogether. He had in mind a new game. He had a plan.

He would save the world.

Instead of diamonds and spades, Ely now played with Europe and Asia. As World War II raged, he thought his move from bidding bridge hands to creating a world peace plan only natural. For most of his life he had been thinking about geopolitics, and constructing systems of all kinds.

He believed he might be the only man alive who could solve the darkest terrors of the times.

Secreted in his hideaway, alone in his silk robe, and with his thoughts, he smoked. He pondered.

After the Lenz match, Ely and Jo lived in material splendor. Commercial opportunities poured in. Ely endorsed Wrigley's chewing gum. Inside three million packs of its cigarettes, Chesterfield distributed free booklets about contract bridge authored by Ely. In 1932, RKO Pictures paid him $270,000 to write, direct, and star in a series of film shorts about bridge. In one, *Murder at the Bridge Table,* a thinly veiled story about the Bennetts, in which a wife shoots and kills her husband in a social game after he botches a contract of four spades, Ely appears as an expert witness called to testify at the wife's murder trial. Using large playing cards on a blackboard, Ely demonstrates for jurors how the husband should have made the contract. Jo appears only briefly in the twenty-one-minute film. She is shown walking into the courtroom with Ely and, in a closeup, watching the trial. In Hollywood, Ely fired scenario writers, directors, and supervisors. RKO found him difficult, obstreperous, impossible. The studio had contracted for a dozen film shorts, but Ely made only six. RKO paid him in full, anyway, happy to be done with him.

Ely and Jo were among America's most conspicuous consumers. At a time when radio was playing the soup-line song "Brother, Can You Spare a Dime?" Ely was spending seven dollars a day on cigarettes. With his tea came caviar. He bought gold watches and gold cigarette cases. "Success in life," Ely said in a speech at the American Club in Paris in July 1933, "depends entirely on whether you know how to handle your own publicity. You have got to sell yourself, your wife, and your children to the world." George Reith of Bridge Headquarters snickered in 1933, saying of Ely, "The greatest showman in the bridge business told me one time that truth was a matter of opinion, and that anyhow the public does not want the truth. They want something that pleases them."

In bridge, Ely remained the center of attention. He made friends with the vanquished Bridge Headquarters (which later dissolved), bullied and underpaid his magazine staffers, became embroiled in lawsuits, and founded his own Crockford's bridge club in New York City, filling it with Flemish tapestries and Louis XVI chairs beside a wide, curving staircase. (The club ultimately failed.) He visited Herbert Hoover in the White House. With the help of ghost writers, he wrote other contract bridge books. His bridge writings were ponderous, at times oppressive. Other bridge stars—Sidney Lenz, for one—wrote about the game in a simpler, more effective style. In 1932, though, Ely outpaced novelist Pearl Buck as America's bestselling author, no doubt a tribute to his marketing and his celebrity, not his skill as a writer. He continued to run from matches against bridge players he knew were his superior. He made a mint from his investment in a company that sold new, longer-lasting plastic playing cards. His publicity machine whirred on: *The Bridge World*'s Sam Fry busily writing fourteen syndicated bridge columns each week, seven under Ely's name and seven under Jo's. Ely and Jo paid $125,000 in December 1934 for an eighty-six-acre estate in Ridgefield, Connecticut, that featured a forty-five-room mansion with detached cottages, a glass-domed swimming pool, gardens, greenhouses bursting with tangerines and grapes, a lake, and miles of paved roads.

In 1935, Ely walked into A. Sulka and Company, the fine haberdashery on Fifth Avenue, and spent $5,000 on pajamas, ties, shirts, and accessories. Hearing him boast of such purchases at *The Bridge World* office, writer Alfred Sheinwold, working for twenty-five dollars weekly, asked, "Then how about a raise to thirty-five dollars per week, Mister Culbertson?" In a fury, Ely fired him (for the second or third time), though Sheinwold soon returned to the staff, only to be fired anew. Ely later wrote that the Scotsman in him saved five cents of every dollar, but the Russian in him spent the remaining ninety-five cents.

In March 1935, he stage-managed one more bridge match following the release of the *Contract Bridge Red Book on Play*. This time, the battle pitted couple versus couple: the Culbertsons against Hal and Dorothy Sims in 150 rubbers at Crockford's. Just as he had hand-selected Buller and Lenz, Ely chose this match for its natural appeal to married couples, and because he knew that Dorothy Sims was little more than an adequate player. The Simses played into the hyperbole, setting up a training camp at Red Bank, New Jersey, where heavyweight Max Baer had trained for the Primo Carnera fight. Hal, Dorothy, and Duke, their Great Dane, wore white turtleneck sweaters, each with a scarlet *S*, as they jogged for cameras along the roadside. Crockford's brought in an oversize table to accommodate the oversize Hal Sims. During the match, Sims playfully called Ely "Professor," and Ely called him "Petronius." After one lost hand, a frustrated Sims chided his wife, "How many times have I told you *not* to think? Just do what I tell you!" Back to his old tricks, Ely arrived to sessions late, and ate spaghetti and spinach at the table. The Culbertsons kept their cool throughout the match, and won by more than sixteen thousand points.

Imperturbable as bridge partners, Ely and Jo were coming undone at home. Jo argued against Ely's micromanagement of their children's lives. Ely applied an eccentric science of conditioning to inure his children against sudden frights. To inure them against common childhood fears, he fed them during storms, forced them to sleep with the lights on and in complete darkness. He demanded they handle crawling creatures, such as lizards and snakes.

Jo had always liked an occasional drink, but now her more

frequent drinking worried Ely. As the marriage foundered, Ely turned to other women who found him charming and charismatic. During a train ride to Chicago in 1935, he boasted to magazine staffer Sam Fry about sex, and how as a young man in Paris he had lacked confidence, but through reading erotic literature he had improved his techniques. Sex, Ely said, was the world's best indoor sport.

Ely planned a memoir. It would be candid, personal, dramatic, and revolutionary. He would write about his early romances, his deflowering in a Russian whorehouse; and of course, he would write about Jo. She asked, "Ely, how could you?"

His answer: their children must know what *not* to do, and besides, his public deserved the full truth, not a bit less. Jo could bear him no more.

On December 1, 1937, their divorce became public. The lead in *The New York Times* read, "The end of a bridge romance was revealed yesterday," rumbling like a major earthquake through the bridge community. Jo obtained the divorce in Reno, citing Ely's "ultra-temperamental moods" and his insistence "on publishing a brutally frank story of his life." Ely deferred to her as his superior in marriage as in bridge, saying in a formal statement, "This is not a case of 'another woman' or 'another man.' Jo has always been my grand romance in life and always will be. Unfortunately I am a married man with bachelor's instincts. Complete solitude is often my most precious and most necessary requirement. In those moments I am a solitary animal, and if disturbed I become unbearable. Any woman who marries a really unsocial man of my type, with his solitary yearnings and attacks of abstract meditation, will sooner or later find her marriage on the rocks. The wonder to me is not that Jo is divorcing me now, but that she was able to stand my temperamental outbursts all these years. Well, anyway, Jo is still my favorite bridge partner." Ely and Jo announced they would retain their business partnership, sharing all assets and future bridge incomes, and maintain equal custody of the children.

Jo and the children remained in the two adjoining fifth-floor apartments on East Sixty-second Street. Ely moved downstairs, to the fourth floor, directly below the children's bedrooms. There, he designed his hideaway, acting as if it were a perfectly normal thing to do.

He published his memoirs in 1940, *The Strange Lives of One Man.* Ely's self-admiration extended 693 pages. Memoir can be unreliable even when the author attempts to tell the truth, let alone when he is burnishing his reputation. For large parts of 1938 and 1939, Ely sat in the Ridgefield mansion and dictated his life story to a secretary taking shorthand, sometimes for as many as eleven hours a day. He believed he wrote at his rhythmic best not with pen or typewriter, but through dictation. He did not review the typed manuscript and left the grammar and fact-checking to editors. Facts mattered little to him, anyway.

Most of the story was beyond independent corroboration. He portrayed himself as an outcast intellectual. It seems never to have occurred to him that he was dysfunctional, especially in his personal life, because he was so skilled in the high arts of bridge and ballyhoo. A man out of touch with reality, he believed that only he understood who he was and what he was doing. Every page swelled with grandiosity. The reader might imagine Ely as Charlie Chaplin, holding the globe in his hands, caressing and spinning it, tossing it into the air with a dictator's malevolent glee.

He envisioned his memoirs as the capstone of his career, a historic chronicle of his triumphs. Instead, in page after page he unwittingly unmasks himself as a liar, psychological bully, and narcissist extraordinaire.

Self-promoters of the age, such as Shipwreck Kelly, shaped their biographies to amaze audiences. But Shipwreck did not pretend to Ely's aura of legitimacy. A sailor on a flagpole is a long remove from a master of a reputable game played by elites. Still, no less a self-promoter than Shipwreck, Ely told stories about his life that stretched credibility.

All that was known of Ely's early life came from Ely himself. His story sparkled with adventure, romance, and drama, and seemed to compress the lives of at least ten brilliant, brave men all into one. He crossed continents, joined revolutions, stared down death. He was jailed as an anarchist in Russia. In Spain a bomb planted by his revolutionist friends failed to kill King Alfonso. He found himself on a rooftop in Mexico with Zapata's revolutionaries, cartridge belts slung over his back and a rifle in his hands. Instead of shooting at government soldiers, he ran, and then boarded a boat to Cuba.

He claimed to have been in a church with monks and in a brothel with whores. Despite his professed awkwardness with women, he wrote of lovers who satisfied his physical impulses: a governess, a French actress, and a Russian revolutionary named Nadya, who was murdered by the Black Hundred. Ely said he carried a revolver then and was slashed in the back by a Cossack's saber. He faced an angry mob of social revolutionists in 1907 in Russia, announcing his shame that he was a son of an American capitalist. Such stories: He played poker, plafond, ecarte, and auction bridge in clubs, cafés, and in jail. In jail with seven Russian revolutionaries in Sochi, he joined their card game of vint. At each dawn, another cellmate was taken away, to a firing squad, and one said, "Good-by, Illiusha. There is no sense in these revolutions. Concentrate on vint!" He said he had attended fine universities across the globe, including the University of Geneva, Yale, and the Sorbonne. As a besotted bohemian in Paris during the war, he said he consumed oysters and snails, tripe à la mode de Caen, a nightly bottle of old Burgundy, and three or four glasses of Armagnac, and played cards with sophisticated friends in clubs, their group surrounded by women who wanted to be just like them. But these women were constantly replaced, "like the water in a well-kept swimming pool." Ely wrote, "We looked upon women not as mates or allies—that was bourgeois romanticism—but as amusing or fascinating, though lower, forms of life." Later, he became a hobo on New York's Bowery, hawked newspapers, befriended a dope fiend, and then stowed away on trains out west. He worked as a common laborer building railroads near Edmonton, washed dishes and planted corn in Oregon, picked fruit near Fresno, and then—what a traveler!—he was back in Paris in 1914 when the Archduke was shot, then left for Germany and then Geneva. He idealized his Russian mother, and struggled to meet the perfection demanded by his American father. In his idle moments, he read Balzac, Flaubert, Shelley, Keats, Tolstoy, Dostoyevsky, Pushkin, Lermontov, Gogol, Turgenev, Gorky, Volga, Twain, Poe, Goethe, Schiller, Heine. And when he arrived in Hoboken, a thief stole his bag of books.

All this—he claimed—before the age of twenty-five.

Four decades later, Alfred Sheinwold, a grand old man of bridge as an author, card theorist, and the *Los Angeles Times*'s syndicated columnist, laughed at Ely's autobiography. "It's a good book *of fiction*," Sheinwold told the British author John Clay. "Typical autobiography is written with some pretense of giving a truthful narrative," Sheinwold said. "But I think in Culbertson's case he consciously set out to write fiction in which he was the central character."

Book reviewers raised a brow, perhaps to stifle laughter.

"It seems, indeed, that [Culbertson] has done and been almost everything there is to do and be except to turn murderer and kill somebody. In point of fact, as a youth he had even that idea in mind," a reviewer wrote in *The New York Times*. "Certain of the chapters appear to be exceedingly shrewd; others might have been extracted from almost any true-confessions magazine; others yet, if cast in wax, should appeal to the heirs of Mme. Tussaud. Card players will be interested in it naturally. Also psychiatrists, psychologists and both amateurs and experts in the art of kidding the public along."

The *New York World-Telegram* wrote that Ely "has managed in 48 crowded years to make Casanova look like a piker. . . . For some unfortunate reason his demon makes him tell the world a lot of things about himself that had been better left unsaid."

As I read Ely's memoirs, I imagined poor Jo. He trampled with cruel insensitivity upon her wishes for privacy, writing in detail about the failure of their marriage. The breaking point, he wrote, came in Budapest in June 1937, at the first World Championship of bridge. As nerves and stomach ulcers tore at his insides, he had no stomach for bridge, or for Jo. They played miserably and lost to a team of Austrians, at which point Ely turned to his favorite partner and said, "It was your fault." At that night's closing banquet, Jo sat beside Archduke Frederick, honorary president of the Hungarian Bridge League.

Champagne was "at flood tide," Ely wrote, and Jo carried an air of "wild resolve." There was a respectful introduction of the Culbertsons as "the king and queen of bridge, to whom millions of players owe an unforgettable debt of gratitude."

Ely stood for the ovation. He addressed the great hall. "Your Highness, ladies and gentlemen: I am most deeply touched . . ."

"Applesauce!" The voice, small and tinny, from the head table, was Jo's.

Ely kept on: ". . . by this undeserved welcome to me and . . ."

"Quite undeserved." Again, it was Jo, mocking him.

Ely smiled at her: ". . . and my wife." The audience applauded, Ely continued, until he heard Jo say, "Don't believe a word of it!"

Ely smiled at her still, as if their repartee had been planned.

". . . when we lost the match," he said.

Jo chimed in: "When *you* lost the match."

"When *we* lost the match," Ely restated.

"*You* lost the match," Jo said, this time louder.

". . . when *I* lost the match," Ely agreed.

It had come to this, a public demise of the most celebrated bridge marriage of all. No Bennett-like slapping or gunshots, not even a bridge table, only a wife's frustrations from fourteen years of Ely.

Ely switched to speaking in French, hoping Jo would not understand most of what he said, but he heard her mutter loudly enough for the Archduke to hear, *"C'est terrible!"* Ely closed in English, saying, "Hungary is a little country. But it has a big heart . . ."

"Which is more than you have," Jo said.

Ely finished with glass raised in a toast to his wife. "Mrs. Culbertson is not only my partner in life but in bridge as well. And I'm sure I won't be violating the bounds of good taste if I propose a toast to the person to whom I am more indebted than anyone else on this earth; whose patience, kindness, and love made my work possible; the greatest woman bridge player and my favorite partner. To my Jo!"

Everyone in the hall stood and applauded, save for Jo, who remained silent and seated. For Ely, this closing proved a masterstroke, at least for the moment. The First Couple of Bridge would never again play together in a competitive tournament.

The structure and chronology of Ely's life as depicted in his memoirs (that is, his birthplace, parentage, and his arrival in the United States in 1921 on the SS *Brookline*) were factually accurate. But the intricately nuanced anecdotes he told provided circumstantial evidence of a master salesman creating product. Ely admitted fictionalizing aspects of his personality to make himself more memorable and marketable. It would be only a small step for a man who did that to also fictionalize aspects of his biography. "The basic technique in influencing the mass mind is sincerity," Ely once said. "The crowd mind is suspicious and, while it admits exaggerations, there must be a kernel of truth." The life story he told was built on the smallest of such kernels. His depiction of his education suggests as much. Despite his claims otherwise, he never attended Yale (his brother Eugene did), and though Ely spent a semester at the University of Geneva in the fall of 1914, school records indicate that he merely audited courses and opted out of final examinations. Exaggerations abounded. In 1931, he told a newspaper feature writer that once, down to his last 100 francs in wartime Paris, he put 20 francs on a baccarat table and by glorious luck it grew to 20,000. Now, in his memoirs, he suggested his baccarat winnings that day grew to 40,960 francs. I wondered: did he embellish all of his stories in this way, doubling the truth, or worse?

The carefully constructed mythology of Ely Culbertson's life became so strong it overwhelmed the facts. Besides, as he well knew, Americans liked mythology more than facts.

Ely's world peace plan was his gift to humanity, and he spent nearly all his time and money to sell it. He met with congressmen and senators, sent telegrams to Harry Truman in the White House. He would seek world peace with another Galatea as his second wife, Dorothy Baehne, a blonde out of Vassar, so young even her mother was a dozen years *younger* than Ely. Expenses at Ridgefield caused him to give up the estate. His intensity pushed him more deeply into secrecy and solitude, and ultimately to the fringe of madness. Dorothy left him, too, and blamed his mental cruelty. Contract bridge's incandescent man had been reduced to a fringe figure, irrelevant and alone.

Bridge had a new celebrated star, Charles Goren, a Philadelphia lawyer once Milton Work's ghostwriter. Goren had accepted Ely's open challenge to all comers in 1936, but Ely withdrew his offer. By the mid-1940s, even with the emergence of gin rummy as a rival game, the Association of American Playing Card Manufacturers reported that contract bridge was played in 44 percent of American homes. More Americans were playing bridge than ever before. In April 1946, First Lady Bess Truman brought her bridge club from Jackson County, Missouri, to the White House, amid great fanfare. Lucy, Mary G., Adelaide, Mag, and Linda came from Independence to share a bridge cruise on the Potomac River on the presidential yacht, the *Williamsburg*. By this time, Goren's syndicated column appeared in more American newspapers than Ely's. Goren created his own bidding system, and would sell millions of books. His seminal *Point Count Bidding in Contract Bridge* in 1949 obliterated Ely's honor tricks and, with them, the Culbertson System. Goren put Ely into total eclipse. Now social players asked, "Do you play *Goren*?"

Ely's World Federation Plan of 1940, one of several such plans floated as the League of Nations withered, was designed to prohibit war. He subdivided the globe into eleven federations, each with its own constitution and government, and proposed armed forces supplied by each and a police force from smaller nations to confront hot spots. He used his bestselling clout in 1943 to publish *Total Peace*, a book outlining the plan. Then he lobbied journalists and politicians. Ely knew that many in Washington did not regard him seriously. He wrote, "I succeeded much too well, and became a victim of my own technique of publicity. Later, because I was 'typed,' like a Hollywood actor, it would be difficult to convince some people that a bridge authority could also be passionately and intelligently interested in the destiny of the country that showered him with fame and wealth far beyond his humble origins."

As the United Nations charter was drafted in San Francisco in spring 1945, Ely holed up in that city at the Palace Hotel, desperate to be involved. He mailed five copies of *Total Peace* to President Truman and suggested to the president's secretary, Charles Ross, that Truman devote two hours to consider his plan. "Though Native American,"

Ely wrote to Ross, he reminded him that he was "brought up in Russia, knew intimately Russian revolutionists, and knows Russia as well as his own country. In urging President Truman to read this booklet now, I am only moved by conviction that I hold the practical solutions to some of the terrifying problems we are now facing."

His plan went nowhere, though, in July 1945, he appeared before the Senate Foreign Relations Committee to discuss his views on the UN Charter. In December, with writer Dorothy Thompson, he met with Truman at the White House. By early 1948, Ely had created a revised peace plan. He spent five months in a Washington hotel lobbying members of Congress. Spending more than $400,000 (his estimate), he gained some support from politicians, but his plan, like many others, died on committee shelves.

In 1946 Ely had delivered a speech in Chicago on "Tomorrow's World Today," and when young Dorothy Baehne approached him afterward, he might have been forgiven for thinking she had answered his advertisement in an Italian newspaper more than thirty years before, seeking Galatea. Baehne was blond and beautiful, only twenty and refined, having studied in Germany and China.

The starstruck Dorothy saw wisdom and greatness in Culbertson. She heard him speak of world peace, and of the role she might play in helping him achieve it. She married Ely, then fifty-five years old, in January 1947.

Unknowingly, she had entered a family nightmare. Ely still looked after Jo. Following their divorce, Jo made only the occasional celebrity stop at a bridge tournament. She lived alone, in poor health and sadness, drinking too much. Their daughter, Joyce, replaced now in her father's eyes by a wife roughly her age, had rebelled against Ely by engaging in an affair with an older man. She became pregnant, married the man, and was divorced soon after. She would need psychiatric help, and her young son, Steve, moved in to live with Ely and Dorothy. Ely's son, Bruce, meanwhile, had engaged in teenage high jinks that cost him a spot at Harvard. Ely and Dorothy would have a son, Peter (who died by drowning), and then a second son, Alex.

I traced Alex to Florida. We spoke several times by phone, and he seemed excited to learn more about Ely. Later, on vacation with his wife in Northern California, Alex came to see me. Just three years old when his father died in 1955, Alex has Ely's smooth facial features, high hairline, and expressive eyes. Modest and self-effacing, and a windsurfing outdoorsman in his spare time, he is a professor of psychology at a junior college in Florida, where he teaches a course on abnormal psychology. Over lunch, he told me he had first read Ely's memoirs when he was fourteen, sneaking the book from the shelf of his grandmother, who despised Ely. He thrilled to his father's exploits as a teenage revolutionary, but wondered about the character flaws beneath the words. Alex asked himself, "Have I caught this? Am I also completely self-absorbed?"

Our meeting prompted Alex to reread Ely's memoirs. I also showed him a 1933 RKO film short, *Three Knaves and a Queen,* capturing Ely at the height of his powers. Ely's Russian accent was less pronounced than his son had imagined, his voice higher pitched, his presence less intimidating. He thanked me for the "great gift" of the film and said he felt newly proud to be Ely's son. Still, he said, "He fits all the clinical criteria for a narcissistic personality disorder." Later he sent me the link to a website that defined the disorder as "a pervasive pattern of grandiosity (in fantasy or behavior), a need for attention, and a lack of empathy." He said that Ely had lived in abstractions, and had had difficulty connecting with people on an intimate level. He wondered if, in Ely's attempt to save the world, he sounded to politicians, as he must have sounded at times to some in the bridge world, *stark raving bonkers.* "It all ties in to megalomania," Alex said. He expressed horror in the way Ely shattered the lives of Jo and their two children, and gratitude for his own "narrow escape."

He asked, "What if I had been brought up by the man?"

He showed me letters exchanged between his parents that revealed the magnitude of Ely's dysfunction and despair near the end of his life. Alex's grandmother, Hildegarde Baehne, had given him the letters so that he would know Ely's true nature. She included a letter from Dorothy's attorney, who described Ely as "a man of great intellect, very domineering," and Jo, his ex-wife, as "an alcoholic and sometime resident of mental institutions."

In the spring of 1954, Dorothy told Ely by phone that she wanted a divorce. He asked, "Why?"

"You'll see it in a letter," Dorothy said.

"Is it another man?"

"Of course not. You know me better than that."

"Is it sex?"

"No."

"But why, then?"

In her letter Dorothy explained that she wanted her own identity:

I, your Galatea, have thought, despaired, wept, and come to know that my own salvation lies in making my life apart from yours. This is not a frivolous decision, nor is it entirely new . . . Do you remember once our talking about the meaning of love? I said that I wasn't sure what it was, but that I believed I must love you because I feared to displease you. That was a wrong definition, Illiusha, as you must have known. Somehow, the fear is gone now, but the affection and tenderness remain. I hope that, similarly, you will not cease to have regard and affection for me.

In a small handwritten scrawl filling six pages, Ely wrote back, professing shock over her letter: "Your demand was a thunder clap in the blue sky." He accepted her decision and promised to provide financially for her and Alex. He made the same offer he had made to Jo: if, after a year of living alone, Dorothy wanted to reunite with him, he would remarry her. He said he was ashamed by their divorce.

Then his venom and ego poured forth. "You write to me: 'Your Galatea has grown, my dear, and is searching within herself to find her own purposes, goals, ideals, values, and strivings.' And what are these, your own ideals that you search [for] within yourself, my dear?" He added:

You are married to a man who holds the key to the solutions of the most terrifying problems of our time; or, at least, the man who is nearer to these solutions than anyone else; or, at least, a man with an altogether extraordinary and valuable political mind. He is your Teacher. You saw that man attack, advance, retreat and advance again in the greatest battle of all time. You linked with his hopes and frustrations and you shared his small victories and bitter defeats. And now when the greatest crisis of humanity is rapidly approaching you decide to leave him—for what? . . . No, my dear, that is not my Galatea. I wanted a modern Jeanne d'Arc, not some dark Jeanne. If this man were a drunkard, a wife beater and filled the cup with the gall of life, my Galatea would stand by to serve in all humility—for the man she is serving is of the very few whose ideals might save the world. Even a small part of his creative work (for so much is at stake) would be worth a hundred great paintings or symphonies. And what did you do? You abandoned me when you could be of the greatest help to me, in the name of what?

Ely's unraveling was complete. Alex told me, "Normal people don't speak about wives as if they are formless lumps of clay. It makes the hair stand up on the back of my neck."

Dorothy divorced Ely in 1954, after more than seven years of marriage, and took custody of Alex, then a toddler. (Dorothy later remarried, but died tragically in 1963, at thirty-eight, from complications following childbirth. Alex was adopted by her second husband, John Marvin, and today uses the name Alex Marvin.)

In the final year of his life, Ely worked on a second memoir, designed to cover the last decade and a half. He dictated several hundred disjointed pages, but did not finish. The manuscript, which is held at the American Contract Bridge League library in Memphis, includes Ely's notes at the bottom of some pages. Mostly, he wrote about women and sex. After his divorce from Jo, he returned to brothels and generally engaged in "big-game hunting of unusual women." One woman, he wrote, became pregnant by him. She had set him up as part of her plan to seek a "superior individual"—Ely, naturally—to father her child.

What was his purpose in writing this? Was *all* of it true? Was *any* of it true? On one page, Ely wrote a note to himself: "Maybe the above description is too good for Margot and should be kept for Sophia." This suggests conflation or fabrication. Is this what Ely did in writing *The Strange Lives of One Man*?

Through Alex I found Steve Culbertson, the son of Ely and Jo's daughter, Joyce. In a bit of serendipity, he lived not far from me. We met in a coffeehouse in the North Beach district of San Francisco. Steve spoke softly, his eyes downcast. At sixty, tall and blond, he seemed uneasy and nervous talking about Ely. "I have a lot of anger—*had* a lot of anger," he said, self-correcting—"against my grandfather for what he did to my uncle and my mother." Ely's grand experiment to shape the lives of his children failed miserably. Steve says his mother, Joyce, "ended up going to a mental institution. I would see her on holidays— just Christmas, really." His uncle Bruce, meanwhile, worked for a technology company, married and divorced, and was throughout his adult life "a functional alcoholic. He was very neurotic." Steve said that Joyce and Bruce rebelled against their parents. Of Jo, he remembered his grandmother as "elegant, noble, cool, reserved, aloof . . . sort of distant, sad. Being a grandmother was sort of a duty."

He retained a young boy's memories—and fears—of Ely as a stern and stooped old man. "Very dark eyes," Steve Culbertson recalled. "I always remember him as a frightening character. Yeah, I was scared of him. He was not somebody a child felt comfortable with. He was very imperious and autocratic." He said Ely forbade him from playing cowboys and Indians with cap guns. "He thought that way he would coerce world peace," Steve said, rolling his eyes. Our conversation seemed for him not cathartic, but painful, an old wound reopened. Steve Culbertson does not play contract bridge, and he said, "That is intentional."

On December 27, 1955, Ely died at sixty-four in Brattleboro, his lungs desiccated from more than forty years of Turkish tobacco. Eighty-seven days later, Jo died in New York City, apparently of a stroke. She was fifty-eight.

Contract bridge went on, if less colorfully, without them.

SEVENTEEN

San Francisco

I sought to immerse myself in bridge today, to measure the game's changes during the past three quarters of a century, and to see if human nature at the table had changed.

Over time, the Culbertson craze, like Culbertson himself, faded. Following the war, America returned to high prosperity, and while contract bridge was widely played (a Gallup poll in 1947 named bridge America's favorite card game), young people with money sought new distractions. Automobiles put them on the road, their families more mobile than ever before. Goren's reign was long and prosperous, and from 1959 to 1964 he hosted a popular television program on bridge. But television steepened bridge's decline. The computer age dawned, American culture became faster, more hectic and impersonal, and for the younger generation, bridge, a game requiring study and patience, dried up like an old riverbed.

The American Contract Bridge League today claims about 160,000 members. The typical ACBL member is older than sixty, college educated, and financially secure. A 2005 ACBL survey suggested that 25 million Americans know how to play bridge—roughly the same number Ely claimed in the early thirties, except the nation's population was 120 million then and more than 300 million now. The Internet has been a boon to bridge players across the world, who can find a game now at almost any time. The ACBL survey indicated that 4.1 million Americans play over the Internet, with 12 percent of them playing daily. But the Internet has also depersonalized bridge, and harmed local clubs and minor tournaments, reducing attendance. Poker, a gambler's game of bravado and bluff, which takes comparatively little time to learn, has gained wide popularity with the younger generation to a degree bridge has not. Contract bridge still has its patron saints: where once it was Vanderbilt and Schwab, now it is the billionaire bridge aficionados Warren Buffett and Bill Gates, who jointly fund a program to teach bridge to teens in schools.

In autumn 2007, I observed the ACBL's North American Bridge Championship in San Francisco, where more than six thousand people filled tables at a downtown hotel. I kibitzed for hours at a time, observing players, moving from table to table. I interviewed some of the game's best players. They knew only a little about Ely and Jo, and the Knickerbocker Whist Club (which shut its doors long ago), and judged the overall quality of bidding in the age of Culbertson as wooden and simplistic. The rich history of the bridge craze era has lived on in bidding conventions known as Josephine and the Jacoby Transfer, and also in the von Zedtwitz Award, given annually to a player from the past nominated by the ACBL Hall of Fame Veterans Committee. (The remarkable Waldemar von Zedtwitz secured his bridge legend by winning the World Mixed Pairs title in 1970, when he was seventy-four years old—and legally blind.) In 1964, when America's leading bridge writers voted for the inaugural members of the Bridge Hall of Fame, Ely topped them all, outpolling Goren and Vanderbilt. Years later he was joined in enshrinement by his "favorite partner." Almost without exception, today's leading players have heard about Myrtle and Jack, and many have read the supposed Fatal Hand in bridge anthologies. One insisted to me that Myrtle was acquitted only because of her beauty, which, he explained, "did not escape the judge's notice. She got on the witness stand and cried, and showed a little leg."

In each interview, I asked about married couples playing as bridge partners. The subject invariably prompted raised eyebrows, smiles, and a few snickers. The real trouble, these players agreed, occurs when one spouse is a far superior player to the other; the marital power dynamics kick in and the partnership inevitably burns with irritation and frustration. I read a delightful little book, *How to Play Bridge with Your Spouse . . . and Survive!*, regaled by author Roselyn Teukolsky's stories about the clash of wills that have come from playing with her husband. "My feminist sensibilities bristle at his 'In-this-partnership-I-am-always-right' mentality," Teukolsky wrote in 2002. "I resent his masculine lack of self-doubt. Somehow, without saying it, he manages to convey to me this message: 'If the little woman would only be quiet and listen occasionally, she might learn how to play bridge.'"

We are three-quarters of a century past the night when Myrtle called Jack a bum bridge player.

I am listening to Frank Bessing talk about married couples who play bridge as partners, one of his favorite topics. A self-professed "bridge addict" of more than forty years, and with a Ph.D. in family therapy, Bessing is animated and intense in our discussion over lunch. He says, "I actually feel like I am loaded with testosterone after a successful bridge game. I just feel"—here he growls playfully— "Arrrgggghhh! All pumped up, like I took three Viagra." Bessing, who is divorced, says nearly all of his long-term bridge partners have been women. "Mostly they have been lovers also," he says. "My women bridge partners tend to have a pretty highly developed masculine side. They are really competitive and they really hang in there." Bessing shows me a callused nub at the tip of a finger. A bridge player's finger, he calls it. During play, he bites that nub—and it hurts. "It's a hypnotic technique," Bessing says. "It serves as an anchor to retain in my memory what I am seeing."

Now Bessing says, "The very first time you play bridge with somebody may be the best game you'll ever have together. It's very much like a courtship period in a relationship. You live in that area people call 'Love is Blind.' Frequently it brings out the very best in your partner and yourself.

"But in bridge partnerships, as is marriage," he adds, "frequently the expectations start to get too high and then there are disappointments. In bridge, as in marriage and in relationships, some of it is,

'How is my partner treating me?' And as in marriage the main conflict is often, 'Who is in charge?'"

Herein lies the rub, Bessing says: "When there is a conflict at the
bridge table where you think your partner has violated an agreement
you have, try as you might, you feel kind of like you just got betrayed.
When your identity and sense of self is caught up with being successful and being good at what you do and then your partner ruins this
for you because they don't follow your agreements, you feel attacked
on a very primitive level.

"I think it pushes the button where you get this big shot of adren-
aline. You are ready for this fight or flight. You really can't get up and
run from the table, although I have seen others do it more than once.

"But in one way or another you are physiologically responding
as if there is an enemy across the table from you."

In some instances, the enemy across the table would apply to the
person you married.

Myrtle Bennett (aka "Auntie Mame") was eighty-seven years old in 1982 when she visited with her cousin Carolyn Scruggs (*at right*).
Personal files of Carolyn Scruggs

EIGHTEEN

Little Rock

My search for what became of Myrtle seemed at times like an archae-
ological dig to find a dark truth long buried. But at other moments,
shafts of light and gaiety broke through, such as when Carolyn
Scruggs, the only living beneficiary of Myrtle's who knew her, said, "I
really loved Auntie Mame." That was Scruggs's nickname for Myrtle,
coined after she saw the 1958 movie that starred Rosalind Russell as
a madcap New York party girl, circa 1929, who drank martinis,
smoked from long cigarette holders, and hosted ribald parties where
her adolescent nephew learned words such as *libido*, *Blotto*, *narcissistic*, and *Cubism*, and served cocktails to guests with a smile, promising, "I'll make it like I do for Mister Woollcott!"

Scruggs adored Myrtle, and once asked, "How am I related to
you, Auntie Mame?" Myrtle answered, "Oh, I don't know," and they
laughed. They agreed they were cousins, sharing a great-aunt,
Maude, cotton fields, and Briar's Point, Mississippi. Myrtle signed
letters and cards to Scruggs, "Auntie Mayme," once explaining the
misspelling by saying that she had an old friend by that name
(Mayme Hofman, undoubtedly). She called Scruggs *Caroline*, not her
name, but it was all part of their relationship, their silly fun. Auntie
Mame phoned her late at night to ask, "How's your love life?" "Not
good, Auntie Mame," replied Scruggs, who never married.

I sit in Scruggs's neatly appointed home in Little Rock, listening
to a southern storyteller's richly textured stories. Scruggs was two
months old in 1929 when Myrtle shot Jack. She heard nothing about
the killing during her formative years, even as Cousin Myrtle visited

Little Rock and sent Christmas cards from New York accompanied by photos of her lively bridge parties. Scruggs knew only that Cousin Myrtle was tall, funny, well dressed, and that her parents invited friends over to meet her.

En route to Europe in the summer of 1951, Scruggs and college classmates gathered in New York, where Scruggs spent a few nights with Myrtle at The Carlyle. They shopped and saw a Broadway show. Myrtle issued a safety precaution to the young woman: "The taxi driver may *not* drive you through Central Park. He must drive you around it, even if it costs more." Scruggs saw Myrtle's regular bridge group, women holding similar positions at The Pierre and other elite New York hotels. The women arrived on Sunday morning and drank gin fizzes into the night as they played cutthroat bridge. Myrtle's pet peeve: inferior players. When Scruggs and her classmates boarded their ship in New York Harbor, Myrtle saw them off with a celebratory bottle of champagne.

The following year, when Scruggs was a twenty-three-year-old airline stewardess, she learned the unspoken truth. She went on a date arranged by Myrtle with a military flyer named Al Ebert, whose mother, Elmena, was an old bridge friend of Myrtle's from San Antonio. That night, Elmena Ebert told Scruggs, "We so love Myrtle! She was one of our dearest friends. We were all just so sad about *that dreadful episode.*" Scruggs had no idea that Mrs. Ebert had been a character witness at Myrtle's trial or even that there had been a trial. Neither did she know that Elmena Ebert had told her son Al, "Jack Bennett really did Myrtle wrong." Scruggs only nodded, as if she knew all about *that dreadful episode.* Later Scruggs phoned home, recounted the exchange, and said, "Mother, there's something about Auntie Mame that I don't know, isn't there?" Scruggs's mother said she had never intended for Carolyn to hear the story about "that unfortunate chapter in Myrtle's life." (Scruggs smiled and told me, "It was a scandal, and Southerners are, well, you know, we tend to make life work out the way we want it to . . . We shade the truth a little.") Her mother told her that Cousin Myrtle always had a temper, especially as a spoiled young girl in Memphis, and that Myrtle had learned, perhaps even that night in September 1929, that Jack was having an affair with a woman in St. Joe. So the shooting was not really about that bridge game but about Jack's terrible behavior, and when Jack fell dead, it was an *unfortunate chapter*.

Scruggs delighted in Myrtle's company even after knowing that Auntie Mame had chased Jack with a gun in her hand and shot him dead. She handed me two old photos of Myrtle. In the first, from 1938, Myrtle smiled broadly—her teeth white, perfect—and her face considerably heavier in the seven years since the trial. The second, from 1982, with Scruggs at her side, showed Myrtle at eighty-seven years old, wearing pearls and silver earrings, her hair white, her posture still erect and impressive. When Scruggs's mother died in 1979, Auntie Mame phoned to say, "Well, babe, it looks like it's just the two of us. Don't you worry, your old Auntie Mame is going to take good care of you." Scruggs says Auntie Mame once had a boyfriend—she wore a gorgeous ring with emeralds and diamonds—but he drank too much, or so the story went, and they broke up. She said after Auntie Mame left The Carlyle, she worked during the 1960s for a hotel chain, setting up interior design and housekeeping in new hotels in Europe and Asia. Along the way, she met women at the bridge table, and a few became lifelong friends. She played bridge always, on cruise ships and, once, on a houseboat in Kashmir.

Scruggs joined Auntie Mame in Wiesbaden, Germany, in 1964. There, at a hotel front desk, Scruggs overheard a military man say he was from Arkansas. Scruggs introduced herself—she and this colonel had common friends in Little Rock, naturally—and that night she and Auntie Mame dined at an old German castle with the colonel and another officer. By night's end, the colonel had given Myrtle a kiss on the cheek. "Well, Auntie Mame's my kissin' cousin now," he boasted, and Myrtle blushed. A few days later, Scruggs saw Myrtle leave with the colonel in a military plane for Paris.

Bridge, vitality, world travels, and gin fizzes carried Myrtle to her ninetieth birthday and beyond. In an undated handwritten letter (likely from the early 1980s) to Ada Mae and Eddie Simpson, Oklahoma cousins who had cared for Alice Adkins until her death in 1936, Myrtle's freewheeling nature and keen attention to her personal finances emerge.

"July 11—Under the Dryer getting a Perm," she wrote from Florida. She added:

> *Hi Folks, Well, I had to get a Perm. Wish I could be at your house. It wouldn't be half as expensive, says I.*
>
> *Eddie, I have changed all my Securities to your address there. Have also made some switches in Securities & Bank accounts. Have bought some bonds, both tax free & otherwise. As soon as I get them all in, will send you a list of each & all as you should have all this information on your files.*
>
> *I have no plans at the moment to go any place—is too Hot to travel tho you can never tell about me. May drive up to your door at any time. Are you expecting the kids from Calif. at any time.*
>
> *Don't work too hard. Let me hear from you folks & love to all.*
>
> *Aunt Myrtle*

Inevitably, her health began to fail. She suffered mini-strokes, with their resulting slurred speech, and a fall that broke her leg. Her Oklahoma cousins came to get Auntie Mame.

At ninety-one, imprisoned by physical limitations, her personality darkened. She became cantankerous. From Florida to Oklahoma, Eddie and Ada Mae Simpson drove their station wagon and pulled a trailer filled with Myrtle's belongings. Eddie's younger brother Walter drove Myrtle in her Olds '98. Myrtle asked Walter to stop in Memphis. She said she wanted to see the church where she and Jack were married. But Walter missed the Memphis turnoff, and Myrtle exploded with rage, until he pulled over and said, "Eddie, you can take this car and I'll take the station wagon."

She spent four years with the Simpsons, and by their account made them miserable in their own home. Finally, at wit's end, they put her in a nearby nursing home. Myrtle never forgave them for it, and took immediate corrective action.

In the summer of 1990, Bill Armshaw's phone rang. Secretly, using a medical taxi, the resourceful Myrtle had left the Oklahoma nursing home and returned to Florida. She told her stockbroker she had checked into a nearby home. Armshaw told her, "Don't sign a thing, I'll be right over." Amazed, he rushed to see his ninety-five-year-old client and friend. She seemed of sound mind, and determined to return to her North Miami Beach apartment.

Then Armshaw's phone rang a second time. Ada Mae Simpson was calling from Oklahoma. Myrtle was *gone*, she said, and no one knew where. Armshaw heard genuine worry in Ada Mae's voice. "She's here," Armshaw told her.

Back in her high-rise apartment overlooking the water, living with a caretaker, Myrtle soon had visitors from California. They were reminders of her past life, relatives of her late husband. Jack Bennett's nieces, Mary and Helen, had visited Myrtle in the late 1970s. Now Mary came with her husband, Walter Jacobs. During their visit, Myrtle's vitality surged, if only briefly. She took Mary and Walter to a duplicate bridge tournament, where the couple finished second.

Meanwhile, still furious with her Oklahoma cousins, Myrtle rewrote her will in August 1990. She removed Eddie and Ada Mae Simpson, punishment, no doubt, for having sentenced her to a nursing home.

Yet her declining health left few options. In November 1991, she returned to a Miami nursing home. The Arkansas cousin Scruggs, visiting her, once spoke with Auntie Mame's attorney as they stood together near her bed. As Myrtle slept, the attorney told Scruggs to persuade Myrtle to sign a power of attorney giving Scruggs decision-making authority over Myrtle's care. Both the attorney and Scruggs believed Myrtle needed the nursing home's twenty-four-hour care. Scruggs did not think Myrtle would sign any such document, but she would ask.

Myrtle opened her eyes. The attorney advised her to sign the paperwork. "Just leave it here," Myrtle said.

When Scruggs and the attorney left her room, Myrtle phoned Armshaw and said, "I'm furious."

Armshaw laughed. He asked, "What are you furious about *now*?"

She told him what her attorney and Scruggs had said while she was *feigning* sleep. Myrtle thought they cared about her, but now she knew the real truth: they cared only about her money.

"Get me a new lawyer," Myrtle said. "I want to draw up a new will."

On December 3, 1991, she created her third will in a five-year period. This time she added her caretaker ("my trusted companion") and reduced Scruggs's share to a nominal amount of Oklahoma Gas and Electric Company stock.

NINETEEN

Santa Rosa, California

On the day Myrtle Bennett died, her caretaker, newly named in her will, phoned the emergency contact posted on Myrtle's refrigerator—no longer Carolyn Scruggs, but Mary Jacobs, in Northern California.

Later that day, Jacobs called Armshaw. In the decade and a half that he had known Myrtle, the stockbroker had heard her mention Mary Jacobs only once—when redrawing her will in 1990. He thought Jacobs's phone call was more mercenary than familial. She "didn't talk about Myrtle, she talked about the money, and how fast she was going to get it, and how much she was going to get," Armshaw said. "There was some ambiguity in the will on the Putnam Funds and [Mary] Jacobs threatened to sue unless she got all the Putnam Funds."

Myrtle's estate was valued at $1,062,144, mostly in bonds and securities. After taxes and legal fees, the payout to beneficiaries was $840,203. According to federal tax returns filed by accountants for Myrtle's estate, Jack Bennett's niece, Mary Jacobs, received stocks and bonds valued at $656,000, and another niece, Jacobs's sister, Helen Fugina, got stock worth $16,000.

A longtime bridge friend who had helped Myrtle escape the Oklahoma nursing home received securities worth nearly $89,000. Armshaw's three children received a combined total of stock worth $65,000. Myrtle gave her caretaker bonds worth $9,000, and Scruggs's stock was valued at $3,400.

At her instruction, Myrtle was cremated and her remains were sent to Eddie and Ada Mae Simpson in Miami, Oklahoma. There, per her wishes, the Simpsons buried her ashes in an urn beside Alice Adkins in the Grand Army of the Republic Cemetery. The Simpsons were reimbursed for burial costs—$276.13—the only money they received from Myrtle's estate. Eddie and Ada Mae have since died, but I spoke by phone with their son, Leroy Simpson, who later sent me an e-mail from Colorado saying he had found an envelope with papers that Myrtle had left in a weather-battered trunk during her stay with his parents in Oklahoma. Ten days later a large envelope arrived on my desk, and out tumbled Jack Bennett's official World War I service record, a Jackson County court filing from Myrtle's murder trial, checks signed by Jack and Myrtle in 1919 and 1920 from banks in Sioux Falls, South Dakota, and San Antonio, Texas. The contents also included a 1992 letter from a woman in Florida named Marion Randall, an old friend of Myrtle's, who several weeks after Myrtle's death wrote to Ada Mae Simpson, "I'm so happy and thankful to you for arranging a funeral for Myrtle, which she really didn't deserve. It was such a shame that Myrtle had words with you because I think she had all intentions of leaving everything to you and Eddie . . . After 72 years, Myrtle didn't even leave me a pleasant smile."

In death as in life, Myrtle Bennett created more puzzles than she solved. No one knew with certainty why she bequeathed her own family less than one half of 1 percent of her estate while leaving 80 percent to the family of the husband she shot dead. Mary Jacobs, the primary benefactor of Myrtle's will, who lived with her husband in Santa Rosa, California, died in 1996, four years after Myrtle's death. The will had specified that if Mary died before Myrtle, the $656,000 would go to her husband, Walter.

When I phoned him in Santa Rosa, Walter Jacobs, then ninety-five years old, cordially agreed to meet me and discuss Myrtle. He warned me that he had not really known her. I asked if Mary had been close with her. "Moderately close," he said. They visited Myrtle in Florida "two or three times," Walter told me, but then he remembered that one of those trips came *after* Myrtle's death. Only a few hours after our brief telephone conversation, though, Walter Jacobs called back to cancel any interview. A family member, he said, had advised him against talking.

The words *moderately close* rang odd to me. If Jack's niece and Myrtle were no closer than that, why lavish riches on her and pennies on her own relatives? Armshaw asked Myrtle that question as she rewrote her will in August 1990. "Why are you giving all this money to Jacobs and not your own family in Oklahoma?" He heard Myrtle say, "Well, first off, my own family doesn't need it." Armshaw never met Mary Jacobs, but he understood she had visited Myrtle during her final year. "And Myrtle felt Mrs. Jacobs really cared for her," he said.

I drove an hour north to Santa Rosa. I wanted to know why Myrtle had given most of her money to the Jacobses. Walter Jacobs lived still in a retirement community in the heart of Sonoma County. I knocked on his door. Months had passed since our unsatisfying phone conversation. Now I identified myself, and he eyed me for a moment, warily. I asked for a few minutes of his time. He led me inside. We sat in his living room, the late morning sun warming the otherwise cool reception. I asked about a dozen questions. His answers were brief, uncomfortable. He said he barely knew Myrtle, and had heard about Jack's killing only in passing. He said he knew nothing about Myrtle's trial. He did not talk about Myrtle's $656,000 gift. He only wanted to know why Myrtle was of any interest to me.

Armshaw offered another answer as to why Myrtle had given the lion's share of her money to Jack's family. He thought the will's stipulations were Myrtle's attempt at atoning for the killing of her husband. He thought she felt the guilt of that night even sixty-two years later. The will was her way of saying she was sorry. "I can't think of any other reason for it," Armshaw told me. "There is no way I could prove that. It's just my gut feeling."

Scruggs believes Myrtle felt a genuine regret and love for Jack. "She still loved him," Scruggs said, "and she didn't want me to think ill of him." Once, Myrtle gave Scruggs two photographs of herself to keep. Then she began to give her a photo of Jack, but pulled it back. Myrtle said she wanted to hold on to that one.

Scruggs told me she once saw an article in a national women's magazine with the headline THE BENNETT MURDER HAND and showed it to Auntie Mame. "Maybe you should sue them," Scruggs said, but the response was only a wave of the hand. "That was a long time ago . . ." On another occasion, traveling together in Geneva in 1964, Scruggs finally summoned the courage to say, "Oh, Auntie Mame, I sometimes think of your life—" Myrtle interjected: "Well, my dear, it was a great tragedy and a great mistake." She studied Carolyn Scruggs's face for a moment, and said, "I was just about your age when it happened." Scruggs replied, "Well, you know, we've never talked about it but I guess"—Scruggs stammered to say it just right—"I guess I want you to know that I understand it." Auntie Mame said, "No, my dear, you don't understand it." Scruggs said this was the only time Auntie Mame ever discussed the shooting with her.

One view of Myrtle Bennett is that her story began and ended on that night in 1929. In an age of increasing female assertion, at the end of the Roaring Twenties, taking part in the American craze of the moment (contract bridge) with a handsome husband involved in a timeless game (adultery), she reached, in alcohol-infused fury, for a Colt .32. But that view is wrongly limited. In truth, Myrtle Bennett's story continued on the same narrative path for another sixty-two years. I believe the humiliation, rage, and impetuosity that moved young Myrtle to shoot Jack were the same fires that moved her at the age of ninety-six to strike from her will those relatives who sent her to a nursing home and those whom she believed plotted at her bedside. I believe Myrtle's will was shaped by guilt finally resolved in the redemptive act of making right with Jack's memory and his family.

The woman born on the hardscrabble farm of nineteenth-century Arkansas, the lead character in the most famous Kansas City murder trial of her time, a survivor who left behind her four spades bid and the melancholy of her past and built a new life among New York's

rich and famous, a life of gin fizzes, bridge games, and world travel—
this singular, stubborn, bold, exasperating, difficult, and remarkable
woman—stepped into the Miami airport terminal in 1982.

There, Scruggs and an old friend waited for her. As Scruggs
retrieved her luggage, she advised her friend, "You wait here for Auntie Mame." "But, honey," said the old friend, who had known Myrtle in Memphis, "I haven't seen Myrtle since 1924!" Scruggs
laughed—it had been fifty-eight years, after all—but she knew there
was only one Auntie Mame, so she replied, "I think you'll know her."
Just then, an eighty-seven-year-old woman approached, moving
briskly, just as she had moved upon first spotting Jack Bennett on an
Illinois Central train during World War I. She wore a fine navy blue
outfit, a red-white-and-blue scarf and high-heeled Spectator shoes.
Noticing boldness in her gait still, the old friend said, "Why, of
course! I'd know Myrtle anywhere." Later, at a hotel restaurant, here
came Auntie Mame into the room, and the piano man, on cue from
Carolyn Scruggs, struck up the theme song from the long-ago Broadway musical. Myrtle Bennett, in the twilight of a robust life, sang
aloud the lyrics:

> *You make our black-eyed peas and our grits, Mame,*
> *Seem like the bill of fare at the Ritz, Mame,*
> *You came, you saw, you conquered*
> *And absolutely nothing is the same.*

Like a burst of light, Myrtle danced a jig in the restaurant and
sang about a 1929 party girl who coaxed the blues out of a horn and
charmed the husks off the corn.

She never changed. She was always Lorelei Lee, always Auntie
Mame, forever Myrtle.

A partnership game for four, two against two, contract bridge starts so innocently. In each hand, all fifty-two cards are dealt face-down, thirteen to each player. Players sort the cards into suits and study their hands. How nice it is to fan your cards out and discover those six high spades, one at a time, a king here, a jack there, and the ace hiding under that club on the far right, or nicer still, to find a treasure trove of the most valuable high cards in multiple suits—four aces, three kings, two queens.

Now the auction, the bidding phase, begins, with the two sides competing for the right to play the hand. One by one, beginning with the dealer, players bid aloud using a strictly prescribed shorthand to explain to their partner the distribution of cards and suit strength in their own hand. Through bids, players try to discover their partnership's greatest interlocking strength. Each bid is a statement to one's partner, and a query, to discover how strong they are together and which suit the partnership has in abundance and might control.

The bidding vocabulary comprises fifteen terms: the numbers one through seven; the four suits (clubs, diamonds, hearts, spades); and the words *no trump, pass, double,* and *redouble.* Bids sound cryptic: "one spade" or "three hearts" or "six no trump." Extraneous words, voice inflections, and arched eyebrows are not permitted. That would be cheating.

At stake in the play of the hand are thirteen *tricks,* each created with one card put down by the four players. Bids specify how many tricks the partnership pledges to win in the hand and what suit, if any, will be the *trump suit.* The thirteen cards in the trump suit are akin to wild cards in poker and have special value over all others. A lowly deuce or trey from the trump suit defeats all cards from other suits.

The hand may also be played at no trump, meaning without wild card power.

In typical auction fashion, each bid must be higher than the previous one. To facilitate matters, suits are ranked in a hierarchical order, starting at the bottom with clubs, up to diamonds, then to hearts, spades, and highest of all, no trump. Thus, during the auction one diamond outranks one club. Two spades outranks two hearts. But nothing outranks seven no trump. Once the play begins, however, the ranking of the suits has no further relevance.

Bidding moves in a clockwise direction, sometimes making several full rotations around the table, until three consecutive players decide to pass. When this happens, there is a tacit understanding that everyone is content, for their own reasons, and not prepared to go any higher. The last bid made—that is, the one followed by three passes—constitutes the *final contract*.

Every bid in bridge has an automatic six tricks built into it. That means a bid of one heart is a pledge to win not one but seven tricks (six plus one), with hearts as the trump suit. A bid of four diamonds is a pledge to win ten tricks (six plus four), with diamonds as the trump suit, and so on. Just to start, then, the first bidder must have a good hand, as he is committing his partnership to taking more than half the available tricks.

In order to succeed, the partnership that captures the final contract must win at least as many tricks as it bid. Failing that, it will suffer penalty points for overbidding. (For instance, with their contract of four spades, Myrtle and Jack Bennett needed to take ten tricks, but Jack only got eight and failed.)

The bidding done, the play of the hand begins. The player who first named the trump suit—and now vies to make the final contract—becomes *declarer*. The opponent to his left puts down the first card, face up. Now the declarer's partner, called the *dummy*, exposes his thirteen cards on the table, in four neat rows, the cards aligned by suits for all to see. The dummy thus bows out of the hand entirely. Only three will play the hand. The declarer plays alone for the partnership, drawing cards from the dummy's exposed hand, and his own.

The other players are obliged to play a card from the suit led, if they can. If not, they can play another card, including one from the trump suit. The highest card of the suit led (or the highest trump) wins the trick and earns the right to lead the next trick.

The role of declarer can be exhilarating or exasperating, depending on the experience of the player. With the partnership's fate in his grip, a confident player relishes the opportunity to showcase his playing skills. An unsure declarer, however, now flying solo, can be consumed by nerves, anticipating criticism, should he fail to make the contract. All the while, the dummy looks on, approvingly or icily, as the situation might warrant.

Social players typically play rubber bridge, a rubber being the best of three games. A side needs to score 100 points to win a game (that might require one hand or several deals), and two games to win a rubber, and the handsome bonus that comes with taking the rubber.

The first six tricks are nonscoring. Only those from the seventh one on count toward fulfillment of a contract. No-trump tricks score the highest: 40 points for the first trick and 30 points for each trick thereafter. Hearts and spades, as the major suits, score 30 points per successful trick after the first six. Clubs and diamonds, as the minor suits, score the lowest, 20 points per trick. Thus, bidding and making a four spades contract (4 times 30 points) would give a partnership enough for game.

The opponents, of course, will be doing all they can to beat declarer. For their efforts, however, all they can earn is penalty points (none of which count toward a game for their side) and the satisfaction that they have prevented declarer from getting a plus score.

A partnership becomes *vulnerable* after winning one game in a rubber, meaning the rewards and penalties for making or failing in the next contract are all the greater. If both sides have won one game in the rubber, then both are vulnerable.

Like chess, contract is a kaleidoscope of possibilities that multiply with every turn of thought. For the eager novice, those possibilities are both daunting and seductive. For the serious player, such is the endless charm of the classic game.

A CONTRACT BRIDGE GLOSSARY

Adapted from *The Encyclopedia of Bridge* (New York: The Bridge World, Inc., 1935), edited by Ely Culbertson, et al.

AUCTION: Known loosely as *the bidding*, the period during which players may bid in rotation for the contract, beginning when the deal is finished and ending when three consecutive players have passed.

DECLARER: The player who for his side first made a bid of the denomination that became part of the final contract. For example, if the contract is four hearts, the player who first named the heart suit is declarer. The declarer plays both his own (closed) hand and that of his partner (the dummy hand), the latter being placed face up on the table for all players to see.

DEFENDING HAND: The hand that makes a call after one of the opponents has opened the bidding, or, in the play, one of the opponents of the declarer; loosely, any player who is defending against an adverse contract, either in the bidding or the play.

DOUBLE: The call made in bridge which would double or otherwise increase certain points won or lost in the event the last preceding bid becomes the contract. A double call may be made only by an opponent of the last preceding bidder. It may be redoubled by an opponent of the doubler, thereby further increasing the points won or lost.

DUMMY: The declarer's partner. After the opening lead is made by the opponent on the declarer's left, the dummy places his cards face up on the table. The dummy takes no part in the play. He may not suggest by word or gesture any lead or play, but may call attention to errors of play or violations of law. The term originated in Dummy Whist, in which there were only three players, the fourth hand being exposed as the "dummy," an imaginary and silent player.

DUPLICATE BRIDGE: The form of bridge in which the same hand is played more than once. It is the form played in tournaments since it reduces the amount of luck, scores being based on a comparison of the results achieved with the same cards.

FINAL CONTRACT: The last bid in the auction followed by three passes, or by a double or redouble, and three passes. The final bid becomes the final contract. If a suit is named in it, that suit becomes trump suit for the hand.

GAME: The side first to score a minimum of 100 points for tricks bid and made wins a game. The game score may be made in one deal or in more than one. As soon as a side wins a game, both sides start afresh (no score) toward the next game.

MAJOR SUITS: The two higher-ranking suits, spades and hearts, so called because, in bidding, they are higher ranked than the two other suits, diamonds and clubs. In either major suit, a four-bid (30 points per trick) is required for game.

MINOR SUITS: The two lower-ranking suits, diamonds and clubs, so-called because, in bidding, they are inferior in rank to the two major suits, spades and hearts. In either minor suit, a five-bid (20 points per trick) is required for game.

NO TRUMP: One of the five denominations of calls at bridge, the other four being suit calls. The characteristic of a no trump contract which distinguishes it from a suit is that there is no trump suit; all four suits have equal trick-taking value in the play.

OPENING BID: The first bid made in any deal. The opening hand may select any bid he wishes to open the auction, from one to seven in a suit or in no trump. By far the great majority of opening bids are one-bids in a suit.

PASS: A call which indicates that the player does not on that occasion bid, double, or redouble, made by saying "Pass" or "No bid." Whenever a player passes, he should observe the same form of indicating every time, not first saying "Pass" and on another hand saying "No bid." Individual variations of indicating a pass by knocking on the table, or using any other expression, may be regarded as unethical.

PSYCHIC BID: A bid which violates established conventions, or agreements, usually made for the purpose of deceiving opponents.

RESPONDING HAND: The partner of the player who has opened the auction.

RUBBER BRIDGE: Contract bridge played with a view to winning rubbers, or best-of-three game sets. A side that wins two consecutive games at the start of a rubber wins the premium of 700 bonus points, or 500 bonus points if the rubber extends to a full three games. These premiums are not affected by vulnerability, doubling, or redoubling.

SLAM: The bidding and making of a contract of six-odd (12 tricks) constitutes a Small Slam, or seven-odd (all 13 tricks) a Grand Slam. However, if 12 or 13 tricks are taken, but have not been contracted for, there is no slam, the tricks above the contract being scored only as extra tricks.

Trick: A card led from one hand, and followed by one card played from the three remaining hands. In the struggle for suits in bridge, the trick is a symbolic gesture signifying the capture of an enemy.

Trump Suit: The suit, if any, to which a higher trick-taking power attaches during the play of the hand. Each of its cards ranks above any card of any other suit. The trump suit, if any, is named in the final contract.

Vulnerable: A scoring term applied to a side that has won a game in a rubber. A vulnerable side runs the risk of incurring greater penalties for defeated contracts, offset by the possibility of making greater premiums for making contracts and slams.

NOTES

vii   **"Don't forget that man"**: Jerome Beatty, "What Is Your Wife Worth to You?" *American Magazine*, October 1931, p. 137.

vii   **"We played perfectly—except Jo"**: John Clay, *Culbertson: The Man Who Made Contract Bridge* (London: Weidenfeld and Nicolson, 1985), p. 192.

INTRODUCTION

xiii   **"Treat it like the measles"**: Steven Watts, *The People's Tycoon: Henry Ford and the American Century* (New York: Alfred A. Knopf, 2005), p. 339. Ford was quoted in the *Ladies' Home Journal* magazine in September 1923, p. 8.

xiii   **Henry L. Mencken, so favored blondes**: Anita Loos, *Kiss Hollywood Good-By* (New York: The Viking Press, 1974). See also Anita Loos, *Gentlemen Prefer Blondes* and *But Gentlemen Marry Brunettes* (New York: Penguin Books, 1998), pp. xxxvii–xxxviii.

xiii   **meets the famous Austrian psychiatrist "Dr. Froyd"**: Loos, *Gentlemen Prefer Blondes*, pp. 88–90.

xiv   **one arrangement of the 635,013,559,600 possibilities**: Edward McPherson, *The Backwash Squeeze and Other Improbable Feats: A Newcomer's Journey into the World of Bridge* (New York: HarperCollins Publishers, 2007), p. 39; and Marvin Reznikoff and Tannah Hirsch, "Over Troubled Water," *Psychology Today*, May 1970, pp. 36–39.

xv   **cards dates to China in or before the thirteenth century**: Catherine Perry Hargrave, *A History of Playing Cards and a Bibliography of Cards and Gaming* (New York: Dover Publications, Inc., 1966), p. 6.

xv   **encountered such fearsome weather that they threw**: Ibid., p. 279.

xv   **They called them *the devil's tickets***: Henry G. Francis, editor in chief, and Alan F. Truscott and Dorothy A. Francis, *The Official Encyclopedia of Bridge*, 6th ed. (Memphis, Tenn.: American Contract Bridge League, 2001), p. 115.

xvii   **"When you write a love scene"**: Loos, *Kiss Hollywood Good-By*, pp. 190–91.

ONE: ELY AND JO

3 **"all the iridescence of the beginning"**: Nathan Miller, *New World Coming: The 1920s and the Making of Modern America* (Cambridge, Mass.: Da Capo Press, 2003), p. 9; and F. Scott Fitzgerald and Edmund Wilson, ed., *The Crack-Up* (New York: New Directions Publishing Corporation, 1993), p. 25.

3 **pancake makeup and jangling jewelry**: Stanley Walker, *The Night Club Era* (Baltimore, Md.: Johns Hopkins University Press, 1999), pp. 95–96, 240–43.

4 **roller-skated the Charleston**: Ibid., pp. 95–96.

4 **"the pleasure of not giving a damn"**: Ben Hecht, *A Child of the Century* (New York: Simon & Schuster, 1954), pp. 357–58, 383.

5 **"90 percent entertainment, 10 percent"**: Neal Gabler, *Winchell: Gossip, Power and the Culture of Celebrity* (New York: Alfred A. Knopf, 1994), p. 73.

5 **" 'Are you Dorothy Parker?' "**: *Daily Mirror* (New York), March 9, 1931.

5 **"seemed to purr with delight"**: Gabler, *Winchell*, p. 80.

6 **Founded in 1891 by twenty enthusiasts of whist**: August R. Ohman, *Historical Sketch of the Knickerbocker Whist Club: Playing Cards, Whist, Bridge, Auction* (New York: Knickerbocker Whist Club, 1926), p. 3.

7 **ladylike, her long, supple fingers dropping**: Ely Culbertson, *The Strange Lives of One Man* (Chicago: The John C. Winston Company, 1940), pp. 424–26; and *New York Sun*, December 17, 1931.

7 **called her the Duchess for her regal**: *Daily News* (New York), December 23, 1931.

7 **she played the adolescent game of basketball**: Ibid.

8 **whispers that she had been his mistress**: Clay, *Culbertson: The Man Who Made Contract Bridge*, p. 60.

8 **from Selma, Alabama, who once tried to irrigate the Congo**: Dorothy Rice Sims, *Curiouser and Curiouser: A Book in the Jugular Vein* (New York: Simon & Schuster, 1940), p. 123.

9 **"a brain of so perfect an organization"**: George Walker, *Chess and Chess Players: Consisting of Original Stories and Sketches* (London: Charles J. Skeet, Publisher, 1850), p. 40.

9 **march with the spirited youth of Paris**: Ibid.

9 **agreed to deposit a quarter million francs**: Ibid., pp. 43–44.

9 **the quick trick table of card values**: *New York Times*, June 28, 1931.

10 **José Capablanca, and spent a year in India studying magic**: *Bridge Magazine*, March 1932, p. 8; also *New York Times*, July 18, 1948, April 17, 1960; also John A. Garraty, ed., *Dictionary of American Biography*, suppl. 6, 1956–

1960 (New York: Charles Scribner's Sons, 1980), pp. 379–80; also *Bridge World*, March 1932, p. 27.

10 **blue bathrobe while settling into a wide armchair**: Sims, *Curiouser and Curiouser*, p. 128.

10 **officer on the USS *Montana* during the war, convoying American soldiers**: *New York World-Telegram*, February 17, 1932.

10 **had died in a yachting accident**: *New York Times*, October 8, 1964.

11 **guardianship of an uncle in Berlin, who later enlisted him**: *Ripley v. Von Zedtwitz*, 201 Ky. 513 (Ky. App. 1923); *Von Zedtwitz v. Sutherland*, 40 F.2nd 785 (D.C. Cir. 1930); *Commonwealth v. Von Zedwitz*, 215 Ky. 413 (Ky 1926).

11 **He had pulled on his earlobes**: *New York Times*, October 21, 1984.

11 **"Intellectually, and almost emotionally"**: *New York World-Telegram*, February 23, 1932.

12 **intending to catch a train Saturday morning**: Commander Winfield Liggett, Jr., "Memories of Fortieth Street," *Contract Bridge*, October 1931, p. 3.

12 **playing bridge, dining out, and attending dance parties**: Madeleine Kerwin, "Jo Culbertson, My Friend," *Bridge World*, April 1956, p. 6.

12 **her husband was a Princeton boy**: Clay, *Culbertson*, p. 60.

12 **former husband was dead, perhaps by suicide**: Ibid.

13 **Ely and Mrs. Shelton won top score**: Culbertson, *The Strange Lives*, pp. 418–19.

13 **the famed 1732 Guarnari del Gesù violin**: *New York Times*, December 30, 1924, and April 2, 1929. *NY Herald-Tribune*, April 2, 1929; also Culbertson, *The Strange Lives*, pp. 424–25.

14 **"Well, then, let's drink a toast"**: Culbertson, *The Strange Lives*, p. 416.

15 **Pygmalion's love, and Aphrodite's spark, Galatea springs**: Louis Herbert Gray, ed., and George Foot Moore, William Sherwood Fox, *The Mythology of All Races: Greek and Roman*, Vol. 1 (New York: Cooper Square Publishers, Inc., 1964), p. 200; and Richard P. Martin, *Bulfinch's Mythology: The Age of Fable, The Age of Chivalry, Legends of Charlemagne* (New York: Harper-Collins Publishers, 1991), pp. 56–57.

16 **Must be between 18 and 21 years old**: Culbertson, *The Strange Lives*, pp. 319–20. The ad was published in Italian; the translation to English is Culbertson's.

16 **"No, signorina"**: Ibid., p. 321.

16 **"It isn't your ideas"**: Ibid., p. 431.

17 **ambition was to create the Modern Theory**: Ely Culbertson, *Contract Bridge Blue Book* (New York: The Bridge World, Inc., 1930), p. xvii.

17 **"You could be a revolutionist, a monk"**: Culbertson, *The Strange Lives*, p. 436.

18 **"You're a bridge monster!"**: Ibid., p. 444.

18 **those who quarreled everywhere, including**: *Bridge World*, July 1930, pp. 44–45.

19 **"oil business"**: Ely Culbertson–Josephine Dillon Affadavit for License to Marry, June 9, 1923, New York City Department of Records and Information Services, Municipal Archives, New York.

19 **Father Duffy presiding**: Marriage Certificate for Ely Culbertson and Josephine M. Dillon, married on June 11, 1923, signed on August 30, 1930, New York City Department of Records and Information Services, Municipal Archives, New York.

19 **the isle of Capri, a lovely country home**: Culbertson. *The Strange Lives*, pp. 453.

20 **young Yale man playing a casual game**: Matthew J. Bruccoli, ed., *The Short Stories of F. Scott Fitzgerald* (New York: Scribner, 1989), p. 326. Originally published as a short story, "The Rich Boy," in a two-part series in *Red Book*, January and February 1926.

20 **plays three-handed bridge with friends**: Ernest Hemingway, *The Sun Also Rises* (New York: Scribner Trade Paperback Edition, 2006), p. 130.

20 **On a cruise ship voyage through the Panama Canal**: Alan Truscott and Dorothy Truscott, *The New York Times Bridge Book: An Anecdotal History of the Development, Personalities and Strategies of the World's Most Popular Card Game* (New York: St. Martin's Press, 2002), pp. 22–24; also Rex Mackey, *The Walk of the Oysters* (London: W. H. Allen, 1964), pp. 12–14.

21 **"Contract will sweep the country"**: Culbertson, *The Strange Lives*, p. 497.

22 **von Zedtwitz came, and so did Ted Lightner**: Ibid., p. 501.

22 **"Here's to the most wonderful wife"**: Ibid., p. 503.

23 **"Whose bid is it?"**: Sims, *Curiouser and Curiouser*, pp. 153–54.

23 GUESTS AND FISH STINK: Ibid., p. 152.

23 **"Bridge sharks multiply like rabbits"**: Ibid., p. 149.

TWO: MYRTLE AND JACK

24 **Her young cousins would wait on the front porch**: Carolyn Scruggs interview.

25 **"i was glad to hear that you enjoyed"**: Letter from H. F. Adkins to his wife, Alice B. Adkins, June 27, 1889, personal files of Myrtle Bennett at the time of her 1992 death, courtesy of a lawyer for the Bennett estate, who asked not to be identified.

25 **The lawyer Abner McGehee, Jr., whose father founded**: *Arkansas Gazette*, June 13, 1938; also *Kansas City Times*, March 3, 1931, and *Kansas City Journal-Post*, February 28, 1931.

25 **In a club car on the Illinois Central**: *Kansas City Star*, October 1, 1929.

26 **completed his infantry work**: Certificate of Graduation, Fourth Officers Training School, Camp Grant, Illinois, August 26, 1918, Myrtle Bennett personal files, courtesy of LeRoy Simpson.

26 **A pharmacist attached to a medical division**: Favorable Discharge from Army of the United States for John G. Bennett, 2061946, Sgt. Medical Division, 161st Depot Brigade upon acceptance of commission as Second Lieutenant at Camp Grant, Illinois, August 26, 1918, Myrtle Bennett personal files, courtesy of LeRoy Simpson.

26 **worked as a clerk at the W. A. Ball drugstore**: *White County* (Illinois) *Democrat*, October 3, 1929.

26 **"a tall bold slugger set vivid"**: Carl Sandburg, *The Complete Poems of Carl Sandburg*, revised and expanded ed. (New York: Harcourt Brace Jovanovich, 1969), p. 3.

27 **[A woman] searches out his weaknesses**: H. L. Mencken, *In Defense of Women* (Garden City, N.J.: Garden City Publishing Company, 1922), pp. 29–30.

27 **"FLASH: The Armistice Has Been Signed"**: *Memphis News-Scimitar*, November 11, 1918.

27 **"HUNS MADE POWERLESS"**: Ibid.

28 **the Shrine band, the Boy Scout Drum Corps**: Ibid.

28 **in the business term of the day, "a producer"**: *Kansas City Star*, October 1, 1929.

28 **a stenographer for a tire company, a doctor**: *Kansas City Star*, March 1, 1931.

28 **Jack was earning $6,000 a year**: *Kansas City Journal-Post*, February 28, 1931.

28 **stitching his trousers**: *Kansas City Journal-Post*, March 3, 1931.

30 **Myrtle had twice lost babies**: *Kansas City Journal-Post*, October 1, 1931.

30 **"broad-verandahed country places"**: *Auction Bridge Magazine*, July 1929, p. 23.

31   **Jack hoping to be perceived as a lavish host:** *Kansas City Journal-Post,* October 1, 1931.

31   **KMBC, broadcasting live from the El Torreon:** Chuck Haddix interview.

31   **"Men have more psychology":** *Bridge World,* October 1929, pp. 18–19.

32   **"*Ships made Carthage*":** William Reddig, *Tom's Town: Kansas City and the Pendergast Legend* (Columbia: University of Missouri Press, 1986), p. 23.

32   **Its downtown skyline took impressive shape:** Rick Montgomery and Shirl Kasper, *Kansas City: An American Story* (Kansas City, Mo.: Kansas City Star Books, 1999), p. 200.

32   **forged iron, milled flour, turned corn into sugar:** *Kansas City Star,* February 12, 1931.

32   **North of the city nearly seven hundred acres:** "At the Municipal Airport," *Kansas Citian,* July 23, 1929.

33   **"In a waiting room a block long":** *Kansas City Star,* February 12, 1931.

33   **"I have seen the streets of Paris":** *St. Joseph* (Missouri) *News-Press,* September 19, 1934; and *Time,* October 1, 1934.

33   **challenged God to strike him dead:** *Kansas City Times,* April 19, 1926; also Richard Lingeman, *Sinclair Lewis: Rebel from Main Street* (New York: Random House, 2002), p. 277; also Mark Schorer, *Sinclair Lewis: An American Life* (New York: McGraw-Hill, 1961), p. 447.

33   **Lewis held "Sunday school classes":** *Kansas City Star,* May 17, 1926.

33   **"What the hell right has the church":** *Kansas City Times,* March 16, 1927.

34   **"Sit down, my son":** Lingeman, *Sinclair Lewis: Rebel from Main Street,* p. 276; also Schorer, *Sinclair Lewis: An American Life,* p. 450.

34   **"I've had huge and delightful reglimpses":** Lingeman, *Sinclair Lewis: Rebel from Main Street,* p. 270.

34   **"It is a good booster town":** *Kansas City Times,* April 1, 1926.

34   **sat on an inverted motorcar brake drum:** *Kansas City Journal-Post,* February 21, 1927.

35   **He placed his thumbs inside holes in the flagpole's shaft:** *New York Times,* October 12, 1952.

35   **he saw a bootlegger deliver four bottles to a man:** *Kansas City Journal-Post,* February 21, 1927.

36   **French gilt and glitter of the Louis XV period:** Lawrence H. Larsen and Nancy J. Hulston, *Pendergast!* (Columbia: University of Missouri Press, 1997), p. 79.

36   **ambience of a fraternal lodge: spare:** William Reddig, *Tom's Town: Kansas City and the Pendergast Legend* (Columbia: University of Missouri Press, 1986), pp. 131–32.

36 **old steamboat pilot named Captain Elijah Matheus**: Ibid.

36 **"They was" or "I seen"**: Larsen and Hulston, *Pendergast!*, p. 5.

37 **"When we had the controversy with Longwell"**: Letter from James A. Reed to Honorable T. J. Pendergast, October 29, 1927, James A. Reed Papers, Western Historical Manuscript Collection, University of Missouri, Kansas City, KC443: Box 13.

37 **"What's government for if it isn't"**: Larsen and Hulston, *Pendergast!*, p. 72.

38 **called it an "incomparable development"**: *Kansas City Times*, January 25, 1926.

38 **"It gives you the comfort"**: *"Ward and Roanoake Parkway Building Corporation: 100% Cooperative Plan,"* sales brochure of Park Manor Development, Kansas City: C. O. Jones Bldg. Co., 1929.

39 **Jack Bennett put down $4,890**: Ibid.

39 **Jack joined the downtown Kansas City Athletic Club**: *Blue Diamond*, newsletter of the Kansas City Athletic Club, Kansas City, Missouri, February 1927, p. 32.

39 **swimming pool, a cigar stand, card rooms**: "Let's Take a Trip Through the Club," *Blue Diamond*, newsletter of the Kansas City Athletic Club, Kansas City, Missouri, December 1930, pp. 12–15.

40 **"They simply let themselves be clouded"**: *Chicago Tribune*, December 19, 1931.

40 **"We have the vote, we have all the liberty"**: *Kansas City Star*, September 23, 1929.

THREE: ELY'S GRAND SCHEME

41 **Every human being floats**: Ely Culbertson, *Contract Bridge Blue Book* (New York: The Bridge World, Inc., 1930), p. 261.

41 **"Whenever a hand contains a biddable"**: Ibid., p.75.

42 **puffs on a cigarette demanded a lead in spades**: Ibid., p. 482.

42 **they offered Ely only a few hundred dollars**: Culbertson, *The Strange Lives of One Man*, p. 519.

43 **big houses that rent for $12,000**: F. Scott Fitzgerald, *The Great Gatsby: The Cambridge Edition of the Works of F. Scott Fitzgerald* (New York: Cambridge University Press, 1991), p. 8.

43 **overgrown garden with stucco monsters**: Culbertson, *The Strange Lives of One Man*, p. 519.

44 **51 percent for him and Jo, and 49 percent divided**: Ibid., p. 520.

44 **to the ego, to fear, and to sex**: Ibid., p. 689. In an eleven-page appendix

entitled "The Mass Mind," Culbertson presents his views on marketing in America, and describes how he sculpted his advertising pitch to sell contract bridge.

47 **"vigorous thinking of a high intellectual order"**: *Bridge World*, October 1929, p. 9.

47 **"From the heights of his masculine egotism"**: Ibid., p. 18.

48 **Ely and P. Hal Sims won**: *Time*, December 2, 1929.

48 **THE BRIDGE WORLD will fill, we confidently**: *Bridge World*, October 1929, p. 5.

49 **Culbertson had his name appear 164 times**: Andrew A. Freeman, "Culbertson: Soldier of Fortune," *Outlook*, December 9, 1931, p. 461.

50 **"More married couples should hear"**: *New York Times*, December 12, 1928; and *Time*, December 24, 1928.

FOUR: FOUR SPADES SHE BID

In this chapter, the intimate details of the fatal bridge game are drawn largely from Kansas City's newspapers: the *Star*, the *Times*, and the *Journal-Post*. There were few discrepancies in the reports, although, true to form, the *Journal-Post* (desperate for circulation gains) was racier, more sensational. I also have used testimony from Myrtle's 1931 murder trial to enrich the depiction of the bridge game and the wee hours of the following morning. In notes for Chapter 4, I cite only sources other than Kansas City's newspapers on the Bennett killing and immediate aftermath.

53 **living room that measured eleven by eighteen feet**: Architectural blueprint: First-floor Plan, Ward Parkway Apartment Building. C.O. Jones Building Company. Personal files of current resident of Ward Parkway, who asked not to be identified.

54 **"The club is proud of the way its members"**: *Blue Diamond*, newsletter of the Kansas City Athletic Club, Kansas City, Missouri, November 1928, p. 10.

55 **feminine moods—Romance, Gaiety, Sophistication**: *New York Times*, November 20, 1927.

55 **"Here's the new generation of Americans"**: Sinclair Lewis, *Babbitt* (New York: Harcourt Brace Jovanovich, 1922), p. 149.

56 **"way out there in the blue"**: Arthur Miller, *Death of a Salesman: Certain Private Conversations in Two Acts and a Requiem* (New York: The Viking Press, 1949), p. 138.

57 **developed the concept of compounding toilet preparations**: *New York Times*, March 18, 1930.

57 "Many a woman has looked at the long array": *St. Louis Post-Dispatch*, March 4, 1931.

57 "an almost fairy-like loveliness": *New York Times*, November 20, 1927.

57 "The moment you take the cover off the box": *New York Times*, September 22, 1929.

57 "gay little *compactes*, topped with genuine": *New York Times*, December 9, 1928.

57 "The initials of a friend": Richard M. Fried, *The Man Everybody Knew: Bruce Barton and the Making of Modern America* (Chicago: Ivan R. Dee, 2005), p. 61.

57 "Any woman who does anything": Ibid.

58 "We build of imperishable materials": Ibid., pp. 66–67.

58 Sears and Montgomery Ward sold by mail order: Timothy B. Spears, *100 Years on the Road: The Traveling Salesman in American Culture* (New Haven, Conn.: Yale University Press, 1997), p. 1.

58 "As influential factors in the creation": Ibid.

58 "victims and martyrs, creatures touchingly": Ibid., p. xv.

58 "curb our tendency to flirt": Ibid., p. 4.

60 two million rubber condoms were used daily: Gerald Leinwand, *1927: High Tide of the 1920s* (New York: Four Walls Eight Windows, 2001), p. 8.

60 flappers shaved their pubic hair: Anita Loos, *Kiss Hollywood Good-by* (New York: The Viking Press, 1974), p. 194.

60 "of kissing every Tom, Dick and Harry": Stephanie Coontz, *Marriage: A History* (New York: Viking, 2005), p. 200.

60 "Psychologists assert that sex": Silas Bent, *Ballyhoo: The Voice of the Press* (New York: Boni and Liveright, 1927), p. 21.

FIVE: MYRTLE'S BLUR

65 "You will leave me, will you?": *Kansas City Times*, October 16, 1929.

66 "Won't you give me your revolver?": *Kansas City Journal-Post*, September 30, 1929.

66 "I shot him. I went into mother's": *Kansas City Times*, February 28, 1931.

66 Hofman brought J. Francis O'Sullivan: *Kansas City Journal-Post*, September 30, 1929.

67 "He and mother were all I had": *Kansas City Times*, October 2, 1929.

68 "Perhaps from the tragedy": *Bridge World*, November 1929, p. 8.

68   "We shudder at the thought": Ibid., p. 64.

68   "Tragedies, comedies, and the broadest farce": *Bridge World*, December 1929, p. 52.

68   "This innocuous-looking deal": Ibid., p. 53.

69   Her nerves shot, Mayme required rest: *Kansas City Journal-Post*, October 2, 1929.

SIX: SENATOR REED COMES HOME

70   he preferred a hearty game of Red Dog: *Kansas City Star*, July 21, 1929.

70   JIM'S HOME, HURRAH: This scene of Senator Jim Reed's return at Union Station is drawn from coverage in the *Kansas City Star*, *Kansas City Journal-Post*, and *Kansas City Times* on March 9–10, 1929.

71   Reed's verbal assaults as "chemical": George Wharton Pepper, *Philadelphia Lawyer: An Autobiography* (Philadelphia: J. B. Lippincott Company, 1944), p. 149.

71   "We will vote on the resolution": *New York Times*, August 8, 1926.

72   "nature's law of love and life": "The Suffragrette Crusader," 1918 speech by Senator James A. Reed of Missouri, James A. Reed Papers, Western Historical Manuscript Collection, University of Missouri–Kansas City, KC443: Box 41.

72   "Now we find a petticoat brigade": Speech by Senator James A. Reed of Missouri in the Senate of the United States, Sixty-fifth Congress, Second Session, September 27, 1918, *Congressional Record*, James A. Reed Papers, Western Historical Manuscript Collection, University of Missouri–Kansas City, KC443: Box 41.

72   "Rid Us of Reed" clubs: Dixon Merritt, "James A. Reed—Fighter,"*Outlook*, vol. CXLVIII (March 21, 1928), p. 468.

72   "some of the leading 'political prohibitionists'": *Washington Star*, February 17, 1929.

72   "magnificent bellicosity": Paul V. Anderson, "Jim Reed: Himself," *North American Review* CCXXV (April 1928).

73   "Like [Daniel] Webster it is impossible": Oswald Garrison Villard, "James A. Reed," *Nation* CXXVI (March 28, 1928), p. 343.

73   requested his office to mail out 750,000 copies: *Kansas City Star*, February 27, 1929.

73   "the most monstrous doctrine ever": Jack M. Bain, "A Rhetorical Criticism

of the Speeches of James A. Reed," Ph.D. dissertation, University of Missouri, 1953, p. 98.

74 **"He may talk of retiring"**: *Kansas City Journal-Post*, March 3, 1929.

74 **Southern breakfast of hot corn bread, fried chicken**: *New York Telegram*, May 25, 1928.

74 **"I'm sure you are mistaken"**: *Kansas City Star*, September 29, 1929.

75 **"We thought of a tiny bit of a mouse"**: *Kansas City Star*, February 25, 1931.

75 **pronounced it, *Eye-oh-way***: James A. Reed speech on election night, November 1, 1940, United Broadcasting Company, James A Reed Papers, Western Historical Manuscript Collection, University of Missouri–Kansas City, 771 KC, Phonograph Recordings Accession 1236kc, Box 1, Folder 2A.

75 **Nancy cold, "vinegary"**: Bain, "A Rhetorical Criticism of the Speeches of James A. Reed," p. 10.

75 **townspeople came to hear the boy orator**: Ibid., p. 13.

75 **he ran for alderman (and lost)**: Ibid., p. 18.

76 **Reed would win all but two of his 287 cases**: Anderson, "Jim Reed: Himself."

76 **"It would hardly be possible for Mr. Reed"**: *Kansas City Star*, March 12, 1900.

76 **"There is no more compromise in Jim Reed"**: *Kansas City Star*, April 21, 1902.

76 **"We find him nearly always occupying"**: Anderson, "Jim Reed: Himself."

77 **"Dare we reject it"**: Margaret MacMillan, *Paris, 1919* (New York: Random House, 2003), p. 489.

77 **"So spoke the creator of this republic"**: Bain, "A Rhetorical Criticism of the Speeches of James A. Reed," p. 98.

77 **"The trouble with you gentlemen"**: Speech by Senator James A. Reed of Missouri about the League of Nations in the Senate of the United States, September 22, 1919, James A Reed Papers, Western Historical Manuscript Collection, University of Missouri–Kansas City, KC443. Box 41 (Speeches), Transcript, p. 40.

77 **"Not at all, sir. Let me puncture"**: Ibid., p. 43.

78 **with such force that the crutch broke in half**: Lee Meriwether, *Jim Reed, Senatorial Immortal: A Biography,* (Webster Groves, Mo.: International Mark Twain Society, 1948), p. 89.

78 the audience hissed in disapproval: *Kansas City Journal*, September 23, 1919; and *Kansas City Star*, September 22, 1919.

78 delivered forty speeches in three weeks: MacMillan, *Paris, 1919*, p. 491.

79 "I just feel as if I am going to pieces": Ibid.

79 "Doctor, the devil is a busy man": MacMillan, *Paris, 1919*, p. 492.

79 "It means this is the greatest day in American history": *New York Evening World*, March 21, 1928.

79 "marplot": *New York Times*, August 8, 1926.

80 crossover Republicans in St. Louis: *Kansas City Star*, November 8, 1922.

80 "Gentlemen, I appreciate the compliment": Undated newspaper review of the 1948 book *Jim Reed: Senatorial Immortal: A Biography*, by Lee Meriwether. James A. Reed Papers, Western Historical Manuscript Collection, University of Missouri–Kansas City, KC443, "Meriwether, Lee, 1920–1944," Box 13.

80 "[Reed] would laugh himself to death": *American Mercury* XVI (April 12, 1929).

80 an anachronistic and disquieting reminder: Ibid.

81 to collect the three remaining $10,000 policies: *Kansas City Star*, March 9, 1931.

SEVEN: ELY AND JO: STARS ON THE RISE

82 Adaptability is a basic law: Culbertson, *Contract Bridge Blue Book*, p. 241.

83 "Instead of carrying the person away": *New York Times*, November 24, 1935.

83 "Social talking presents far more risks": Robert S. Lynd and Helen Merrell Lynd, *Middletown in Transition* (New York: Harcourt Brace and Company, 1937), pp. 269–71.

84 "fraction infinitestimal": Lt. Col. Walter Buller, *Reflections of a Bridge Player* (London: Methuen and Co. Ltd., 1929), pp. 7–8.

84 a wife threw an alarm clock: *Bridge World*, June 1930, p. 26.

84 "Personally, I have always deplored": *Bridge World*, August 1930, p. 28.

84 "is a game in which superiority in play": Ibid., p. 4.

84 "Now and then a wife does throw": Maude Weatherly Beamish, "Clubs and Daggers," *Saturday Evening Post*, March 29, 1930, pp. 12, 83.

85 "If Germany and England and America": Ibid.

85 "Bridge players are usually suffering": *Bridge World*, April 1930, p. 3.

85 **"like his books, but half truth"**: Ibid.

86 **"Mr. Wilbur C. Whitehead describes himself"**: Buller, *Reflections of a Bridge Player*, p. 88.

87 **Each hand dealt in the first room would be reproduced**: *Manchester Guardian* (U.K.), September 13, 1930.

87 **"the first purely intellectual"**: *Bridge World*, June 1930, p. 42.

87 **"The overwhelming majority of America's"**: Ibid.

88 **Ely told Jo they would need $5,000**: Culbertson, *The Strange Lives of One Man*, p. 539.

88 **"Suppose you don't write it?"**: Ibid.

88 **in advance of regular trade channels**: *Bridge World*, May 1930, p. 3.

89 **" . . . And now to England!"**: *Bridge World*, August 1930, p. 9.

89 **"the absence of errors in their defensive play"**: *New York Times*, September 2, 1930.

89 **"When a team-of-four is defeated"**: *Bridge World*, September 1930, p. 14.

90 **"*To my wife and favorite*"**: Culbertson, *The Strange Lives of One Man*, p. 547.

90 **four Americans weighed a combined 520 pounds**: *London Evening Star*, September 12, 1930.

90 **"She is a very beautiful woman"**: *London Evening Star*, September 13, 1930.

90 **quiet voice and *miraculously* delicate hands**: *Bridge World*, November 1930, p. 9; reprinted from *London Evening Standard*.

91 **The Brits assumed a lead of 960 points**: *Manchester Guardian*, September 16, 1930.

91 **England leading by 595 points**: This number might look strange to the modern bridge player since nowadays all point totals are divisible by ten. In the time of the Culbertson-Buller match, though, a no trump trick contract was worth thirty-five points.

91 **the hand cost his team 1,400 points**: *London Star*, September 16, 1930; also *London Daily Telegraph*, September 27, 1930.

91 **"machine-guns were working with deadly"**: *Manchester Guardian*, September 18, 1930.

91 **"In the middle of this match"**: *London Evening Star*, September 22, 1930.

92 **would win "hands down"**: *London Evening Star*, September 29, 1930.

92 **"more informative, more certain and more exact"**: *Bridge World*, October 1930, pp. 9–10.

92   **"The matches at Almack's and Crockfords"**: *Bridge Magazine* (U.K.), V, no. 55 (November 1930), p. 259.

92   **"The New Best Seller of All Bridge Books"**: *Bridge World*, November 1930, p. 3.

93   **"Nowhere else in the modern"**: *New York World-Telegram*, January 8, 1932.

EIGHT: THE SENATOR AND MRS. DONNELLY

94   **he'd climb the back stairs to the master bedroom**: Peter Reed interview, Reed is a grandson of Jim Reed and Nell Donnelly.

95   **protect patent rights on the Handy-Dandy Apron**: *St. Louis Post-Dispatch*, December 15, 1933.

95   **Peck's Dry Goods Store in Kansas City sold**: Terence Michael O'Malley, *Nelly Don: A Stitch in Time* (Companion to the film *Nelly Don: A Stitch in Time*) (Kansas City, Mo.: The Covington Group, Inc., 2006), p. 2.

95   **a thousand workers, nearly all women, and producing five thousand**: Ibid., p. 30.

95   **"Honestly, I would be happier here"**: *Kansas City Post*, November 10, 1910.

95   **"The game is not worth the candle"**: Ibid.

95   **"People often express surprise"**: *Nelly Don: A Stitch in Time,* documentary film of ninety-four minutes, by Terence Michael O'Malley. (Kansas City, Mo.: O'Malley Preferred Media Production, 2006). The "national magazine" quoting Nell Donnelly is not named in the documentary.

96   **Paul Donnelly once threw an ashtray**: O'Malley, *Nelly Don,* p. 50.

96   **he tried to sweat out his late-night carousing**: Peter Reed interview.

96   **she dropped thirty of Paul's guns**: Terence Michael O'Malley interview.

96   **the twelfth child in the family**: *Kansas City Star Magazine*, May 24, 1987.

96   **domestic science at Lindenwood**: *St. Louis Post-Dispatch*, December 15, 1933.

97   **to find Paul sharing intimacies**: Peter Reed interview.

97   **wrong for this woman to be wearing *her* pajamas**: Ibid.

97   **"The dresses are a little shorter"**: James A Reed, "The Pestilence of Fanaticism," American Mercury V, no. 17 (May 1925), p 5.

97   **"That was *before* I met you, Nell"**: Terence Michael O'Malley and Peter Reed interviews.

97   **she no longer was interested in having sex**: Peter Reed interview.

97   **senator told all of this to Roberts**: Ibid.

98   **"if Nelson ever supported James A. Reed"**: Bain, "A Rhetorical Criticism of the Speeches of James A. Reed," p. 156.

98   **"Down at Eleventh and Grand"**: Ibid., p. 134.

98   **he gave speeches in thirteen states**: Ibid., p. 193.

98   **"Throw the rascals out!"**: *St. Louis Post-Dispatch*, June 29, 1928.

98   **making a $1,000 contribution**: O'Malley, *Nelly Don,* p. 39.

99   **senator's standing order to his secretary**: Peter Reed interview.

NINE: MYRTLE'S MURDER TRIAL, PART 1

The trial coverage in the three Kansas City dailies was voluminous with extensive excerpts drawn from transcripts of testimony. In Notes for this chapter and chapters 11 and 13, I cite only sources other than direct trial coverage of the Kansas City newspapers.

101   **"Comrades, don't starve—FIGHT!"**: *Kansas City Star,* February 10, 1931.

101   **"He defied the criminal code"**: *Kansas City Star,* February 22, 1931.

101   **Kansas City as the center of far-reaching**: *Kansas City Star*, February 21, 1931.

101   **"You're a'gin everything—the Bible"**: *Kansas City Star*, March 1, 1931.

102   **"The situation is so terrible"**: Gabler, *Winchell*, p. 108.

102   **to make order out of chaos in that person's life**: Peter Reed interview.

103   **had poured $750,000 into Reed's pockets**: *New York Times*, January 8, 1931.

103   **borrowed heavily and lost nearly everything**: Peter Reed interview.

103   **Reed was contesting his fee from the Universal**: *Kansas City Star*, March 26, 1931.

103   **"Mrs. Waterstradt just insisted"**: *Kansas City Star*, February 22, 1931.

103   **Ely Culbertson, now world champion"**: *Kansas City Star*, February 21, 1931.

104   **"a man who loves fairness as the sun"**: A. E. Montgomery, ed., *Great Speeches by Famous Lawyers of Southwest U.S.A.* (Tulsa, Okla.: Southwest Publishing Company, Inc., 1961), p. 49.

104   **"I am asking, gentlemen"**: Ibid., p. 71.

106   **including Missouri, still categorically excluded women**: Joanna L. Grossman, "Women's Jury Service: Right of Citizenship or Privilege of Difference?" *Stanford Law Review* 46, no. 5 (May 1994): 1136–37.

107   **murder a libertine who had had sex with his wife**: Jeffrey S. Adler, "'I

Loved Joe, But I Had to Shoot Him': Homicide by Women in Turn-of-the-Century Chicago," *Journal of Criminal Law and Criminology* (Northwestern University School of Law) 92, nos. 3–4(2003): 882.

107 **"I look upon my act as a morally"**: Ibid., p. 881.

107 **"to join the great army of boob"**: Ibid., p. 883.

108 **"I suppose if I had been young"**: Ibid., p. 885.

108 **would never marry an Irishwoman**: Peter Reed interview. Nell Donnelly told this story to her grandson during a conversation in the 1970s.

109 **emigrated from County Cork, Ireland**: O'Malley, *Nelly Don*, p. 26.

109 **would have to wait for Lura to die**: Peter Reed interview.

110 **"I have never tried to appeal"**: Montgomery, *Great Speeches by Famous Lawyers of Southwest U.S.A.*, p. 70.

TEN: ELY IN THE CRUCIBLE

120 **Hard Times and Bridge**: *Bridge World*, January 1931, p. 28.

120 **write weekly letters to their parents**: *New York Times*, February 13, 1933.

120 **He decided his son would become a scientist**: Culbertson, *The Strange Lives of One Man*, pp. 515–16.

121 **He preferred frozen meats, four**: *New York Daily News*, November 17, 1931.

121 **On radio, the United States Playing**: *Bridge World*, October 1929, p. 34.

121 **Goldwyn, Irving Thalberg, and Louis B. Mayer**: McPherson, *The Backwash Squeeze and Other Improbable Feats*, p. 102.

121 **"That's the only time this afternoon"**: Clay, *Culbertson*, p. 140.

121 **Lou Gehrig regularly partnered with sports columnist Rice**: Charles Fountain, *Sportswriter: The Life and Times of Grantland Rice* (New York: Oxford University Press, 1993), pp. 238, 258.

121 **"kneaded, rough thumbed"**: Paul Gallico, *Farewell to Sport* (New York: Alfred A. Knopf, 1938), p. 32.

122 **"So long, kid"**: Jerome Holtzman, *No Cheering in the Press Box* (New York: Holt, Rinehart and Winston, 1973), p. 105.

122 **"than on any other activity except"**: Shepard Barclay, "Contract Bridge," *Saturday Evening Post*, April 26, 1930, p. 60.

122 **"Ladies and gentlemen, I am sorry"**: *Bridge World*, April 1931, p. 21.

122 **"I'm half Russian and entirely American"**: *Bridge World*, June 1931, p. 15.

122 **748 were women**: *Boston Evening Transcript*, April 1, 1931.

123 **Nearly 3,000 showed up for Ely's lecture in Oakland**: Clay, *Culbertson*, p. 142.

124 "His bid was one spade": *Bridge World*, June 1931, pp. 14–15.

124 "We have heard of lives depending on the play": *Bridge World*, April 1931, p. 7.

125 refused to be photographed with a pretty woman: *San Francisco Call-Bulletin*, April 24, 1931.

125 "I'd be president by an electoral grand slam": *San Francisco Chronicle*, April 22, 1931.

125 "women trust less to intuition": Ibid.

125 "I'm all for bridge fights": *Bridge World*, June 1931, p. 15.

125 "Had Husband Been Good Player": *San Francisco Call-Bulletin*, April 24, 1931.

125 "All married people": *San Francisco Chronicle*, April 22, 1931.

126 His maid found him there, slumped: These details of Elwell's lifestyle, and of his killing, are drawn from coverage in *The New York Times*, *New York Sun*, *New York American*, and *New York Herald*, from June 12, 1920, through July 12, 1920.

126 "I live in a strictly rural": E. B. White, *One Man's Meat* (New York: Harper and Row, 1944), p. 51. This quote is drawn from White's story "Sabbath Morn."

127 German air raids on Paris were so amateurish: Culbertson, *The Strange Lives of One Man*, p. 333.

127 his twenty francs had grown to more than twenty thousand: Freeman, "Culbertson: Soldier of Fortune," *Outlook*, December 9, 1931, p. 461.

127 "He had the gray matter": *New York Sun*, December 17, 1931.

127 each teacher spending sixty dollars for three days: Beatty, "What Is Your Wife Worth to You?" *American Magazine*, October 1931, p. 134.

128 "sensational and universal success": *Bridge World*, May 1931, p. 27.

128 "at the unheard of rate" of four thousand copies: Ibid., p. 16.

128 "This new [Culbertson] Contract system has splashes: *Bridge World*, May 1931, p. 16.

128 "to preserve the game of contract bridge": *Bridge World*, July 1931, p. 18.

129 "Elder Statesmen and Minor Luminaries": Ibid., p. 13.

129 "This will be Mr. Lenz's system No. 5": Ibid.

129 wager $5,000 against $1,000: *New York Times*, June 24, 1931.

130 "If we can pull down Lenz": Culbertson, *The Strange Lives of One Man*, p. 587.

130 "ephemeral little bridge gods": Ibid., p. 585.

130 "good until the cows come home": *New York World-Telegram*, June 25, 1931.

130 "My lady listeners": Ibid., p. 22.

131 Ely reportedly was earning $200,000: "The Bonaparte of the Bridge War," *Literary Digest*, October 17, 1931, pp. 30–31; also *New York Daily News*, November 17, 1931, *New York Sun*, September 24, 1931.

132 "An irreparable loss to bridge": *Bridge World*, July 1931, p. 8.

132 Mr. or Mrs. Ely Culbertson challenge: Ibid., p. 1.

133 "Our reaction to the combination": Ibid., p. 4.

133 "And if Mr. Culbertson means business": *New York Sun*, July 10, 1931.

ELEVEN: MYRTLE'S MURDER TRIAL, PART 2

134 wonderful city, he said, with lovely Spanish: *Kansas City Times*, March 3, 1931.

134 "What a sober town": Ibid.

136 Darrow spoke to the press every bit as much: Richard J. Jensen, *Clarence Darrow: The Creation of an American Myth* (Westport, Conn.: Greenwood Press, 1992), p. 24.

136 They were often edited *after* he'd delivered them: Ibid.

137 denigrated Sapiro, and consistently mispronounced: Watts, *The People's Tycoon*, pp. 393–94.

147 "his courageous, forceful and honest stand": *Kansas City Star*, March 20, 1919.

TWELVE: BRIDGE BATTLE OF THE CENTURY

155 The practical attitude toward all: Culbertson, *Contract Bridge Blue Book*, pp. 261–62.

155 "Their so-called system": *New York Times*, September 18, 1931.

155 Ely taught a weekly bridge class: Beatty, "What Is Your Wife Worth?" *American Magazine*, October 1931, pp. 136–37; also Culbertson, *The Strange Lives of One Man*, pp. 579–80.

156 "a youngish David": Ibid.

156 "He's grand!": Beatty, "What Is Your Wife Worth?" *American Magazine*, October 1931, p. 27.

156 He once was offered $1,000: *Bridge World*, November 1931, p. 29.

156 traveled to India to study magic and Hindu: Ibid., also *Bridge World*, March 1932, p. 27.

157 "lays down all the conditions": *New York Times*, October 15, 1931.

158 "Whom will I choose as my partner?": *Bridge World*, November 1931, p. 6.

158 "A Culbertson Christmas": *Publishers Weekly*, November 14, 1931, p. 2203.

158 ABSOLUTE SILENCE: *New York Herald-Tribune*, December 8, 1931; also *Chicago Tribune*, January 9, 1932.

159 Americans would spend an estimated $100 million: "A foursome for bridge," *Vanity Fair*, March 1932, p. 38.

159 "The Greatest Peep Show in History": Clay, *Culbertson*, p. 125.

159 a "crack reporter": H. Allen Smith, "Culbertson's Coup," *Sports Illustrated*, December 20, 1954, p. 62.

159 "Who's pickin' up the tab?" Ibid.

160 More than two million words (by Ely's count): Culbertson, *The Strange Lives of One Man*, p. 601.

160 "the most amazing card battle in history": *New York World-Telegram*, December 7, 1931.

160 "the contract championship of the world": *New York Sun*, December 5, 1931.

160 Goldman Sachs stock plummeting from $121: Grantland Rice, *The Tumult and the Shouting: My Life in Sport* (New York: A. S. Barnes and Company, 1954), p. 309.

160 "So, if there were room enough": *Atlanta Constitution*, December 8, 1931.

161 luck would not equalize itself: *Bridge Magazine* 1, no. 4, January 1932, p. 4.

161 "now I know why it's called the Battle": *Brooklyn Daily Eagle*, December 8, 1931.

161 President Dwight Eisenhower's partner: *Time*, September 29, 1958.

161 "Gentlemen of the press!": *Sacramento Bee*, December 8, 1931.

162 He contracted for game at no trump: *New York Herald-Tribune*, December 8, 1931.

162 "I'm sorry, Jo": December 8, 1931, *New York World-Telegram;* also William Ashby, *SLAM! A Ga-Ga History of the Culbertson-Lenz Bridge War* (New York: The Bridge World, 1932), p. 25.

162 to the nearest bellhop, who told the elevator boy: *Atlanta Constitution*, December 10, 1931.

162 Lenz-Jacoby led by 1,715 points: This number might look strange to the modern bridge player since nowadays all point totals are divisible by 10. In the time of the Bridge Battle of the Century, though, a no trump contract was worth 35 points per trick.

162 "According to the diffident Mr. Culbertson": *New York Times*, December 8, 1931.

162 players named "Reno," Mike Cohen, Artie Adelman: *New York American*, December 24, 1931.

163 in an auditorium with an electronic scoreboard: *New York Sun*, December 19, 1931.

163 I wish you'd have been there: *Sacramento Bee*, December 8, 1931.

164 "Mr. Culbertson is by far and away": *Atlanta Constitution*, December 10, 1931.

164 "My God, Ely, you're getting grease": *Sports Illustrated*, December 20, 1954. p. 63.

164 "My vast public won't let me": Ibid.

164 "Ely, that's getting awfully monotonous": *New York Times*, December 12, 1931.

164 He hung a large wishbone: *Atlanta Constitution*, December 11, 1931.

165 He also offered to autograph it: *New York Times*, December 12, 1931.

165 "He's been sitting there for 10": *New York Sun*, December 11, 1931.

165 "It's just like letting out a yell": Ibid.

165 "Hamlet required a shorter interval": *New York World-Telegram*, December 12, 1931.

165 "we have the reformed Culbertsonians": Ibid.

165 "Now I am prepared to acquit": *New York World-Telegram*, December 19, 1931.

166 "neither side has yet demonstrated": *New York Times*, December 14, 1931.

166 "I always lead this way for no trump": *New York Sun*, December 15, 1931.

166 "an express-train and a hansom cab": *Bridge World*, February 1932, p. 15.

166 youngest ever to pass the Society of Actuaries: J. Patrick Dunne and Albert A. Ostrow, *Championship Bridge: As Played by the Experts* (New York: McGraw-Hill Book Company, Inc., 1949), p. 61.

166 "Darling, you are wonderful": *St. Louis Post-Dispatch*, December 15, 1931.

167 "At the conventional suburban": *New York World-Telegram*, December 16, 1931.

167 "She seems detached": *New York Sun*, December 17, 1931.

167 "If Lightner smiles, is it a signal?" *New York Times*, December 18, 1931.

168 "one of the most grotesque hands": Ely Culbertson, analyst, with Josephine Culbertson, Theodore A. Lightner, and Waldermar von Zedtwitz, *Famous Hands of the Culbertson-Lenz Match* (New York: The Bridge World, 1932), p. 355.

168 "Ozzie promised me faithfully": *New York World-Telegram*, December 18, 1931.

168 "Another session like tonight's": *New York Times*, December 18, 1931.

168 "The whole thing is a publicity stunt": Ibid.

168 "I believe I may safely allow": *New York Times*, December 19, 1931.

169 "Baron, you played a perfect game": *Atlanta Constitution*, December 23, 1931.

169 "Why don't you read my *Blue Book?*": *New York Times*, December 22, 1931.

169 "I haven't!": Ibid.

169 sixty white men lynched two black men: *New York Times*, December 11, 1931.

169 "the fires of suffering": *New York Times*, January 4, 1932.

169 "the right of the individual": *New York Times*, January 7, 1932.

169 The Chicago Crime Commission declared: *New York Times*, December 21, 1931.

169 Adolf Hitler promised a day of reckoning: *New York Times*, December 17, 1931.

169 "Who does he think he is?": *New York World-Telegram*, December 4, 1931.

170 John "Legs" Diamond was shot to death: *New York Herald-Tribune*, December 18, 1931.

170 suffered head injuries and two broken ribs: William Manchester, *The Last Lion: Visions of Glory, 1874–1932* (New York: Dell Publishing, Co., Inc. 1984), pp. 878–80; also *New York Times*, December 21, 1931. The accident occurred on December 13, 1931.

170 "Germany has declared war against Russia": Manchester, *The Last Lion*, p. 472.

170 Mrs. Marshall Field III, Mrs. Vincent Astor: *Bridge World*, February 1932. p. 12.

170 "You're going down with flying colors": *Brooklyn Daily Eagle*, December 23, 1931.

170 "Why do you make these rotten bids?": *New York Times*, December 29, 1931.

171 "Well—well, sir, well, sir": *New York Sun*, December 29, 1931.

171 "I was criticized merely to cover": *New York Herald-Tribune*, December 29, 1931.

171 Lenz had believed, incorrectly, that Liggett preferred: *Brooklyn Eagle*, January 9, 1932.

172 **"Looking at you, how can I?"**: *Atlanta Constitution*, January 9, 1932.

172 **"Looks like I'm the goat"**: Ibid.

172 **Ely's side held 1,745 aces**: *Atlanta Constitution*, January 9, 1932.

172 **"that Lenz is just as apt to bid"**: "The Revolt Against Bridge Systems and Ballyhoo," *Literary Digest*, January 2, 1932, p. 32.

173 **Ely "is to contract what John D. Rockefeller"**: Ibid.

173 **"More citizens than ever are now talking"**: *Brooklyn Eagle*, January 11, 1932.

173 **"No such excitement has been felt"**: Uncle Henry, "Sound the Trump," *Collier's*, February 6, 1932, p. 16.

173 **"It has been stated several times"**: *Bridge World*, February 1932, p. 19.

174 **"To women the most satisfying feature"**: Ibid.

THIRTEEN: MYRTLE'S MURDER TRIAL, PART 3

179 **"Queen of the West and Southwest"**: Letter written in 1901 from Kansas City mayor James A. Reed to the Kansas City mayor in the year 2001, James A. Reed Papers, Western Historical Manuscript Collection, University of Missouri–Kansas City, KC443: Box 43.

179 **"In 2001 you may have greater concourse"**: Ibid.

189 VERDICT IN BENNETT CASE: Western Union telegram from James A. Reed to his wife, Lura Reed, March 6, 1931, James A. Reed Papers, Western Historical Manuscript Collection, University of Missouri, Kansas City, KC443: Box 3.

FOURTEEN: MIAMI

193 **"Why go to Arkansas"**: *Kansas City Star*, March 13, 1931.

193 **"The senator should have snapped"**: Ibid.

194 **"has deliberately obstructed the introduction"**: *Kansas City Star*, March 9, 1931.

194 **"Some people are preordained"**: Ibid.

194 **"It was representative of a good many"**: *Kansas City Times*, March 7, 1931.

194 **Hickok held two pair, aces and eights**: Joseph C. Rosa, *Wild Bill Hickok: The Man and His Myth* (Lawrence: University Press of Kansas, 1996), pp. 193–95.

194 **shot through the stomach with a Colt .38**: Nick Tosches, *King of the Jews* (New York: HarperCollins Publishers, 2005), pp. 142–50, 316.

195 **"four shots heard round the world"**: Alexander Woollcott, *While Rome Burns* (New York: The Viking Press, 1934), pp. 191–96. Woollcott's 1931 story originally appeared in *The New Yorker*.

195 "There was probably not a literate": Ibid.

195 "I'm afraid you'll want to shoot me for this": Ibid.

195 Myrtle settled out of court: *Kansas City Star*, July 6, 1931; July 7, 1931.

195 7 men were hanged and 3,088 were sentenced: *Kansas City Star*, November 21, 1934.

195 "ran around on his wife for years": *Kansas City Star*, March 18, 1993.

196 "There can be no more terrible accidents": Peter Reed interview.

196 "He was such a gentleman": Interview with Becky Rice Stanley. A granddaughter of Annie Rice, Stanley lives in Carmi, Illinois. I had placed a notice about my book project in the Carmi newspaper, seeking to interview any remaining members of Jack Bennett's extended family. Ms. Stanley contacted me after reading that notice.

196 "Can you imagine someone": Ibid.

196 I searched online for "Myrtle A. Bennett": Number 489-07-3621; Issue state Missouri; Issue date: Before 1951. Social Security Administration, Social Security Death Index, Master File, Social Security Administration.

196 I located Myrtle in the 1930 Census: Year: 1930; Census Place: Kansas City, Jackson, Missouri; Roll: 1196; Page: 29A; Enumeration District: 111. United States of America, Bureau of the Census, Fifteenth Census of the United States, 1930, Washington, D.C.: National Archives and Records Administration, 1930, T626, 2,667 rolls.

196 a remarkable finding: a will for "Myrtle A. Bennett": Myrtle A. Bennett, signed December 3, 1991, filed January 22, 1992, case number 1992-338-CP-02, 11th Judicial Circuit Court, Dade County, Fla.

197 died at her apartment at 5:27 A.M.: Myrtle A. Bennett, Certificate of Death, January 21, 1992, Local File No. 001011, Office of Vital Statistics, Florida Department of Health.

197 distribute an estimated $850,000: Myrtle A. Bennett, signed December 3, 1991, filed January 22, 1992, case number 1992-338-CP-02, 11th Judicial Circuit Court, Dade County, Fla., Petition for Administration.

198 "She was a fascinating woman": William Armshaw interview.

198 "one of the most domineering women": Ibid.

198 "Did someone die?" Ibid.

FIFTEEN: KANSAS CITY

201 designed by John Browning, weighed just twenty-three: Garry James, "Colt Model M Pocket Auto," *Guns and Ammo*, January 2002, pp. 46–48;

also Colt Automatic Pistol, Pocket Model, Calibers .32 and .380 Hammerless Owner's Manual, Colt's Patent Fire Arms Manufacturing, Co., Hartford, Conn., 2001.

201 **"Equipped with safety features"**: Advertisement on the inside of the manufacturer's box of the Colt Model 1903 Hammerless .32 Pocket Automatic, Courtesy of Alan Henry, owner of Marin Firearms, Novato, Calif.

201 **"Abe Lincoln may have freed all men"**: Kathleen Hoyt interview; Hoyt, a Colt company historian and archivist, believes this phrase first circulated during, or perhaps soon after, the Civil War.

204 **"The Secrets of Nelly Don"**: *Kansas City Star Magazine*, May 7, 2006.

205 **husband, Paul, telling him to get $75,000**: *Kansas City Journal-Post*, December 17, 1931.

205 **"I will say this, if a single hair"**: *Kansas City Star*, December 17, 1931.

205 **That was a ruse. She returned from Europe**: Terence Michael O'Malley and Peter Reed interviews.

206 **Reed presented Lazia an ultimatum**: O'Malley, *Nelly Don*, pp. 52–53.

206 **found Nell and her chauffeur walking**: *Kansas City Star*, December 18, 1931.

206 **"You go and sit down"**: William Reddig, *Tom's Town: Kansas City and the Pendergast Legend* (Columbia: University of Missouri Press, 1986), pp. 212–13.

207 **"crushed by the sudden loss"**: *Kansas City Star*, October 12, 1932.

207 **"Heartfelt sympathy from your old friend"**: *Kansas City Times*, October 13, 1932.

207 **Thirty-four days later Nell filed for divorce**: *Kansas City Times*, December 14, 1933.

207 **She purchased Paul's half-interest**: O'Malley, *Nelly Don*, p. 61.

207 **"Wonder if there is anything to the buzz"**: *Minneapolis Tribune*, November 27, 1932, James A. Reed Papers, Western Historical Manuscript Collection, University of Missouri, Kansas City, 771KC: Box 4.

207 **"You may think what you said was witty"**: Letter from James A. Reed to Walter Winchell, December 28, 1932, James A. Reed Papers, Western Historical Manuscript Collection, University of Missouri–Kansas City, 771KC: Box 4.

207 **The Walnuts, she and the Senator married**: *Kansas City Times*, December 14, 1933.

207 **placed metal bars on the second-story**: Peter Reed interview.

208 **he hanged himself**: O'Malley, *Nelly Don*, p. 61.

208 **"If Mr. Reed gets smart"**: Letter from U.S. senator Harry S. Truman to his wife, Bess, July 4, 1935, Robert H. Ferrell, ed., *Dear Bess: The Letters from Harry to Bess Truman, 1910–1959* (New York: W.W. Norton and Company, 1983), p. 368.

208 **"I am happy you find my logic infallible"**: Letter from U.S. senator Harry S. Truman to James A Reed, May 20, 1937, James A. Reed Papers, Western Historical Manuscript Collection, University of Missouri–Kansas City, KC443: Box 13.

208 **"There's Reed. Don't you want"**: Ferrell, ed., *Dear Bess: The Letters from Harry to Bess Truman*, p. 491.

208 **"the old so-and-so"**: Ibid.

209 **had promised Nell not to disclose the story**: Peter Reed interview.

209 **"They were drunk as skunks"**: Ibid.

210 **"We expected them to figure it out"**: Ibid.

210 **"There were some things"**: Ibid.

SIXTEEN: NEW YORK

211 **"Mrs. Bennett was so good-lookin'"**: Michael O'Connell interview.

212 **touting "pleasant working conditions"**: These advertisements for The Carlyle ran intermittently in *The New York Times* from September 1945 through July 1955.

212 **"Well, I'll give them a hell of a walk"**: Michael O'Connell interview.

212 **leaving for dinner with film stars Mary Pickford**: Ibid.

214 **the bookcase swung backward, revealing**: "Seven Keys to Culbertson," *The New Yorker*, April 27, 1940, pp. 16–17; also *Philadelphia Inquirer*, February 5, 1939.

215 **Chesterfield distributed free booklets**: Clay, *Culbertson*, p. 137.

215 **RKO Pictures paid him $270,000**: Ibid., p. 141.

215 **Ely appears as an expert witness**: *Variety*, October 24, 1933.

215 **Ely fired scenario writers, directors**: *New York Sun*, October 24, 1933.

216 **"Success in life"**: *New York Times*, July 14, 1933.

216 **"The greatest showman in the bridge"**: *Bridge Forum*, February 1933.

216 **filling it with Flemish tapestries**: Clay, *Culbertson*, p. 147.

216 **In 1932, though, outpaced novelist Pearl Buck**: *New York Times*, January 17, 1933.

216 **Ely and Jo paid $125,000**: Clay, *Culbertson*, pp. 173–74.

217 **spent $5,000 on pajamas, ties**: Alfred Sheinwold interview by author John Clay, as research for Clay's 1985 biography, *Culbertson*. Courtesy of John Clay.

217 "Then how about a raise to thirty-five dollars": Ibid.

217 Hal, Dorothy and Duke, their Great Dane, wore: Clay, *Culbertson*, p. 181.

217 "How many times have I told you *not*": Ibid., p. 183.

217 he fed them during storms, forced them to sleep: Ibid., p. 190.

218 boasted to magazine staffer Sam Fry about sex: Ibid., p. 193.

218 "The end of a bridge romance": *New York Times*, December 1, 1937.

218 "This is not a case of 'another woman'": Ibid.

219 in the Ridgefield mansion and dictated: *New Yorker*, April 27, 1940, p. 17.

220 "Good-by, Illiusha": Culbertson, *The Strange Lives of One Man*, p. 223.

220 consumed oysters and snails, tripe à la mode de Caen: Ibid., p. 344.

220 "We looked upon women not as mates": Ibid., p. 345.

221 "It's a good book *of fiction*": Alfred Sheinwold interview by author John Clay, as research for Clay's 1985 biography, *Culbertson*. Courtesy of John Clay.

221 "It seems, indeed, that [Culbertson] has done": *New York Times*, April 9, 1940.

221 Ely "has managed in 48 crowded years": *New York World-Telegram*, April 10, 1940.

221 "It was your fault": Culbertson, *The Strange Lives of One Man*, p. 656.

222 "Your Highness, ladies and gentlemen": Ibid. This scene is drawn from Culbertson's description on pages 656–59.

223 in 1921 on the SS *Brookline*: Microfilm roll T715 3019, page 72, line 16, Passenger and Crew Lists of Vessels Arriving at New York, N.Y., 1897–1957 (National Archives Microfilm Publication T715, 8892 rolls), Records of the Immigration and Naturalization Service, National Archives, Washington, D.C.

223 he merely audited courses and opted out: This information was provided by Dominique Anne Torrione-Vouilloz of Archives de l'Université (at the University of Geneva) in e-mail correspondence in October 2007.

223 by glorious luck it grew to 20,000: Andrew A. Freeman, "Culbertson: Soldier of Fortune," *Outlook*, December 9, 1931, p. 461.

223 winnings that day grew to 40,960 francs: Culbertson, *The Strange Lives of One Man*, pp. 359–60.

223 Expenses at Ridgefield caused him to give up: Clay, *Culbertson*, p. 173.

224 Goren had accepted Ely's open challenge: Jack Olsen, "King of the Aces," *Time*, September 29, 1958.

224 contract bridge was played in 44 percent of American: David Owen, "Turning Tricks," *The New Yorker*, September 17, 2007, pp. 91–93.

224 **Lucy, Mary G., Adelaide, Mag, and Linda . . . to share a bridge**: *Kansas City Star*, April 10, 1946.

224 **He subdivided the globe into eleven federations**: Ely Culbertson, *Total Peace: What Makes Wars and How to Organize Peace* (Garden City, N.Y.: Doubleday, Doran and Company, Inc., 1943), pp. 239–54.

224 **"I succeeded much too well"**: Ibid., p. 9.

224 **He mailed five copies of *Total Peace* to President**: Telegram from Ely Culbertson to White House Secretary Charles Ross, May 25, 1945, Harry S. Truman Library, Independence, Mo., Papers of Harry S. Truman, General File (Cuc-Cullen, C.), Box no. 539.

224 **"Though Native American"**: Ibid.

225 **he appeared before the Senate Foreign Relations**: Clay, *Culbertson*, pp. 216–17.

225 **Spending more than $400,000 (his estimate)**: Ibid., p. 218.

225 **poor health and sadness**: Madeleine Kerwin, "Jo Culbertson, My Friend," *Bridge World*, April 1956, p. 6.

226 **"Have I caught this?"**: Alex Marvin interview.

226 **"He fits all the clinical criteria"**: Ibid.

226 **"a man of great intellect"**: Letter from James L. Oakes, attorney for Dorothy Culbertson, to attorney Frederick V. D. Rogers, March 17, 1954, personal files of Alex Marvin.

226 **"an alcoholic and sometime resident of mental"**: Ibid.

227 **"Is it another man?"**: Letter from Ely Culbertson to his wife, Dorothy Culbertson, April 2, 1954, personal files of Alex Marvin.

227 **I, your Galatea, have thought, despaired**: Letter from Dorothy Culbertson to her husband, Ely Culbertson, March 29, 1954, personal files of Alex Marvin.

227 **"Your demand was a thunder clap"**: Ibid.

227 **You are married to a man who holds the key**: Ibid.

228 **"Normal people don't speak about wives"**: Alex Marvin interview.

228 **"big-game hunting of unusual"**: Ely Culbertson, *Elys, in Corpore: An Autobiography (Years 1938–1954)*, American Contract Bridge League Library, Memphis, Tenn., permission to cite granted by Alex Marvin, Ely Culbertson's son, p. 71-1.

228 **became pregnant by him**: she had set him up: Ibid., pp. 119-1–133-1.

229 **"Maybe the above description is too good"**: Ibid., p. 45-1.

229 **"I have a lot of anger"**: Steve Culbertson interview.

229 **"elegant, noble, cool, reserved, aloof"**: Ibid.

SEVENTEEN: SAN FRANCISCO

230 **Gallup poll in 1947 named bridge**: *New York Times*, December 28, 1947.

230 **A 2005 ACBL survey suggested that 25 million**: Brent Manley interview; also McPherson, *The Backwash Squeeze and Other Improbable Feats*, p. 12.

231 **Buffett and Bill Gates, who jointly fund**: *New York Times*, November 27, 2005.

232 **"My feminist sensibilities"**: Roselyn Teukolsky, *How to Play Bridge with Your Spouse . . . And Survive!* (Toronto: Master Point Press, 2002), p. 55.

232 **"I actually feel like I am loaded"**: Frank Bessing interview.

233 **"When there is a conflict at the bridge table"**: Ibid.

EIGHTEEN: LITTLE ROCK

235 **"I really loved Auntie Mame"**: Carolyn Scruggs interview.

236 **"The taxi driver may *not* drive"**: Ibid.

236 **"Jack Bennett really did Myrtle wrong"**: Al Ebert interview.

236 **"Mother, there's something about Auntie Mame"**: Carolyn Scruggs interview.

237 **"Well, babe, it looks like"**: Ibid.

237 **"Well, Auntie Mame's my kissin' cousin"**: Ibid.

238 **"July 11—Under the Dryer"**: Letter from Myrtle A. Bennett to Ada Mae and Eddie Simpson, undated, from the personal files of their son, LeRoy Simpson.

238 **"Eddie, you can take this car"**: Walter Simpson interview.

238 **made them miserable in their own home**: LeRoy Simpson and LaVerne Simpson Mitchell interviews.

239 **"Don't sign a thing"**: William Armshaw interview.

239 **"She's here"**: Ibid.

239 **She took Mary and Walter to a duplicate**: Walter Jacobs interview.

239 **She removed Eddie and Ada Mae Simpson**: Myrtle A. Bennett, signed December 3, 1991, filed January 22, 1992, case number 1992-338-CP-02, 11th Judicial Circuit Court, Dade County, Fla.; also Carolyn Scruggs provided copies of two earlier wills signed by Myrtle Bennett, one dated September 5, 1986, the other August 16, 1990.

239 **"Just leave it here"**: Henrietta Biscoe and Carolyn Scruggs interviews. Biscoe was Myrtle Bennett's attorney at the time.

240 **"Get me a new lawyer"**: William Armshaw interview.

240 **she added her caretaker**: Myrtle A. Bennett, signed December 3, 1991, filed January 22, 1992, case number 1992-338-CP-02, 11th Judicial Circuit Court, Dade County, Fla.

NINETEEN: SANTA ROSA, CALIFORNIA

241 **emergency contact posted on Myrtle's refrigerator**: Carolyn Scruggs interview.

241 **Jacobs's phone call was more mercenary than familial**: William Armshaw interview.

241 **"didn't talk about Myrtle, she talked about the money"**: Ibid.

241 **Myrtle's estate was valued at $1,062,144**: Courtesy of a lawyer for the Bennett estate who asked not to be identified.

242 **reimbursed for burial costs—$276.13**: Letter to Eddie Simpson from the estate of Myrtle A. Bennett, February 21, 1992, personal files of LeRoy Simpson.

242 **"I'm so happy and thankful to you"**: Letter from Marion Randall to Ada Mae Simpson, February 20, 1992, from the personal files of their son, LeRoy Simpson.

242 **"Moderately close"**: Walter Jacobs interview.

243 **"Why are you giving all this money"**: William Armshaw interview.

243 **"And Myrtle felt Mrs. Jacobs"**: Ibid.

243 **He said he knew nothing about Myrtle's trial**: Walter Jacobs interview.

243 **"I can't think of any other reason"**: William Armshaw interview.

243 **"She still loved him"**: Carolyn Scruggs interview.

244 **"Maybe you should sue them"**: Ibid.

244 **"Well, my dear, it was a great tragedy"**: Ibid.

245 **"I haven't seen Myrtle since 1924!"**: Ibid.

BIBLIOGRAPHY

Allen, Frederick Lewis. *Only Yesterday: An Informal History of the 1920s*. New York: Harper and Row Publishers, 1931.

Ashby, William. *SLAM! A Ga-Ga History of the Culbertson-Lenz Bridge War*. New York: The Bridge World, 1932.

Barton, Bruce. *The Man Nobody Knows*. New York: Bobbs-Merrill Company, 1925.

Bent, Silas. *Ballyhoo: The Voice of the Press*. New York: Boni and Liveright, 1927.

Berg, A. Scott. *Lindbergh*. New York: Berkley Books, 1999.

Bruccoli, Matthew J., ed. *The Short Stories of F. Scott Fitzgerald*. New York: Scribner, 1989.

Buller, Lt. Col. Walter. *Reflections of a Bridge Player*. London: Methuen and Co. Ltd., 1929.

Carey, Gary. *Anita Loos: A Biography*. New York: Alfred A. Knopf, 1988.

Caro, Robert. *Master of the Senate: The Years of Lyndon Johnson*. New York: Alfred A. Knopf, 2002.

Cavanaugh, Jack. *Tunney: Boxing's Brainiest Champ and His Upset of the Great Jack Dempsey*. New York: Random House, 2006.

Clay, John. *Culbertson: The Man Who Made Contract Bridge*. London: Weidenfeld and Nicolson, 1985.

Coleman, Richard P. *The Kansas City Establishment: Leadership Through Two Centuries in a Midwestern Metropolis*. Manhattan, Kan.: KS Publishing, Inc., 2006.

Coontz, Stephanie. *Marriage, A History*. New York: Viking, 2005.

Culbertson, Ely. *Contract Bridge Blue Book*. New York: The Bridge World, Inc., 1930.

———. *Contract Bridge for Auction Players*. Garden City, N.Y.: Garden City Publishing Company, Inc., 1932.

———. *The Strange Lives of One Man*. Chicago: The John C. Winston Company, 1940.

———. *Total Peace: What Makes Wars and How to Organize Peace*. Garden City, N.Y.: Doubleday, Doran and Company, Inc., 1943.

Culbertson, Ely, analyst, with Josephine Culbertson, Theodore A. Lightner, and Waldemar Von Zedtwitz. *Famous Hands of the Culbertson-Lenz Match*. New York: The Bridge World, 1932.

Culbertson, Ely, ed., and Albert H. Morehead, Lloyd E. Smith, et al. *The Encyclopedia of Bridge*. New York: The Bridge World, Inc., 1935.

Daniels, David. *The Golden Age of Contract Bridge*. Briarcliff Manor, N.Y.: Scarborough Books, 1982.

Doctorow, E. L. *Ragtime*. New York: Plume Books, 1996.

Dos Passos, John. *1919*. Boston: Houghton Mifflin Company, 2000.

Driggs, Frank, and Chuck Haddix. *Kansas City Jazz: From Ragtime to Bebop—A History*. New York: Oxford University Press, Inc., 2005.

Dunne, J. Patrick, and Albert A. Ostrow. *Championship Bridge: As Played by the Experts*. New York: McGraw-Hill Book Company, Inc., 1949.

Elwell, Joseph B. *Bridge Axioms and Laws*. New York: E. P. Dutton and Company, 1907.

———. *Elwell on Auction Bridge*. New York: Charles Scribner's Sons, 1911.

Ferrell, Robert H., ed. *Dear Bess: The Letters from Harry to Bess Truman, 1910–1959*. New York: W.W. Norton and Company, 1983.

Fitzgerald, F. Scott. *The Great Gatsby: The Cambridge Edition of the Works of F. Scott Fitzgerald*. New York: Cambridge University Press, 1991.

Fitzgerald, F. Scott, and Edward Wilson, ed. *The Crack-up*. New York: New Directions Publishing Corporation, 1993.

Foster, R. F. *Foster's Bridge Manual: A Complete System of Instruction in the Game*. New York: Brentano's, 1907.

Fountain, Charles. *Sportswriter: The Life and Times of Grantland Rice*. New York: Oxford University Press, 1993.

Francis, Henry G., editor-in-chief, Alan F. Truscott, and Dorothy A. Francis. *The Official Encyclopedia of Bridge*, 6th ed. Memphis, Tenn.: American Contract Bridge League, 2001.

Frey, Richard L. *According to Hoyle: Official Rules of More than 200 Popular Games of Skill and Chance with Expert Advice on Winning Play*. New York: Fawcett Books, 1956.

Fried, Richard M. *The Man Everybody Knew: Bruce Barton and the Making of Modern America*. Chicago: Ivan R. Dee, 2005.

Gabler, Neal. *Winchell: Gossip, Power and the Culture of Celebrity*. New York: Alfred A. Knopf, 1994.

Gallico, Paul. *Farewell to Sport*. New York: Alfred A. Knopf, 1938.

Garraty, John A. ed. *Dictionary of American Biography: Supplement Six, 1956–1960*. New York: Charles Scribner's Sons, 1980.

Garraty, John A., and Mark C. Carnes, eds. *American National Biography*, Vol. 22. New York: Oxford University Press, 1999.

Gladwell, Malcolm. *The Tipping Point: How Little Things Can Make a Big Difference.* Boston: Little, Brown and Company, 2000.

Goren, Charles. *Goren's Hoyle Encyclopedia of Games: With Official Rules and Pointers on Play Including the Latest Laws of Contract Bridge.* New York: Chancellor Hall, Ltd., Greystone Press, 1961.

Gray, Louis Herbert, ed., George Foot Moore, William Sherwood Fox. *The Mythology of All Races: Greek and Roman*, Vol. 1. New York: Cooper Square Publishers, Inc., 1964.

Gurko, Miriam. *Clarence Darrow.* New York: Thomas Y. Crowell Company, 1965.

Hargrave, Catherine Perry. *A History of Playing Cards and a Bibliography of Cards and Gaming.* New York: Dover Publications, Inc., 1966.

Hecht, Ben. *A Child of the Century.* New York: Simon & Schuster, 1954.

Hemingway, Ernest. *The Sun Also Rises.* New York: Scribner Trade Paperback Edition, 2006.

Hessen, Robert. *Steel Titan: The Life of Charles M. Schwab.* Pittsburgh, Penn.: University of Pittsburgh Press, 1975.

Hillenbrand, Laura. *Seabiscuit: An American Legend.* New York: Random House, 2001.

Holtzman, Jerome. *No Cheering in the Press Box.* New York: Holt, Rinehart and Winston, 1973.

James, Jesse, Jr. *Jesse James, My Father: The First and Only True Story of His Adventures Ever Written.* New York: Frederick Fell, Inc., Publishers, 1957.

Jensen, Richard J. *Clarence Darrow: The Creation of an American Myth.* Westport, Conn.: Greenwood Press, 1992.

Kaplan, Edgar. *Bridge Master: The Best of Edgar Kaplan: A Tribute to One of the Game's Leading Personalities and Inventors.* New York: Bridge World Books, 2004.

Karpin, Fred L. *Psychological Strategy in Contract Bridge.* New York: Harper and Row, Publishers, 1960.

Larsen, Lawrence H., and Nancy J. Hulston. *Pendergast!* Columbia: University of Missouri Press, 1997.

Leinwand, Gerald. *1927: High Tide of the 1920s.* New York: Four Walls Eight Windows, 2001.

Lemons, J. Stanley. *The Woman Citizen: Social Feminism in the 1920s.* Charlottesville: University of Virginia Press, 1990.

Lenz, Sidney S. *Lenz on Bridge.* Garden City, N.Y.: Garden City Publishing Company, Inc., 1926.

Lewis, Sinclair. *Babbitt*. New York: Harcourt Brace Jovanovich, 1922.

———. *Elmer Gantry*. Harcourt, Brace and Company, 1927.

Lingeman, Richard. *Sinclair Lewis: Rebel from Main Street*. New York: Random House, 2002.

Link, Arthur. *Wilson: The New Freedom*. Princeton, N.J.: Princeton University Press, 1956.

Loos, Anita. *Kiss Hollywood Good-By*. New York: The Viking Press, 1974.

———. *Gentlemen Prefer Blondes and But Gentlemen Marry Brunettes*. New York: Penguin Books, 1998.

Lynd, Robert S., and Helen Merrell Lynd. *Middletown: A Study in Modern American Culture*. New York: Harcourt Brace Jovanovich, 1929.

———. *Middletown in Transition*. New York: Harcourt Brace and Company, 1937.

Lynn, Kenneth S. *Hemingway*. Cambridge, Mass.: Harvard University Press, 1987.

MacAdams, William. *Ben Hecht: The Man Behind the Legend*. New York: Charles Scribner's Sons, 1990.

McCullough, David. *Truman*. New York: Simon & Schuster, 1992.

Mackey, Rex. *The Walk of the Oysters*. London: W. H. Allen, 1964.

MacMillan, Margaret. *Paris, 1919*. New York: Random House, 2003.

McPherson, Edward. *The Backwash Squeeze and Other Improbable Feats: A Newcomer's Journey into the World of Bridge*. New York: HarperCollins Publishers, 2007.

Manchester, William. *The Last Lion: Visions of Glory, 1874–1932*. New York: Dell Publishing Co., Inc., 1984.

Martin, Richard P. *Bulfinch's Mythology: The Age of Fable, the Age of Chivalry, Legends of Charlemagne*. New York: HarperCollins Publishers, 1991.

Meade, Marion. *Dorothy Parker: What Fresh Hell Is This?* New York: Penguin Books, 1987.

Mencken, H. L. *In Defense of Women*. Garden City, N.J.: Garden City Publishing Company, 1922.

———. *A Religious Orgy in Tennessee: A Reporter's Account of the Scopes Monkey Trial*. Hoboken, N.J.: Melville House Publishing, 2006.

Meriwether, Lee. *Jim Reed, Senatorial Immortal: A Biography*. Webster Groves, Mo.: International Mark Twain Society, 1948.

Miller, Arthur. *Death of a Salesman: Certain Private Conversations in Two Acts and a Requiem*. New York: The Viking Press, 1949.

Miller, David. *The History of Browning Firearms*. Guilford, Conn.: The Lyons Press, 2006.

Miller, Nathan. *New World Coming: The 1920s and the Making of Modern America*. Cambridge, Mass.: Da Capo Press, 2003.

Mitgang, Herbert. *Once Upon a Time in New York: Jimmy Walker, Franklin Roosevelt, and the Last Great Battle of the Jazz Age*. New York: The Free Press, 2000.

Mollo, Victor. *The Bridge Immortals*. New York: Hart Publishing Company, 1968.

Montgomery, A. E., ed. *Great Speeches by Famous Lawyers of Southwest U.S.A.* Tulsa, Okla.: Southwest Publishing Company, Inc., 1961.

Morehead, Albert H., Richard L. Frey, and Geoffrey Mott-Smith. *The New Complete Hoyle Revised: The Authoritative Guide to the Official Rules of All Popular Games of Skill and Chance*. New York: Doubleday, 1991.

Nasaw, David. *Chief: The Life of William Randolph Hearst*. New York: Houghton Mifflin, 2000.

———. *Andrew Carnegie*. New York: The Penguin Press, 2006.

Ohman, August R. *Historical Sketch of the Knickerbocker Whist Club: Playing Cards, Whist, Bridge, Auction*. New York: Knickerbocker Whist Club, 1926.

Olsen, Jack. *The Mad World of Bridge*. New York: Pyramid Books, 1962.

O'Malley, Terence Michael. *Nelly Don: A Stitch in Time* (companion to the film *Nelly Don: A Stitch in Time*). Kansas City. Mo.: The Covington Group, Inc., 2006.

Pepper, George Wharton. *Philadelphia Lawyer: An Autobiography*. Philadelphia: J. B. Lippincott Company, 1944.

Pole, William. *The Evolution of Whist: A Study of the Progressive Changes Which the Game Has Passed Through from Its Origin to the Present Time*. London: Longmans, Green and Co., 1895.

Reddig, William. *Tom's Town: Kansas City and the Pendergast Legend*. Columbia: University of Missouri Press, 1986.

Remarque, Erich Maria. *All Quiet on the Western Front*. New York: Ballantine Books, 1996.

Rice, Grantland. *The Tumult and the Shouting: My Life in Sport*. New York: A. S. Barnes and Company, 1954.

Rosa, Joseph C. *Wild Bill Hickok: The Man and His Myth*. Lawrence: University Press of Kansas, 1996.

Sandburg, Carl. *The Complete Poems of Carl Sandburg: Revised and Expanded Edition*. New York: Harcourt Brace Jovanovich, 1969.

Schenken, Howard. *The Education of a Bridge Player*. New York: Simon & Schuster, 1973.

Schorer, Mark. *Sinclair Lewis: An American Life*. New York: McGraw-Hill, 1961.

Sheinwold, Patricia Fox. *Husbands and Other Men I've Played With*. Boston: Houghton Mifflin Company, 1976.

Silverman, Kenneth. *Houdini!!! The Career of Erich Weiss*. New York: HarperPerennial, 1996.

Sims, Dorothy Rice. *Curioser and Curioser: A Book in the Jugular Vein*. New York: Simon & Schuster, 1940.

Sontag, Alan. *The Bridge Bum: My Life and Play*. New York: William Morrow and Company, Inc., 1977.

———. *Power Precision: A Revolutionary Bridge System from a World Champion Player*. New York: William Morrow and Company, Inc., 1979.

Spears, Timothy B. *100 Years on the Road: The Traveling Salesman in American Culture*. New Haven, Conn.: Yale University Press, 1997.

Steiner, Jesse Frederick. *Americans at Play*. New York: Arno Press, 1970.

Teachout, Terry. *The Skeptic: A Life of H. L. Mencken*. New York: Perennial, 2003.

Teukolsky, Roselyn. *How to Play Bridge with Your Spouse . . . and Survive!* Toronto: Master Point Press, 2002.

Tosches, Nick. *King of the Jews*. New York: HarperCollins Publishers, 2005.

Truscott, Alan, and Dorothy Truscott. *The New York Times Bridge Book: An Anecdotal History of the Development, Personalities and Strategies of the World's Most Popular Card Game*. New York: St. Martin's Press, 2002.

Walker, George. *Chess and Chess Players: Consisting of Original Stories and Sketches*. London: Charles J. Skeet, Publisher, 1850.

Walker, Stanley. *City Editor*. Baltimore: Johns Hopkins University Press, 1999.

———. *The Night Club Era*. Baltimore: John Hopkins University Press, 1999.

Watts, Steven. *The People's Tycoon: Henry Ford and the American Century*. New York: Alfred A. Knopf, 2005.

White, E. B. *One Man's Meat*. New York: Harper and Row, Publishers, 1944.

Woollcott, Alexander. *While Rome Burns*. New York: Viking Press, 1934.

Zeitz, Joshua. *Flapper: A Madcap Story of Sex, Style, Celebrity, and the Women Who Made America Modern*. New York: Crown Publishers, 2006.

DISSERTATIONS

Bain, Jack M. "A Rhetorical Criticism of the Speeches of James A. Reed." Ph.D. diss. University of Missouri, 1953.

Bell, William Jackson. "A Historical Study of The Kansas City Star Since the Death of William Rockhill Nelson, 1915–1949." Ph.D. diss. University of Missouri, 1949.

Hults, Jan E. "The Senatorial Career of James Alexander Reed." Ph.D. diss. University of Kansas, 1987.

Oitzinger, Kathleen D. "Competition Patterns of Married Couples in Tennis and Bridge." Ph.D. diss. Adelphi University, 1979.

ACADEMIC AND LITERARY JOURNALS

Adler, Jeffrey S. "'I Loved Joe, But I Had to Shoot Him': Homicide by Women in Turn-of-the-Century Chicago." *The Journal of Criminal Law and Criminology* (Northwestern University School of Law) 92, nos. 3–4(2003): 867–97.

Crespi, Irving. "The Social Significance of Card Playing as a Leisure Activity." *American Sociological Review* 21, no. 6 (Dec. 1956): 717–21.

Fischer, Claude S. "Change in Leisure Activities, 1890–1940." *Journal of Social History* 27, no. 3 (Spring 1994): 453–75.

Fisher, James J. "History and Newspapering." *Missouri Historical Review* LXX, no. 2 (January 1986): 123–33.

Grossman, Joanna L. "Women's Jury Service: Right of Citizenship or Privilege of Difference?" *Stanford Law Review* 46, no. 5 (May 1994): 1115–60.

GOVERNMENT PUBLICATIONS, ORGANIZATION, AND CLUB JOURNALS

Blue Diamond. Monthly newsletter of Kansas City Athletic Club, Kansas City, Mo., 1927–1930.

Bridge Bulletin. American Contract Bridge League, Memphis, Tenn.

Culbertson Studio Journal. Published by *The Bridge World*, New York, 1933.

Kansas Citian. Journal published by the Chamber of Commerce of Kansas City, Kansas City, Mo., 1929.

Official Bulletin of Bridge Headquarters. Published by Bridge Headquarters, New York, 1932.

The Congressional Record. Official publication of the proceedings, including speeches and debates, of the United States Congress.

Ward and Roanoake Parkway Building Corporation: 100% Cooperative Plan. Sales brochure of Park Manor Development, Kansas City: C.O. Jones Building Company, 1929.

FILM AND VIDEOTAPE

Animal Crackers. Paramount Pictures, 1930.

Auntie Mame. Warner Bros. Pictures, 1958.

Championship Bridge with Charles Goren. Four-disc DVD set of show that aired on ABC from 1959–1964. American Contract Bridge League, 2007.

Kansas City. Fine Line Features, Inc., 1991.

Nelly Don: A Stitch in Time. A documentary film by Terence Michael O'Malley. O'Malley Preferred Media Production, 2006.

Three Knaves and a Queen. A film short, part of Ely Culbertson's series entitled "My Bridge Experiences." RKO Radio Pictures, 1933.

UNPUBLISHED MANUSCRIPTS

Culbertson, Ely. *Elys, in Corpore: An Autobiography (Years 1938–1954)*. Archived at the American Contract Bridge League Library, Memphis, Tenn.

MAGAZINES CONSULTED

American Magazine; American Mercury; Auction Bridge Magazine (U.K.); *Bridge Forum; Bridge Magazine; Bridge World; Collier's; Contract Bridge; Good House-keeping; Guns and Ammo; Ladies' Home Journal; Liberty; Literary Digest; Nation; New Republic; Newsweek; The New Yorker; North American Review; Outlook; Psychology Today; Saturday Evening Post; Saturday Review of Literature; Sports Illustrated; Success; Time; Vanity Fair*

NEWSPAPERS CONSULTED

Arkansas Gazette; Atlanta Constitution; Atlanta Journal; Boston Evening Tran-script; Boston Globe; Brooklyn Daily Eagle; Carmi (Ill.) *Democrat-Tribune; Carmi* (Ill.) *Tribune-Times; Chicago Daily Tribune; Cincinnati Enquirer; Kansas City Jour-nal; Kansas City Journal-Post; Kansas City Post; Kansas City Star; Kansas City Times; London Daily Telegraph* (U.K.); *London Evening Standard* (U.K.); *London Star* (U.K.); *London Times* (U.K.); *Los Angeles Evening Herald and Express; Los Angeles Times; Louisville Courier-Journal; Manchester Guardian* (U.K.); *Memphis Commercial Appeal; Memphis News-Scimitar; Minneapolis Tribune; New York American; New York Daily Mirror; New York Daily News; New York Herald-Tribune; New York Post; New York Sun; New York Times; New York World-Telegram; Philadelphia Evening Bulletin; Philadelphia Inquirer; Sacramento Bee; San Francisco Call-Bulletin; San Francisco Chronicle; San Francisco Examiner; Seattle Times; St. Louis Post-Dispatch; Tampa Daily Times; Variety; Washington Post; Washington Star; White County* (Ill.) *Democrat*.

INTERVIEWS

All interviews were conducted between December 2005 and September 2008. A number of subjects graciously agreed to multiple interviews. Bill Armshaw, Frank Bessing, Henrietta Biscoe, Augie Boehm, Tim Bourke, John Clay, D. J. Cook, Steve Culbertson, Carolyn Davenport, Jim Dean, Al Ebert, Sue Emery, Barbara Fox, Ger-ald Fox, Joan Fugina, Chuck Haddix, Roy Hoppe, Kathleen Hoyt, Walter Jacobs,

Bruce Keidan, John Kranyak, Lisa Laico, Bobby Levin, Jill Levin, David Levy, Cassandra Mani, Brent Manley, Chip Martel, Alex Marvin, Laverne Simpson Mitchell, Kathyrn Mittelberger, Michael O'Connell, Terence O'Malley, Sharon Osberg, James A. Reed II, Peter Reed, Tinker Reed, Carolyn Scruggs, Gene Simpson, LeRoy Simpson, Walter Simpson, Gary Soules, Jan Soules, Rebecca Rice Stanley, Joanna Stansby, Lew Stansby, Peter W. Steinwart, David Treadwell, Anne Marie Vingo, Bill Worley

ACKNOWLEDGMENTS

The idea for this book came indirectly from the billionaire investor Warren Buffett, a man I've never met. Several years ago, in a conversation in Omaha with my literary agent, David Black, Buffett cited his love for bridge and marveled about how once there had been a bridge craze in America.

That night, David phoned me. "I've got a book idea for you," he said. David is, by nature, excitable; his metabolism moves like the second hand on a clock. On the phone his words tumbled out quickly, and I heard him say something about bridge.

Bridge?

I thought he meant *bridge* as in the Brooklyn Bridge. (David McCullough already handled that subject, quite handsomely, in *The Great Bridge*.) "No," David Black clarified, "I mean the card game of bridge." Buffett had told him about a time when contract bridge was all the rage. Buffett said it happened during the Depression. He said bridge hands were analyzed on the radio, and bridge how-to books filled the bestseller lists. He said there was even a bridge-table murder.

A bridge-table murder?

I agreed to take a look, and what I found captivated and stirred me.

My first thank-you, therefore, goes to Warren Buffett and to David Black.

Librarians and archivists are the unsung heroes of historical nonfiction. They know where all the bones (or at least all the documents) are buried. Sherrie Kline Smith, archivist at the Missouri Valley Special Collections at the Kansas City Public Library's central branch, befriended my project early, and stayed late. Her e-mails and phone calls brimmed with energy and optimism. Sherrie is a consummate professional. I also received many kindnesses from David Smith at the

New York Public Library; David Boutros of the Western Historical Manuscript Collection at the University of Missouri–Kansas City; Randy Sowell at the Harry S. Truman Library in Independence, Missouri; Chuck Haddix at the Marr Sound Archives at UMKC; Jim Miller, Brent Manley, and Tracy Yarbro at the American Contract Bridge League in Memphis; editor Jeff Rubens at *The Bridge World*; and Christel Schmidt at the Library of Congress in Washington.

Gerald Fox once taught economics at Smith College and later demography at the University of California–Berkeley. For the past thirty-seven years he has been a bridge instructor, and he's one of the finest. During this project, Gerry became my bridge guru, sharing his wisdom, his bridge books, and his collection of *Bridge World* magazines from the age of Culbertson. Gerry adores bridge and its history, and we discussed all of that, and more, at his home in Napa, over lunches, and on the phone. He introduced me to instructor Cassandra Mani, who taught me bridge in lessons, and Tim Bourke, an Australian now compiling a comprehensive bridge bibliography, who generously shared insights about bridge and its history.

I received research assistance from April White, a database whiz in Philadelphia, Susan Jezak Ford in Kansas City, and from Simi Wilhelm in London. Alan Henry, owner of Marin Firearms in northern California, allowed me to shoot his .32 Colt automatic pistol to learn the sensations of the firing act. Barry Cleveland, editor of *The Carmi* (Illinois) *Times*, the paper of record in what once was Jack Bennett's hometown, published a notice that helped me reach out to Bennett family members still in the area. From London, John Clay, author of a 1984 biography of Ely Culbertson, generously sent cassette tapes of an interview he conducted a quarter century ago with the bridge writer Alfred (Freddy) Sheinwold. I also received support and cooperation from members of the Culbertson and Bennett families. Steve Culbertson and Alex Marvin shared old Culbertson family photographs and letters as did Myrtle's cousins Carolyn Scruggs and Leroy Simpson. I counseled during this project with my esteemed Berkeley history professors from three decades ago—Leon Litwack and Larry Levine. With Levine, it was my final conversation: he passed away in the fall of 2006. In their teachings, Litwack and Levine brought the past to life, and vividly so. Both, in their way, inspired. Because of them, I write history.

I'm indebted to a panel of readers who read all or parts of earlier drafts of this manuscript: Sharon Osberg, two-time world champion bridge player; Don Samuel, noted criminal defense attorney at Garland, Samuel & Loeb in Atlanta; Bill Worley, professor of history at the University of Missouri–Kansas City; the aforementioned Gerry Fox and his wife Barbara; David Levy of San Francisco, a savant of bridge and other games, and a rare books collector who counts among his most cherished tomes a first-edition Hoyle and a Milton Work bridge instruction book that once belonged to the legendary Cavendish (in it, there is a signed letter from Work to Cavendish); also Camille Lefkowitz of Atlanta; Bruce Keidan in Florida; my bridge partner Melanie Haddad in northern California; and, as ever, Dave Kindred, the bard of Locust Grove, Virginia, a wry and economical writer, who over the past seventeen years has sliced his stiletto through my overstuffed early drafts. In the process, Kindred has saved forests, and me.

This is my third book for Crown, where Tina Constable guides the ship; from the start, Tina's friendship and support have been steady, and heartwarming. For this book Kristin Kiser handed the editing baton to Rick Horgan, whose wisdom (and insistence on understanding bridge) made this narrative sharper and more cohesive. Rick's assistant, Nathan Roberson, was a model of efficiency.

At home, our kids, Ross, Win, and Leigh, added new words to their vocabularies during the past three years, including *trump* and *trick*. They know never to pronounce *E-Lee* as *E-lye*. My wife, Carrie, lived this book with me, as she has lived each book with me. Carrie doesn't know how to play bridge, which, I have come to believe, is one of the secrets to marital bliss.

INDEX

ABOUT THE AUTHOR

GARY M. POMERANTZ is an author, journalist, and visiting lecturer in the Department of Communication at Stanford University. His first book, *Where Peachtree Meets Sweet Auburn*, was named a 1996 Notable Book of the Year by the *New York Times*. The *Times* named his third and most recent book, *Wilt, 1962*, a narrative about race, celebrity, and Wilt Chamberlain's legendary 100-point game, a 2005 editors' choice selection. A graduate of the University of California, Berkeley, Pomerantz worked for nearly two decades as a daily journalist, on staff for the *Washington Post* and the *Atlanta Journal-Constitution*, initially as a sportswriter and then writing columns, editorials, and special projects. He later served for two years as Distinguished Visiting Professor of Journalism at Emory University in Atlanta. His second book, *Nine Minutes, Twenty Seconds* (2001), about an air crash, has been published in China, England, and Germany and was termed by *The London Evening Standard* "a masterpiece of nonfiction storytelling." He lives in the San Francisco Bay Area with his wife and their three children. Visit his website at www.garympomerantz.com.